ORCHESTRA

Richard Morrison is chief music critic of *The Times*, and writes a wide-ranging weekly on cultural and social matters, which is noted for its humour and passion. From 1989 to 1999 he also edited the paper's arts pages. He is a music graduate of Cambridge University and former orchestral trombonist and organist.

He was taken to his first London Symphony Orchestra concert in 1960, aged five, and wrote his first professional review of the orchestra 16 years later. Since then he has heard the orchestra perform under most of the world's top conductors.

He lives in London with his wife and three children.

ORCHESTRA

The LSO: A Century of Triumph
and Turbulence

RICHARD MORRISON

faber and faber

First published in 2004
by Faber and Faber Limited
3 Queen Square London WC1N 3AU
Published in the United States by Faber and Faber Inc.
an affiliate of Farrar, Straus and Giroux LLC, New York
This paperback edition first published in 2005

Typeset by Faber and Faber Limited
Printed and bound in Great Briatin by Bookmarque Ltd

A CIP record for this book
is available from the British Library

ISBN 0-571-21584-X

2 4 6 8 10 9 7 5 3 1

Contents

List of Illustrations

Introduction

Deciding to write a book about the London Symphony Orchestra wasn't too difficult. I grew up listening to its LPs on Decca and Mercury, and it was the first orchestra I ever heard in a concert. As a teenager in 1960s London I knew that other orchestras existed, but none exuded the swaggering confidence of the LSO's jaunty virtuosos. Somehow, they matched the era perfectly. Their music-making exuded punch and pizzazz. They had their own TV show. They had a man from Hollywood as their conductor. They sometimes wore polo-necked sweaters. They even made classical music seem a bit groovy. I was hooked.

Then, when I started studying music at university, I became fascinated by the LSO's Edwardian origins – a rebellion by the workers against the established order, no less! – and by its subsequent turbulent history, as captured and, no doubt, fancifully embellished in a thousand musicians' anecdotes. It wasn't just the fact that the players owned and controlled their own orchestra that was interesting – though that had generated a richly entertaining fabric of 'creative tensions' over the years. There was also, I quickly realised, a mythic quality about the LSO.

It seemed to epitomise music-making in London in all its spirited, muddled, stoic, crazy, impoverished, infuriating and yet often magnificent variety. It had been acclaimed across the globe, but also reviled at home. It had survived world wars and recessions, but managed to tear itself apart more than once with bitter internal feuds. It had earned millions from lucrative film sessions, and probably made more recordings than any other orchestra in history, yet it often teetered on the brink of bankruptcy – sometimes in the same year. Its reputation on the concert platform and in the recording studio depended on absolute teamwork. Yet this was an orchestra that had always attracted big, forceful personalities, fiercely and proudly individualistic in their music-making and their outlook on life.

My fascination intensified in the late 1970s when I became a journalist and started writing about London's cultural life. I reported on the LSO's triumphant entry into the long-delayed Barbican Concert Hall; the near-catastrophic losses it incurred in its first months there; the grim struggle to survive in the mid-eighties; and the extraordinary rescue effected by a cellist plucked from the LSO's own ranks. All those things happened nearly 20 years ago, but the LSO's story has become, if anything, even more enthralling since then. What we have seen is the remarkable determination of one man, Clive Gillinson, to transform this venerable orchestra's long-ingrained attitudes and basic principles, and to turn it into an ensemble that points the way forward for all orchestras, in every country, at the start of the twenty-first century.

The story goes on, of course. Indeed, the perennial battles appear bloodier than ever today – for audiences; for sponsorship and subsidy; for the presence of good music in children's lives; for the very existence of orchestras in a 'sound-bite' age. But the LSO's centenary in 2004 seemed as good an opportunity as would ever occur to take stock of this ebullient orchestra's history and achievements, its trials and tribulations – and to produce a book which celebrated its hundred years of superb music-making without being coy or evasive about the darker episodes in its story.

As will quickly become apparent, I have written this chronicle from the perspective of an independent outsider. The views I express are my own, not the LSO's – and so is the tale that I tell. The one thing you quickly learn when you talk to orchestral players is that, if a hundred people perform in the same concert, there will be a hundred conflicting accounts of what really happened. That's just as true of stormy confrontations with conductors, or passionate disputes inside the band. Each participant remembers it differently. The writer has to make a judgement, and I accept complete responsibility for the judgements I make in these pages.

That said, I have received nothing but the fullest co-operation from the players, management and backstage staff of the orchestra. In particular, Clive Gillinson – who, more than any other person, encapsulates the heart and soul of the modern LSO – has given me hours of illuminating conversation. Libby Rice, the LSO's archivist, has also been an invaluable source of documents, programmes and photographs, and a mine of information on all sorts of historic matters. Dvora Lewis, Sue Mallet and their teams have facilitated all my requests for interviews and information.

Many conductors and soloists who have worked regularly with the LSO have provided me with honest assessments and priceless anecdotes. In particular, I must thank Pierre Boulez, Sir Colin Davis, André Previn, Mstislav Rostropovich and Michael Tilson Thomas – all central figures in LSO history who generously allowed me to probe their memories at length. Dozens of LSO players, past and present, have given equally willingly of their time and recollections. I thank them all for supplying me with such entertaining discourse and for going to such trouble to furnish me with facts, figures, recordings and documents. In addition, many other former players and administrators – including some key movers and shakers in LSO affairs – have recorded their memories for the LSO Archive in a series of excellent taped interviews with the broadcaster and journalist Jon Tolansky (himself a former percussionist). For me to have access to such an invaluable and unexpected source of oral history was manna from heaven, and I have drawn on it with immense relief and pleasure.

The editor of my newspaper, *The Times*, kindly allowed me to remove myself from the rough and tumble of daily journalism for a month when it became clear that this book could not be written solely between the hours of midnight and 4a.m., and I am grateful for that. I would also like to thank the staff of *The Times*'s own archives for helping me to pin down vital dates, reviews and news items, sometimes going back ninety years or more.

At Faber and Faber, the expertise, wisdom and encouragement of my editor, Belinda Matthews, has been crucial to this enterprise. I would also like to thank Michael Downes, who discreetly polished my rough pebbles of prose, and Kate Ward and Ron Costley for making the book look attractive.

Finally, I must thank my wife, Marian, and my children for their forbearance. After a year of living with a man obsessed with an orchestra – which sounds like a good subject for a Polish avant-garde film noir – they were fully entitled to be seething with Sturm und Drang. Instead, we still live together in relatively sweet harmony. Further evidence, no doubt, that music has a way of elevating mortals above the petty squabbles and vicissitudes of daily life. Which is, in essence, what this book is all about.

Richard Morrison July 2003

1 Prologue

Members of the LSO

previous page Full orchestra at the Barbican

A grey November morning, 9.30 a.m. Everything is gloomy, even the news. On the streets of London, striking firemen picket their own stations. Two Tube lines have broken down. Thousands wait in bus queues as the drizzle falls. The world seems to be heading towards a new war in the Gulf. And news comes from Australia that the English cricket team is on the brink of losing the Ashes, even earlier than the pundits had predicted. Just another average day in twenty-first-century Britain.

Inside the Barbican Hall, too, an average day is starting. Here the mood is different, though. On the wide wooden platform, dozens of musicians gather. The air fills with an extraordinary sonic anarchy – a hundred or more instruments being warmed up, coaxed back into life; a thousand pieces of vital orchestral gossip being exchanged.

Two days ago those instruments and their owners were playing Russian music in Japan. Next week they will be playing French music in Italy. But today they are at home, and Mahler's Sixth, an Everest of a symphony, looms. It's the unsurpassable frisson of playing massive scores like this in packed halls that binds people to one of the most pressurised and insecure professions on earth.

From the middle of this chattering crowd, virtually invisible between the gleaming ranks of brass and the sea of strings, an oboist sounds an A. This is not just a note to tune to, it's a signal that calls this vast assembly to order. It marks the moment when a hundred individuals prepare to meld into a single entity.

The faces on the platform may change. The surroundings constantly shift. But this precise ritual has been repeated four, five, even six hundred times a year for the past hundred years. It means one thing: the London Symphony Orchestra has arrived for work.

*

But today there is an unexpected frisson. Where's the maestro? Clive Gillinson, the LSO's managing director, has descended from the orchestra's office, tucked high up in the Barbican's hind quarters, and wanders into the hall looking mildly perturbed. 'He's never late,' he mutters.

Since playing its very first notes on 9 June 1904, the LSO has been owned and governed by its own players. They answer to nobody, admit to no higher authority than the board of directors they elect from their own ranks. In theory, Gillinson is their employee. In practice, as everyone cheerfully admits, he runs the show: the LSO without Gillinson would be like a car without a battery. But this morning the battery is slightly overheated. Instructions are issued. Phone calls are made to the hotel of the absent maestro, the revered Latvian conductor Mariss Jansons.

Nothing, however, ruffles the LSO's leader, Gordan Nikolitch, and his invariable platform partner, Lennox Mackenzie ('Bernstein called me "the other Lenny"'). They have been in the profession too long to allow a little unscheduled delay to bother them. They stretch their legs out languidly towards the podium, casually skim through awkward passages from the massive first-violin part that lies open before them, and swap Serbo-Scottish jokes – sometimes all at the same time.

Further back, in the principal clarinet chair, Andrew Marriner warms up even more gently, blowing very soft, long notes into his instrument, until distracted by a horn player. 'What? Oh God, wasn't that awful? An innings and how many? What a shower!'

Marriner – like Goossens, Brain, Cummings, Cruft, Camden and Borsdorf – is a name that has resonated through the LSO, and the London musical world in general, for decades. The life of a top orchestral musician is so stressful, anti-social, intensely focused and insecure that it probably helps if you have the trade in your blood. Andrew Marriner does. Forty years ago, Andrew Marriner's father, Neville, led the LSO's second violins. Whatever became of old Nev after that?

*

A sudden commotion at the front of the platform. The maestro has arrived, only a couple of minutes late after all. He isn't happy with his life. 'I cannot sleep, last night, no night,' he says. Riga-born, St Petersburg-bred, he speaks English with a fervour that more than compensates for any grammatical shortcomings. 'Eight days since I cross Atlantic, and still the jet lag. Thank God the symphony wake me up.'

It wakes everyone up. The LSO loves Jansons, his passionate interpretations, his vitality and professionalism. 'He's one of the few conductors around who knows what to rehearse and what to leave,' says Noel Bradshaw, an LSO cellist for the last twenty years. 'He's a real musician,' says Lennie Mackenzie. An outsider would imagine that everyone who conducted a great orchestra was a real musician. Orchestral players know differently.

And Jansons, too, was steeped in this trade from the cradle. His father, Arvid, was also a much-admired conductor, until he had a fatal coronary conducting the Hallé Orchestra in Manchester. Mariss has also had a massive heart attack while conducting. His doctors constantly urge him not to exert himself unduly on the podium. There is absolutely no chance that he will obey this injunction. Not while he is conducting Mahler Six, anyway. Not even in a rehearsal on a wet Tuesday morning.

The symphony's great opening march begins: a colossal emotional journey. The orchestra hasn't played it for a couple of seasons, yet it sounds stunning. Jansons lets it run for fifteen minutes or so. 'The best conductors', says John Lawley, who has seen them all in his twenty-two years as second oboist, 'are the ones who do it with their hands and their eyes, not their mouths.'

Jansons gives a mesmerising masterclass in the art of doing it with the hands and eyes. But eventually he stops the music and, in a remarkable demonstration of musical recall, lists everything in the previous quarter of an hour that has not been to his liking. 'You are repeating bows? Two before eight? I would like it not! Please!'

His remarks create ripples that spread outwards through the ranks of strings. The best string sections are so closely knit, so unanimous in attack and timbre, that to an outsider it seems as if telepathy binds them together. You can see that in the smallest things. For instance, after the cellos have got carried away with their fearsome Mahlerian *col legno* (hitting the strings of their instruments so hard with the wood of their bows that they produce a rattling effect), they all smooth out the hairs of their bows as if struck by the same thought.

'Believe it or not,' says Paul Silverthorne, principal viola, 'I can actually change our bowing in mid-concert if, say, I feel we aren't loud enough – and the players are with me all the way.' The saying goes that a string player has to keep one eye on the notes, one eye on the conductor and one eye on his section leader. Most of this apparent telepathy, however, is the result of hard graft in rehearsal, hour after hour, day after day. As Jansons speaks, every desk of string players adds his instructions to the hundreds of 'down' and 'up' signs already scattered through their parts.

But the strings are not currently Jansons' major concern. Something else – much more mundane, yet crucial – troubles him. 'The cowbells!' he cries plaintively. 'I don't hear them. They are here?'

The cowbell player is summoned from his offstage post to be instructed. Jansons asks him to play the offending passage by himself, while an assistant opens and closes the door to give the illusion of a crescendo and diminuendo.

The conductor isn't satisfied. 'Please, again.' Still not right. The orchestra is intrigued and amused by this strange jangling interlude. When the cowbells are rehearsed for the third time, some wits in the brass section start making mooing noises. Jansons shushes them, but grins at the same time. Conductors don't get very far with the LSO if they don't develop a keen appreciation of English schoolboy humour.

This time the cowbell virtuoso excels himself. The strings tap their bows on their music stands – perhaps in mock appreciation of his artistry, perhaps out of genuine empathy with a fellow player under pressure. Everyone on this platform knows about pressure. Every orchestral player has his or her symphonic *bête noire* – the piece with the tricky, exposed passage that is the stuff of nightmares. They may make light of it in conversation, they would never let their worry show, but it gnaws away all the same.

'I was feeling very tense the other day and I imagined it was because of the England–Brazil match,' says John Lawley, an ardent football fan. 'But I was kidding myself. We had a Mahler Nine coming up, and once that was over it was amazing how much better I felt.'

The pressure in the LSO doesn't only come from the demands of a constantly changing repertoire. It also comes from colleagues – for in a self-governing orchestra the players themselves are ultimately responsible for the standards and reputation of the ensemble.

And it comes from the next generation. As with athletes, the technical ability of young instrumentalists leaving conservatoires rises with every passing decade. Each year, hundreds will knock on the LSO's door and ask for an audition. Ask any LSO member what they think of these aspiring twenty-two-year-olds, and the word you most often hear is 'terrifying'. 'Every one of my students at the Royal Academy of Music wants my job,' one LSO wind player confides. 'And I think I know which one will get it, too. But not just yet, I hope.'

*

The music has now reached an apocalyptic climax. Searing through it all comes an unmistakable sound: a clarion call so brazen, so thrilling that it proclaims its creator as surely as a signature on an artist's canvas. Maurice Murphy has occupied the hottest seat in British brass – principal trumpet with the LSO – for the past twenty-seven years. He is supposed to have retired, twice. Not a chance. Every orchestra needs its talisman, an embodiment of its collective voice and character. For more than a quarter of a century – whether launching Mahler Five with a fanfare that seems to summon the dead, or soaring over the title-credits of *Star Wars* – Murphy has been the LSO's calling card.

'In my job,' he says, 'you're either scared to death or bored to death.' It's a great remark but, in his case, manifestly untrue. He's been playing the trumpet for sixty-one of his sixty-seven years, and seems simply indestructible. More than that, however, his career is one of the great rags-to-riches stories in orchestral music. Like the LSO's first-ever principal trumpet, John Solomon – who played in East End working men's bands and the orchestra on Southend Pier before breaking into the London orchestral world – Murphy came up the hard way. He left school at fifteen, not to go to some grand conservatoire but to work as an office boy with the National Coal Board. He joined a succession of increasingly distinguished brass bands in the North of England, while earning spare cash as a freelance trumpeter. It is said that Yorkshire choral societies used to stagger the times of their Christmas *Messiah*s so that Murphy could play 'The Trumpet Shall Sound' in all of them.

Only in 1976, after fifteen years in the comparatively humble BBC Northern Orchestra, did the LSO lure him to London. His impact was immediate and dramatic. Murphy would undoubtedly subscribe to Miss Jean Brodie's maxim: 'Safety does *not* come first.' To see that ruddy face peering out from the middle of the brass section is to be assured of a roller-coaster ride. Colin Davis, the LSO's principal conductor, likes to recount how the orchestra was struggling through Sibelius's Second Symphony at the end of an exhausting Russian tour. 'What we desperately needed, with the orchestra and myself so tired, was a lift from somewhere,' he says. 'I looked at Maurice. He gave me this big smile, picked up the LSO, and made me a present of it.'

*

The orchestra have reached the third movement now. Jansons starts it four times. He isn't satisfied that the players have caught the malice and sarcasm of the piece. When his English fails him, he stamps his foot and makes growling noises. Only a few decades ago, orchestras needed five or six full rehearsals simply to master the notes of Mahler's virtuoso scores. Now, not only are the notes in place at the first runthrough – so too are many of Jansons' own ideas: the hesitations, the nuances of phrasing, the subtle things that make the music ebb and flow.

But one rubato catches a clarinettist out. As the other players hold back – responding with mercurial reflexes to Jansons' tiny hand movement – the errant note pops out with comical clarity. Everyone giggles. The clarinettist lifts a hand in apology. He won't make the same mistake again. That's how a great orchestra works.

Jansons ends the rehearsal a courteous five minutes before its scheduled conclusion. Conductor and orchestra will resume this intensive process – polishing, refining, digging deeper and deeper for meaning – in just thirty-five minutes' time. Tomorrow morning they will add finishing touches. Then the accumulated debris of rehearsal will vanish from the platform, the male players will clamber into the penguin-like costumes that have been worn for a century and more, the audience will gather in the Barbican's angular foyers, and a buzz of expectation will fill the air.

Not all of the 5,000-odd concerts in London each year are special, but this one is. Jansons is a hot ticket, and the LSO – which has been through more ups and downs than an elevator in its hundred years of existence – is currently perceived as being on the crest of a wave. People will expect to leave the hall, ninety minutes later, with their souls refreshed and their spirits elevated.

Orchestral players often seem embarrassed at their collective power to inspire profound emotions, usually dismissing it with a shrug or a joke. Yet the evidence must confront them every time they perform. 'A friend of mine came to one of our concerts the other day,' says Christine Pendrill, the LSO's cor anglais player since 1986. 'I told him I didn't think he would like it. The first half was very modern, and then it was Mahler Nine. His idea of classical music is "Spanish Eyes". Anyway, afterwards he was ecstatic. "That was brilliant," he said. "It makes you realise how useless your stereo is."'

Now the doors close and the oboist sounds his A once more. This time the mass tuning ritual is more subdued – a last reassurance that valves aren't sticking, reeds are responsive, fingers supple, brain and sinew absolutely synchronised. Jansons enters, bows, takes a deep breath, then suddenly clenches his right fist and brings it crashing down in the general direction of the cellos. It is not so much a downbeat, more an eruption of the psyche. And the orchestra that has entertained, entranced and inspired Londoners through two world wars, the Blitz and the Depression, strides ferociously away on Mahler's tumultuous journey.

It is probably the last thing on the players' minds at this moment – but a curious historical coincidence links their orchestra with this music. In 1903 and 1904, while Mahler laboured in Austria to pour his hopes and fears into the vast canvas of his Sixth Symphony, a group of disgruntled musicians in London was also struggling to create an epic musical enterprise. And they, too, would invest all their hopes in it. They would call it the London Symphony Orchestra – and this is its turbulent and triumphant tale.

2 The birth of the band
1904–6

left to right Henri van der Meerschen (horn), Adolf Borsdorf (horn), Thomas Busby (horn), John Solomon (trumpet) in 1905

previous page LSO in the Queen's Hall 1905/6 with conductor Artur Nikisch; painting by Richard Jack, RA, Tate Gallery

'Gentlemen, in future there will be no deputies; good morning.' Is there a more famous sentence in the history of orchestral music? It is certainly up there with 'Damn that horn!' – the comment that allegedly infuriated Beethoven when uttered by a well-meaning friend after the celebrated 'wrong' entry in the 'Eroica' Symphony.

Most music-lovers think that it was the conductor Henry Wood who issued the ultimatum about deputies on that momentous spring day in 1904. It wasn't. 'Timbers' had already stomped off the podium in high dudgeon at the end of a rehearsal with what was supposed to be his Queen's Hall Orchestra – but was in fact a motley band of unfamiliar faces and indifferent talents.

No, the tough talking was administered, as it usually is, by the money man. Robert Newman was the visionary impresario who had founded the Proms nine years earlier at the Queen's Hall. The hall itself, built in 1893, was the nearest London ever came to getting its own Musikverein or Concertgebouw. Its architect, Knightley, may have specified that its predominant internal colour should match 'the belly of a London mouse' (and he reputedly hung several dead rodents, appropriately Cockney in origin, in the paint shop to ensure that his wishes were followed to the last whisker). But in every other respect the hall was a brave British stab at *fin-de-siècle* decadence, with mirrors round the stalls, frescos on the ceiling of 'attenuated Cupids clad in sallow pantaloons' (as E. M. Forster memorably recalled), and opulent acoustics to match. It was Victorian public architecture at its sauciest.

And Newman had exploited it brilliantly to put on an audacious series of concerts that were years, perhaps decades, ahead of their time. He had cut ticket prices, engaged the solid and scrupulous Wood as conductor, and attracted a whole new public to programmes that cannily and cheerfully mixed old favourites with novelties, and heavyweight symphonies with parlour-room fripperies. The concoction suited the breezy era; the Proms were fun and fashionable. Everything was turning out well for Newman and Wood – except for one thing. They had to work with that unreliable species of humanity known as orchestral musicians.

The deal in early-twentieth-century London was quite simple. If you were an instrumental player and free on a certain date, you accepted an engagement. But if something more lucrative came along, you dumped the first engagement on a colleague or perhaps one of your students – and 'traded up'. And for the better players, at least, something more lucrative was always coming along.

A glance through the playbills of the era is enough to show why. With Marie Lloyd and Harry Lauder in their prime, this was the heyday of the music hall. There were more than fifty of them in London alone, and each required a pit band. So did the ebullient new 'revues' – bizarre but spirited attempts to combine the traditional British variety show with the eroticism of Paris's Folies Bergère and the thrills of the circus.

That was a fad that would reach its gaudy zenith in the very year that Newman issued his ultimatum to his Queen's Hall musicians – for late in 1904 an incredible new 3,500-seat palace of varieties opened. Designed by the great theatre architect Frank Matcham, it was grandly called the London Coliseum, and would provide well-paid work for forty or fifty musicians a night. (The Coliseum proved to be a dangerous place for musicians to work. On one notorious occasion, real horses were sent galloping over its three revolving stages in an attempt to recreate the Derby. One horse toppled into the orchestra pit, killing its rider and inflicting grievous bodily harm on several players and their instruments.)

The music halls and variety palaces were far from being the only employers of musicians. The West End theatres were also packed with 'musical comedies' and light operas, whether home-grown (Edward German's *Merrie England* was the nostalgia trip of this decade), continental (the waltzes of Oskar Straus and Franz Lehár were sweeping across Europe like a tidal wave of tinsel), or, increasingly, American (the young Jerome Kern had a song called 'Rosalie' included in the 1906 West End hit *Spring Chicken*).

All of these needed sizeable orchestras. Then there were the grand hotels, which required chamber ensembles for their 'palm courts' and restaurants. And, of course, the best players were summoned to the fashionable Belgravia drawing rooms of the rich and well-connected, where they would supply discreet background music while the cream of London society wined and dined, gossiped and flirted.

In short, Edwardian London was a honey pot for wandering minstrels. What's more, there were also rich pickings to be had at the well-endowed choral festivals held annually in cities such as Sheffield, Leeds, Birmingham and Norwich – engagements that could take musicians away from their regular London jobs for several weeks each year.

So there were a hundred and one well-paid reasons why you might want to pass on an engagement for a concert conducted by worthy but dull Henry Wood. The trouble was that your replacement might get as far as doing the rehearsal, and then himself be offered a more lucrative engagement. In which case the original concert would be passed to a third player – who would, of course, come to it completely unrehearsed. And so on. 'On this basis,' recalled Sir Adrian Boult, who was a pupil at Westminster School during the early 1900s, 'were collected the orchestra for the Philharmonic Society, for long the cream of London orchestras, and the orchestra which took part in the Proms, together with Sir Henry Wood's Sunday afternoon concerts and Saturday symphony concerts.'

This ramshackle and anarchic procedure was called the 'deputy system'. It had existed in London's musical life since time immemorial. It still survives today, especially in the West End theatre world and at the semi-professional level of classical music. In 1904, however, Wood and Newman were determined to stamp out the practice, which Wood described as 'disastrously unprincipled'. They believed, correctly, that while such a cavalier attitude towards rehearsal and ensemble virtues existed among players, standards would never rise. Nor could repertoire be repeated later in the concert series in the expectation that the players wouldn't need to rehearse it again: the reality was that a completely different bunch of musical mercenaries would most likely turn up for the repeat performance.

The system insulted the public, because concerts would be unprepared by many of the players. It insulted the conductor, because there could be no such thing as interpretation, only a kind of glorified traffic management. And it insulted the very concept of an orchestra, a term that is usually taken to mean a close-knit team of musicians, unified in style, nuance and aim. True, concerts given by orchestras of 'deps' could (and can) be exciting affairs – but mostly for the wrong reasons, like a journey in a taxi with faulty brakes and unreliable steering.

Wood's players, however, saw things very differently. 'Free trade' was an article of faith for Victorian and Edwardian England. After all, the British Empire had grown rich on it. The musicians regarded Newman's ultimatum as a scandalous attempt to restrict their freedom to sell their skills to the highest bidder. This wasn't simply a matter of principle. The orchestral profession of the early twentieth century had even less security than it does in the early twenty-first, hard to imagine though that is.

'There were no permanent orchestras at all in the whole country, except at Bournemouth,' Boult recalled. 'The life and livelihood of every orchestral player were based on the fact that in those days no decent theatre could exist without an orchestra of at least twenty.' They survived on their wits, their connections – and luck. Be in the right place at the right time. Don't fall out with people who can give you work, especially conductors. Don't get ill. Work like a dog while the work is there; it won't last. Those were the rules of the jungle.

Out of the tension between these two polarised positions – Wood's and the players' – the London Symphony Orchestra was born. It was a rebel band, formed of the dissidents who refused to sign on Newman's dotted line. But the foundation of the new orchestra resolved nothing, least of all within the LSO itself. Within a year the very players who had led the revolt against Wood were reprimanding colleagues who sent deputies to LSO concerts, and the same conflict, in essence, was replayed time and again over the next eighty-odd years. What comes first, the team or the individual? Can any orchestra's aims ever be satisfactorily reconciled with the personal ambitions of the highly skilled people sitting inside it? Are high artistic standards possible without an element of dictatorship?

A hundred years on from Newman's momentous announcement, those basic questions remain pertinent, and explosive. In trying to find their own answers over the course of the intervening century, successive generations of LSO members sometimes expressed themselves with such violent feeling that they almost shook their organisation apart. The supreme irony is that the LSO of today has achieved high standards, consistency and an unusual degree of stability by admitting one thing: Wood and Newman were right all along. 'In point of fact,' says Clive Gillinson, the orchestra's current managing director, 'what we are now is the absolute antithesis of the reason why we were founded.'

*

Newman's ultimatum after that famous rehearsal always strikes me as being slightly pointless, since it was clearly aimed at the musicians who weren't actually present that morning. Perhaps the impresario was confident that the orchestral grapevine would quickly transmit his tough words into all the right quarters, the most important being the pub near the Queen's Hall called The George, though it was universally known by its nickname – 'The Glue Pot' – because of the near-impossibility of dislodging brass players from its snug innards. Because Alexander Graham Bell's outlandish invention, the telephone, was not yet commonly used, The George acted as unofficial clearing house and recruiting office for the music world. It was here that 'deps' were fixed, contacts and contracts made, gossip exchanged, mischief con-cocted, whistles wetted – in short, all the usual essential business conducted by musicians in pubs through the ages. The lunchtime atmosphere must have been raucous indeed: a mixture of Stock Exchange trading floor, school can-teen and boys' club.

Perhaps Newman also realised that everybody already knew what he and Wood were going to announce – for few upheavals in the history of music were more anticipated than this one. Wood was a pragmatist by necessity. No conductor who learnt his trade in the chaotic London musical scene of the 1890s could be anything else. By inclination, however, he was a perfec-tionist. Later in his great fifty-year career he would spend seventeen rehearsals preparing an orchestra for Strauss's *Ein Heldenleben*, and fifty preparing a Liverpool choir for Bach's B minor Mass. This was the level of diligence to which he aspired, so his frustration at what confronted him daily at the Queen's Hall can only be imagined. At one early Prom, he recalled in his memoirs, he found 'an orchestra with seventy or eighty unknown faces in it; even my leader was missing'. They had all disappeared to some regional festival, for twice the money, without telling him.

That was in 1896. At that stage Wood, aged only twenty-seven, could do little except dream about reform. But he did vent his anger by sacking the concertmaster (known as the 'leader' in England) and promoting the deputy leader, Arthur Payne. Not that this secured Payne's loyalty: eight years later he would join the anti-Wood rebels and become the first leader of the LSO.

The situation was rather different by late 1903. Wood and Newman knew that they couldn't outbid the theatre and hotel managements in a straight cash auction. Their Queen's Hall Proms paid orchestral members only £2 10s. a week – for six rehearsals and six concerts of demanding repertoire that changed every night. It was not a mouth-watering prospect, when a player could earn the same weekly wage at a West End theatre, plus a 'white tie allowance' (ostensibly to pay for a fresh, starched white tie and collar each night, but in practice simply pocketed), for six performances of the same show and no rehearsals. Or he could work at a big hotel and earn even more, perhaps £3 10s. a week. Or he could hit the jackpot and be summoned to play for the King at Windsor, as the horn player Henri van der Meerschen was commanded to do in the autumn of 1903. His reward for that? A regal three pounds, for two nights of gentle blowing.

Wood and Newman had one trump card, however: they could guarantee regular and plentiful work. By 1904 they were able to offer Queen's Hall Orchestra players at least a hundred dates in a nine-month season. In return, they felt they had the right to demand first call on a player's time; all absences, they decided, would have to be justified by the production of a doctor's certificate.

There were two problems with that strategy. The first was that Wood and Newman were demanding absolute loyalty but only guaranteeing about a hundred pounds a year – roughly equivalent to the salary of a clerk or junior teacher. That might have satisfied a fresh-faced young fiddler straight out of one of London's many music colleges. But the top-ranking veterans in Wood's orchestra had grander aspirations. To live with even a modest degree of middle-class comfort in Edwardian England, a household needed at least three times that amount. (George Orwell famously described growing up in an Edwardian 'lower-middle-upper-class' household that struggled to keep up genteel appearances on four to five hundred pounds a year.) So forty-six of them resolved to resign and set up what they would later memorably describe as a 'something akin to a Musical Republic'. It would, they decided, be called the London Symphony Orchestra.

*

No veteran was more highly prized than the infallible John Solomon, a forty-eight-year-old East Ender who had risen from the brass band world to become, by general consent, the finest orchestral trumpet player in Edwardian England. ('One has to confess', the composer Ralph Vaughan Williams mischievously noted, 'that he was fully aware of his infallibility.') It was Solomon who, some thirty-four years later, would send a letter to Wood setting out (in rather quaint grammar) the real insecurities and fears that had led the players to make the break:

May I be allowed as a culprit to tell you how deeply sorry we were for it. But the real truth is that all our old players had built up a connection with the best concerts, festivals and many other engagements which we had been forced to accept, not knowing what would happen in the future. You might have been snapped up either abroad or elsewhere, and the Queen's Hall Orchestra would have been abandoned or smashed up. Consequently we would have been stranded.

In other words, the players didn't want to put all their eggs into one basket. Especially this basket. For what Solomon understandably doesn't say in his letter to Wood is that, back in 1904, the conductor was not regarded as a good long-term bet by the orchestral profession. They weren't prepared to tie themselves contractually to a maestro whose star might fade, and whose backers might melt away, in a year or two.

Something else about Solomon's letter is rather revealing. The trumpeter felt that he had to spell out, even to a conductor who was born and bred in London, exactly what the realities of life were like for common-or-garden orchestral players in the early twentieth century. For Wood was on the other side of the great divide. In the hierarchical organisation of its musical life, as in many other matters, Edwardian England was still clinging to the Victorian notion of an 'upstairs–downstairs' society. Conductors – usually knighted, sometimes ennobled, always connected to money – qualified as upper-class figures. Players did not. Indeed, in social terms they scarcely ranked above the thousands of maids, cooks, butlers and valets who kept the grand mansions of Mayfair ticking like clockwork.

The anti-Wood rebels' plan – to seize control of their own destinies, burn their bridges, proclaim their independence and their rights, and accept no master but themselves – was nothing short of a revolution. But London in 1904, oddly enough, was teeming with such heretical notions.

*

The city was enormous – in wealth, power and geographical size. 'One may go east or north or south or west from Charing Cross and almost despair of ever reaching the rim,' an American visitor wrote in the 1890s. It was also, with a population approaching seven million by 1904, the most bustling metropolis on earth: its pavements teeming with people, its streets gridlocked. At precisely the moment when the future LSO players were planning their new venture, the German explorer Carl Peters was writing his celebrated study of England and the English. With Teutonic attention to detail, he decided to stand on London's busiest streets and count the number of passers-by. 'In front of the Mansion House two hundred and forty-eight thousand and fifteen people are passing every day,' he noted with incredulity. 'And the number of those who pass through Cheapside amounts to ninety-one thousand, one hundred and ninety.'

The multitudes that amazed Peters were not unskilled labourers. They were prosperous white-collar workers, securely attached to well-paid jobs in the 'Square Mile' – the City of London, then utterly unchallenged as the powerhouse of capitalism. And in Edwardian England there seemed no limit to how far, or how fast, their living standards could rise. At the turn of the twentieth century Britain's gross national product rose by no less than twenty per cent in a decade.

The LSO's founders could feel confident, then, that London had a sufficiently large and prosperous middle class to support a new cultural venture.

There were other factors in their favour as well. One was jingoism: a naked and unashamed nationalistic fervour which fuelled every branch of Edwardian culture and entertainment. As well as being a rich trading city, London was also an imperial capital, infused with as much grandeur, self-importance and sense of destiny as first-century Rome or twenty-first-century Washington. By 1914, an astonishing two hundred thousand civil servants were employed by the British Government to rule an Empire of four hundred million people, stretching over every continent on the globe except Antarctica. (And a whole string of intrepid if generally rather ill-fated Edwardian heroes were racing to raise the Union Flag even on that icy wasteland.)

Imperial capitals expect to get the best of everything. Yet the mighty British Empire, on which the sun never set, had one gaping cultural hole at its heart: its capital had no world-class orchestra. As rivalry with Germany and the emerging new superpower, the United States, grew more intense, this lack became an increasing source of irritation – at least to music-loving imperialists. Berlin, Vienna, New York, Boston: all had established superb, permanent orchestras decades ago. Surely it was high time that London, the greatest city of them all, did the same?

The LSO's founders played cannily upon this sense of unease: this Achilles heel in the otherwise impregnable self-confidence of Edwardian England. 'This city needs a great orchestra to make its glory complete, and we are it' – that was the underlying message of the LSO's first prospectus. And the language in which it was couched was scarcely less boastful. The new orchestra, the players declared, 'is second to none in Europe'.

Not, you note, 'will be' or 'hopes to be'. It seems a staggeringly arrogant claim, coming from an ensemble that had yet to play a note in public. (Or, if Boult is to be trusted, in private either! 'I believe,' he wrote later, 'these [first] concerts took place with practically no rehearsal.') But anything less assertive would not have matched the spirit of the times, or the blissful belief of the Edwardian English in their God-given destiny to spread enlightenment to lesser races.

The pioneering spirit was another factor in the new LSO's favour. Despite its ossified manners, Edwardian England was by no means hostile to new ideas. That was just as well, since those living through the twenty years between 1890 and 1910 must have felt as if they were trapped inside one of H. G. Wells's futuristic fantasies, so fast and bewildering was the transformation in transport and communications, the workplace and the home. Man learnt to fly in those years, and to construct the 'horseless carriages' that started to chug along London's streets at about the same time as Newman was issuing his ultimatum. Pioneers such as Edison, Marconi and the Lumière brothers were experimenting with the recording and transmission of sound waves and the flickering projection of 'moving pictures' – though virtually nobody in 1900 predicted how comprehensively or how quickly these strange experiments in applied electricity would transform all notions of 'mass entertainment'.

The LSO's founders were no more far-sighted than anyone else. Had they been blessed with prophetic powers, they might have thought twice about casting adrift from Wood in order to maintain their connections with London's theatres. Of the fifty-odd music halls active in London in 1904, only a handful were still operating ten years later. Most of the rest had been converted into cinemas, of which there were already three thousand in Britain by the outbreak of the Great War.

This technological revolution was matched by new ideas about politics and society, even in stuffy, class-bound Edwardian England, and especially in London. In the early 1900s, republican sentiments swirled round the capital like one of its famed 'pea-soupers'. The London County Council was controlled by socialists and radicals, much engaged in the task of improving the early Victorian slums of the East End, providing affordable new housing and transport links, and eradicating the worst pockets of poverty. A gentle, rather idealised version of 'socialism' became acceptable, even rather chic, in many fashionable London drawing rooms – provided that it didn't spread below stairs, of course.

At the same time, the organised labour movement was pushing up from below. The Trades Union Congress had met for the first time fourteen years earlier, the Labour Party was in full flow by 1900, and the Suffragettes were pushing militantly for women's rights by 1903. In 1906 even the British Government caught a mild dose of radicalism: the Liberal Party pushed through a Trades Disputes Act that granted trade unions full legal immunity – a status then unique in Europe.

It is against this background that we must view the public pronouncement of the new LSO's founders that they were forming 'something akin to a Musical Republic'. Yes, it was a bold statement. But its socialist tone was surely also designed to appeal to London's intelligentsia, just as the LSO's boast of being the best in Europe was contrived to appeal to the jingoistic side of the Edwardian temperament.

In short, the LSO's first prospectus – its 'mission statement', as we would now call it – was a subtle, sophisticated and well-targeted piece of marketing. So who wrote it?

There were four ringleaders in the great Queen's Hall mutiny, all of them brass players. One was Solomon, the trumpeter. The other three were horn players – part of a legendary quartet nicknamed 'God's Own', a soubriquet they didn't go out of their way to discourage. Thomas Busby was a military man by birth (son of a Grenadier Guards drum major), upbringing (he was an Army warrant officer before entering the orchestral world via seaside bands and August Mann's impressive Crystal Palace Orchestra) and, by all accounts, disposition: his brand of argument seems to have stopped only a few decibels short of a parade-ground roar. But he undoubtedly had a head for business, and he was elected managing director of the new orchestra, a job he fulfilled (from the horn section) for twenty years.

The other two rebels were both foreigners, which is not as surprising as it might seem. Like New York, London has always been a magnet for immigrants who, particularly in the fields of the arts, design and technology, made a contribution to British life out of all proportion to their numbers. Indeed, one could argue that it was immigrants who have created many of the most quintessentially British facets of British culture. The Germans gave Britain the House of Windsor and Handel's *Messiah*. Refugees from Hitler's Germany were largely responsible for creating Glyndebourne. The Huguenots introduced the English to fish and chips; Pugin, a second-generation French settler, designed the interiors of the Houses of Parliament; and another great family of French immigrants, the Brunels, gave Britain its Great Western Railway, the SS *Great Britain* and most of its best-loved bridges and tunnels.

By 1904 there were more than two hundred thousand continental Europeans, or first-generation descendants, living in London. Most were German, Czech, Italian, or Russian and Polish Jews, recently fled from the pogroms. This expatriate community was a rich source of musical talent; indeed, many of those living in the tightly packed immigrant communities of Soho, Hoxton or Clerkenwell were instrumentalists drawn to London by its multifarious musical opportunities.

Among them were two horn players. One was Henri van der Meerschen (the man who earned thirty shillings a night by playing at Windsor). He had trained in his native Brussels as an opera singer, but found more work playing the horn. Invited to England to join the orchestra of the Carl Rosa Opera Company, he proceeded to marry the company's principal contralto and move to Glasgow. He returned to London to join the Queen's Hall Orchestra and, he hoped, make his fortune freelancing for the likes of King Edward VII.

Clearly, he had a lot to lose if Wood's no-deputies rule went through unchallenged. He would play in the new LSO for nearly thirty years, and became the orchestra's chairman in the 1920s.

The other foreign rebel was an even more significant force in the creation of the new band. Adolf Borsdorf was fifty-two at the time. The son of Saxon peasants, he had learnt the horn (from a village cobbler) and the fiddle in his native Ditmannsdorf, played in local village taverns as a boy, drifted to Leipzig where he financed his musical studies and supported himself by playing viola in the music-hall pit, and then graduated to the Dresden Opera orchestra. There he had met, and grown to know, Hans Richter – soon to become the greatest German conductor of the age. This friendship would prove crucial to the early success of the LSO.

Like Meerschen, Borsdorf was attracted by the bright lights and rich pickings of London's musical life. Though he played regularly at Covent Garden, he had struggled initially, and had to supplement his income by french-polishing coffins in a dingy Soho basement (another skill he had apparently picked up in Saxony). But after a spell in Glasgow this infinitely resourceful musical survivor was finally recognised as the best horn player in Britain, and he secured the principal's chair in Wood's Queen's Hall Orchestra.

He, too, had plenty to lose if his profitable moonlighting activities were curtailed by Wood and Newman. But his general outlook on life was probably a more significant factor in his decision: a man who had already progressed through dozens of different orchestras and theatres in England and Germany would feel no strong ties to any particular organisation. He was tough-minded, proud and independent. The new orchestra would be created in his image.

Borsdorf's later history was almost worthy of an Aeschylean tragedy. In 1911 he would suffer the fate feared by all brass players. He contracted the gum-shrinking disease pyorrhoea, lost virtually all his teeth, and was demoted to second horn – though the LSO board put on 'lasting record' its gratitude at the 'great and valuable services rendered by Mr Borsdorf since the inception of the orchestra'.

This gratitude was short-lived. Three years later, the day after the outbreak of the First World War, a round robin from the LSO players complained to the board that the presence of this German in their ranks – albeit one who had lived in Britain for thirty years and was married to a British woman – was not in the best interests of the orchestra. Borsdorf, though one of the orchestra's four founders and arguably its chief driving force in the early days, was forced to quit.

*

The four founders (or 'flounders', as Solomon self-deprecatingly called them), had clearly discussed the possibility of a breakaway orchestra many times before Newman's announcement, which was probably in January or February 1904. LSO folklore has it that the orchestra was conceived (as the 1950s film-maker Humphrey Jennings put it, after talking to some of the original players) 'in the autumn of 1903 in a railway carriage between Manchester and London'. If this was so, then like all good pregnancies this one lasted nine months, for it wasn't until 19 May 1904 that the rebels held a meeting at St Andrew's Hall in Newman Street. (That month was clearly an auspicious time for starting new British ventures. In Manchester on 4 May the Honourable Charles Rolls – a devotee of the bizarre new sport known as motor racing – signed an agreement with an engineer called Henry Royce to produce automobiles under their joint names.)

At St Andrew's Hall the plans for the new orchestra were laid out. It would be a 'co-operative' venture: all the players would share jointly in its risks and its profits and elect their own board. The board, in turn, would invite suitable conductors and soloists to perform. In short, the usual hierarchy of London's musical life was turned on its head. The servants had become the masters. Or perhaps, as they may have said in the more sceptical corners of the musical world, the lunatics were attempting to run the asylum.

Mad or not, they made a remarkably assured job of organising their début concert and of issuing a prospectus outlining their aims and pleading for public support. It is worth quoting in full:

The recent decision of the Directors of the Queen's Hall Orchestra regarding the employment of Deputies imposes conditions on its most prominent Members that they find it impossible to accept. About half the Band has in consequence found it necessary to resign. These performers being, however, unwilling to lose touch with a public that has for many years showed the most generous appreciation of their abilities, have formed an Organisation of their own under the title of

THE LONDON SYMPHONY ORCHESTRA

and have obtained the co-operation of a sufficient number of other eminent Instrumentalists to complete an Orchestra which they venture to think is second to none in Europe. That this is not too much to claim is evident from the fact that the players are the 'elite' of their profession in London – artists not only of talent, but of experience in the rendering of all kinds and styles of music under the direction of the most eminent conductors of Germany, Hungary, Italy, France and Great Britain.

The objects of the London Symphony Orchestra will be similar to those of the Queen's Hall Orchestra – that is to say, it will give Concerts of its own, and will be open to accept Engagements to play at Concerts given by others. For this latter purpose the Orchestra will be available in its full strength or in smaller contingents, its numbers varying from forty to one hundred.

This new venture will be carried on as in Berlin and in Vienna, where the Members of the Orchestra of the Philharmonic Societies are their own directors. As such they elect their own conductors, and therefore form something akin to a Musical Republic. It is believed that the standing of the artists forming the band of the London Symphony Orchestra is such that the most eminent musicians will not hesitate to allow their names to appear as conductors of its Concerts, and the belief is strengthened by the significant fact that Dr Hans Richter has kindly consented to conduct the First Concert.

Several things about that forthright text are striking. The first is that, unlike the spin-doctored and euphemism-enriched documents that tend to come from arts organisations today, the LSO's prospectus makes no attempts to hide the distressing circumstances that led to the break from Wood and Newman. But perhaps there would have been little point, since the row was already the talk of musical London. Boult recalls how he had discussed one Queen's Hall concert early in 1904 with one of his teachers at Westminster School. The teacher opined that 'it had been "abominably played", a result of the "terrible fight" going on at Queen's Hall – Wood had dismissed half the orchestra.'

Secondly, the mentions of the Philharmonic Societies of Berlin and Vienna were clever, because this immediately bracketed the brash new band with the most exalted orchestras in Europe. But as the players, and particularly the German Borsdorf, would certainly have known, the set-up in Berlin was very different: the players were bound to each other contractually. What the LSO intended was a constitution that enshrined almost the opposite principle: that its members retained the right to accept private engagements elsewhere whenever they wanted.

The most striking point of all is the determination evident in the prospectus that the new orchestra would, in effect, park its tanks on the Queen's Hall lawn: offering precisely the same musical services to the public, and with most of the old Queen's Hall players. The extent to which Henry Wood's larder had been raided only became apparent when patrons of the LSO's first concert, a month later, perused the list of names in the programme. Fifteen out of sixteen first violins, the entire brass section, and all the oboes, clarinets and percussion were rebels or past members of the Queen's Hall Orchestra. Its stars, besides those already mentioned, included the horn player A. E. Brain (father of Aubrey, who joined the LSO in 1912, and grandfather of Dennis, arguably the greatest horn player of them all), and the imperious timpanist C. Henderson. Tucked innocuously at the back of the first fiddles, meanwhile, was one W. H. Reed. Within four years young Billy Reed would rise through the ranks to lead the occasional concert, and in 1913 he was officially appointed the LSO's leader – a position he held for twenty-three years. In all he played in the orchestra for thirty-eight years, until just before his death in 1942. But his main claim to fame was the close friendship that grew between him and Elgar; a friendship partly responsible for the long relationship between the composer and the LSO. Fittingly, when Reed died in 1942, his ashes were buried under the Elgar Window in Worcester Cathedral. The violinist had led the LSO's performance of 'Nimrod' at the dedication of the window six years earlier.

Wood must have been bitterly upset at the grand larceny perpetrated on his Queen's Hall Orchestra. It would be another twelve years before the wounds had healed sufficiently for him to conduct the rival orchestra, by which time many of the original rebels had gone. But in classic Edwardian manner, he exhibited an impeccably stiff upper lip in public. He turned up in the audience at the LSO's first concert, and apparently declared that it was an excellent thing for London to have 'two first-rate orchestras where previously it only had one'.

It is unlikely that any LSO board members copied his gracious attitude in 1929, 1932, 1945 or 1946, when their own pool of talent was in turn ruthlessly trawled. They probably did not declare it an excellent thing that London now had three, four or five orchestras where previously it only had one. But by the mid-twentieth century the world had become rather less courteous, and the dash for survival in the music business was even more frenetic.

*

The oddest thing about that first LSO concert, in the Queen's Hall on 9 June 1904, was the hour at which it took place: three in the afternoon, on a Thursday. There was a pragmatic reason for that. Many of the new orchestra's players had to be in the Covent Garden Opera House pit by seven p.m. for an evening performance. Presumably they hopped on the new 'Tuppenny Tube' (the Central Line of London's underground railway system, which had opened three years earlier). They could have boarded a train at Oxford Circus, close to the Queen's Hall in Langham Place, and alighted at Holborn, a few minutes' dash from Covent Garden for a fleet-footed fiddler.

But the timing is also an indication of the sort of middle-class patrons, prosperous and leisured, that the new orchestra expected to attract. They certainly had to be well-heeled to sit in the best seats, priced at 7s. 6d. – the equivalent to two days' wages for the average working man. Standing tickets, however, could be bought for one shilling.

And the orchestra gave its first audience plenty of excitement for their money. Hans Richter demanded one hundred players, and got ninety-nine! That figure was not untypical of the period. The standard romantic orchestra that had sufficed for Beethoven, Schubert and Brahms – perhaps fifty string players, plus pairs of woodwinds, four horns, two trumpets, three trombones, tuba and timpani – had been expanded enormously when Wagner decided that his magnificent operatic spectacles needed to be matched by an equally opulent sound from the orchestra pit. By the early twentieth century audiences expected to hear the same rich sound in the concert hall as in the opera house.

The scope of the programme, however, was exceptional, even for the time. A stupendous first half contained the prelude from Wagner's *Die Meistersinger*, Bach's Suite in D, the overture to Mozart's *Magic Flute*, Elgar's *Enigma Variations* (premièred by Richter in the St James's Hall in Piccadilly just five years earlier) and Liszt's First Hungarian Rhapsody. And as if this formidable array of schools and styles didn't show off the new orchestra's prowess sufficiently, Beethoven's Fifth Symphony was rolled out after the interval.

But the real fascination for the packed audience was in hearing how this new ensemble performed with one of the truly great European maestros on the podium. The vast, prodigiously bearded Richter was then sixty-one, and in every sense a towering presence in the musical life of both Germany and England, the country he virtually adopted as his second homeland. He was a man with decided musical tastes, which certainly included Wagner (Richter had been involved in the very first Bayreuth Festival), and definitely did not include anything emanating from France – 'There is no French music,' he once declared.

English music and musicians, however, he adored. In Germany and Austria he had championed the music of Hubert Parry, Charles Villiers Stanford, Frederick Cowen and, most of all, the rising young star Edward Elgar. Indeed, so energetic were his Anglophile musical exertions that the acerbic Viennese critic Eduard Hanslick took him to task for turning Vienna Philharmonic concerts into 'a little English colony'. In an age of rising nationalist fervour – particularly when it came to the rivalry between Britain and Germany – Richter's bilateral sympathies were unusual.

Not surprisingly, then, he soon gravitated towards England itself. As early as 1879 he was conducting an annual series in London that became known simply as the 'Richter Concerts'. Twenty years later he accepted the chief conductor's post at the well-funded and ambitious Hallé Society in Manchester (an organisation, ironically, that many British music-lovers in the 1890s would have considered to be a 'little German colony').

To have recruited this giant to their cause was a real coup for the LSO's founders, and Richter, who became the orchestra's principal conductor, proved to be a staunch ally. Of course, he could be ferocious towards players who made careless mistakes. Once, conducting Dvořák's 'New World' Symphony in Manchester, he was infuriated by a wrong entry from a cymbal player. Years later, rehearsing the same work with the same orchestra (minus the unfortunate percussionist, who had 'moved on'), he stopped the music just before the offending moment, and growled: 'Iss he shtill alife?'

Yet this kind of rigour was exactly what the new LSO needed. 'Gentlemen,' he told the orchestra just before that first concert, 'for you to be successful there must be discipline, artistic discipline.' That afternoon, by all accounts, there was. The brilliance of that concert 'staggered all those that knew the London orchestral world at that time,' Boult recalled. His words are confirmed by the review that appeared in *The Times* the next morning. Though it was unsigned (no journalists' names appeared in *The Times* until well into the 1960s) it was written by the chief music critic, J. A. Fuller-Maitland:

Nothing could have been more propitious than the inaugural performance of the newly-constituted 'London Symphony Orchestra' yesterday afternoon in the Queen's-hall; and the large audience, feeling, no doubt, that whatever may be the ultimate fate of the undertaking, it is for the public good that first-rate orchestras should be multiplied, applauded the orchestra with the utmost enthusiasm. As everybody knows, the new band has been formed by those who felt unable to agree to the stipulations made by the directors of the Queen's-hall Orchestra in regard to the employment of deputies; these players have been joined by a smaller body of former members of the Queen's-hall band who left it on another matter now well-nigh forgotten . . . Thus . . . much more than three-quarters of the players have enjoyed the advantages of working with Mr. Wood for longer or shorter periods. This of itself brings about a satisfactory unanimity in the matter of phrasing, &c., and as none of the prominent players availed themselves of the privilege of sending deputies as substitutes – the privilege for which they had seceded from the other organization – the volume of tone was magnificent, and the effect of the performance under Dr. Richter was truly memorable. It is clearly impossible that the great conductor can accept the post of permanent conductor, and it is to be hoped that some Englishman will be found to possess the skill and experience to lead the new institution to the success for which every one must hope.

On the strength of such acclaim the LSO took the plunge and announced a season of six self-promoted concerts for the following autumn and spring. But Richter's wise words about discipline were not always heeded in the decades to come.

The rivalry between the new LSO and the Queen's Hall Orchestra must have been cut-throat in the winter of 1904–5. Wood did not necessarily have to trawl 'The Glue-Pot' to find second-string replacements for the star players who had deserted him. Thanks to music-education pioneers such as George Grove, London had no fewer than ten musical conservatoires by 1904, producing hundreds of eager young instrumentalists each year, better trained than ever before. But the leap needed to progress from student to professional music-making was – and remains – immense. Students learn by making mistakes acceptable in colleges but not in concert halls. Professionals, especially in London where plentiful rehearsal time is as rare as a brilliant blue sky, must get nearly everything right first time.

'The position for the first few months was that Henry Wood had a great public following but a poor orchestra; and that the LSO had no public at all but certainly was a splendid body of instrumentalists.' That was the recollection of Sir Landon Ronald, who by that time had graduated from being Nellie Melba's pet piano accompanist into an ambitious young conductor. But Ronald's self-serving 1931 memoirs, aptly named *Myself and Others*, are not entirely trustworthy on LSO matters – as we shall see. He believed, like *The Times*'s critic, that the new orchestra should appoint an 'Englishman of skill and experience' to be its permanent maestro – and that he himself fitted the description like a glove.

More objective, perhaps, are the comments of William Maitland Strutt, an astute amateur observer of the London scene, though only eighteen at the time. 'Wood set about training a new Queen's Hall Orchestra, and succeeded tolerably well, though the new organisation was vastly inferior to the old,' he wrote. 'But the spheres of activity of the two orchestras very shortly became more or less clearly separated. The London Symphony undertook the performances of the standard masterpieces under men like Richter and Nikisch, and ignored the drawing power of great soloists and "popular" music.' Consequently, he concludes, the LSO attracted a 'far more cultivated and discriminating public'.

In its determination not to become the personal fiefdom of a single maestro, the LSO hit almost by accident on the concept of the 'guest conductor'. Until that time, the opportunity to compare the interpretations and styles of different conductors at work with the same orchestra was virtually unknown in Britain. That all changed with the LSO's early seasons in which (with the exception of Richter, who usually directed four or five concerts each year) nearly every programme brought with it a different hand on the baton.

They were impressive hands, too. Included as conductors in the 1904–5 season were three eminent British composers – Elgar, Stanford and Frederick Cowen – as well as the mercurial Hungarian Artur Nikisch (who would assume an increasingly important role in the orchestra's life), the German Fritz Steinbach and a Frenchman, Edouard Colonne. The latter leavened the predominantly Germanic repertoire of those early years (Brahms, Bach and Beethoven) by conducting large chunks of Berlioz – presumably infuriating Richter in the process.

During the next few seasons, the list of conductors would broaden still further. The young but already monstrously self-assured Thomas Beecham shared the podium with Richter at one concert. A Russian double-bass virtuoso turned conductor, who then billed himself as 'Sergius Kussewitzky', but who later would achieve worldwide fame with the Boston Symphony Orchestra as Serge Koussevitzky, made a cataclysmic impression by conducting the British première of Skryabin's 1907 *Poem of Ecstasy* – a work little heard today, but then regarded as the last word in decadence, excess and degeneracy. (Even as late as 1921, when the LSO played it at the Three Choirs Festival, Elgar wrote: 'To think that Gloucester Cathedral should ever echo to such music. It's a wonder the gargoyles don't fall off the tower.')

In rather more austere style, Felix Weingartner first appeared with the LSO in 1908 – the year he succeeded Mahler as conductor of the Vienna Opera. Dignified, scrupulous and courteous, he would return to the orchestra constantly over the next thirty years. And what of Mahler himself, generally regarded then as the finest conductor of the age, rather than as a composer? The great man wrote to the LSO and asked for an engagement in 1907, the year he went to New York to conduct the Metropolitan Opera and the New York Philharmonic. Oddly, the LSO directors appear to have turned him down. Perhaps his reputation for chewing up orchestral players in rehearsal had spread to London.

However, that same year the LSO board did decide to invite the forty-year-old Arturo Toscanini (then known chiefly as an opera conductor, with La Scala, Milan) to conduct a concert. Not surprisingly, nothing came of the invitation. Toscanini was wise to the way London's musical life worked, and he wanted nothing to do with it. Two years earlier he had written to an agent who had clearly made a similar offer:

I fear working abroad because of the dizzying rush in the preparation of both opera productions and concerts, but I especially fear London because I remember a performance of *Götterdämmerung* [probably in 1898 or 1900] in which the orchestra was sightreading the opera's final scene before an audience. The audience noticed nothing, and the press found the performance superb. Under no circumstances would I want to find myself in such a situation.

It would be nearly thirty years before the fiery Italian struck up a close relationship with a London orchestra. And then it was with the BBC Symphony Orchestra – very much to the LSO's annoyance and discomfort.

3 Tours and tribulations
1906–25

top On the SS *Baltic*, LSO American Tour, 1912
Sightseeing in Washington DC, LSO American Tour, 1912

previous page LSO, Hereford Festival, 1921

George Anderson, who played second clarinet in the very first LSO concert and was on the orchestra's board for many years, once uttered one of the great understatements of music history. From the outset, he recalled, the LSO had been 'a difficult and outlandish company to run, especially from the auditing point of view'. Nobody who has had any financial dealings with any London orchestra at virtually any period in the past century would doubt the truth of that. The very first LSO programme contained a plea for financial support. And it would be no great exaggeration to claim that the orchestra lived hand-to-mouth for the next eighty-five-odd years.

In a salaried orchestra it is the management and the chief funding authority – the city, the broadcasting organisation, or the endowment trust – that takes responsibility for keeping the outfit solvent and the players in work. But the LSO players had opted for something much more dangerous. They were their own management, their own shareholders, their own fundraisers. In good years, this was wonderful. Overheads were minimal, since there were no non-playing office staff to pay. (Even today, the back-up staff employed by the London orchestras are a tiny fraction of the clerical multitudes that American orchestras of quite modest artistic accomplishments seem to find necessary.) So the profits went directly to the players.

In 1908, for instance, when the orchestra found, somewhat to its surprise, that it had amassed a bank balance of £1,600, the board decided to distribute £1,000 between the members as a bonus on top of their concert fees. (Indeed, so flush with funds did the board feel in that year that it turned down Newman's offer for the LSO to replace the Queen's Hall Orchestra at the Proms.) Much the same distribution of yearly bonuses went on in the mid-1920s when, for a few prosperous seasons between war and slump, the British economy was strong, people had money to spend, and the LSO had virtually no competition in the London musical world.

But those were the good years. They were far outnumbered by the indifferent or the plain awful ones. Right from the start, the LSO's founders had to immerse themselves in the labyrinthine calculations and slippery negotiations that have characterised the 'business side' of music since little David played on his harp. That was especially the case when it came to hiring soloists and conductors for its own concert series – in which, of course, the players themselves bore the brunt of any box-office shortfall. In 1904, as in 2004, there was a breed of star soloist who was fully aware of his own worth, and determined to extract every penny of it from those bold enough, wealthy enough, or rash enough to hire him. One such was Ignacy Jan Paderewski, virtuoso pianist and, later, Prime Minister of his beloved Poland. His fee was a hundred pounds a night – an astonishing demand at a time when top conductors usually settled for a gentlemanly fifty guineas, or else (as often happened in the LSO's early days) ended up paying for the concert themselves, on the grounds that conducting this orchestra in the Queen's Hall was an excellent showcase for their talents.

But if the orchestra could sell five hundred extra five-shilling seats on the strength of Paderewski's name, the hundred pounds 'invested' in his fee could be said to have produced a twenty-five per cent return. Better still, if it could sell five hundred annual subscriptions to its whole concert series (priced at £3, £2 and £1) on the strength of the great Polish pianist's appearance, the profit would be enormous. The marketing tactics that American orchestras imagined they had invented in the 1970s (and British orchestras imagined they had pinched from the Americans in the 1980s) would have been regarded as rather old hat to the impresarios of Edwardian London.

There was little room for sentiment in this crude calculation of a conductor or soloist's box-office worth. Hence the orchestra brutally and hurtfully dropped Elgar as its principal conductor in 1911, and later did the same to Hamilton Harty. For all their superb musicality, such figures simply didn't pull in the crowds in sufficient numbers for the LSO to stay solvent.

The real financial danger, however, was over-ambition. The new orchestra needed to prove itself, to keep on making a splash, if it was to stay ahead of the competition, and this meant taking risks. But risks sometimes proved costly. A big Wagner concert in the second season brought in a handsome £271 at the box office, but cost £330 to mount, whereas a normal Richter concert might take £265 but cost only £165. And so on. No wonder that members were told at the 1906 annual general meeting that the orchestra had entered into 'various speculations, some of which, in the nature of things, proved disastrous'.

One such speculation was the orchestra's agreement to play some concerts at the Crystal Palace. The huge glass barn in South London, built for the 1851 Great Exhibition and destroyed by fire in 1936, had reached its musical zenith – if 'musical' is the right word – with the incredible Handel celebrations of the 1880s, involving four-thousand-strong choruses and five-hundred-strong orchestras. (Not, perhaps, the last word in authenticity – but the performance must have been heard in Calais.) By the early twentieth century, however, its best days were over, and the LSO's decision to put on a concert series there in tandem with the resident promoter turned into a nightmare. A bad debt of £200 was still being chased a year later.

The LSO's first foreign tour was another problematic venture. The players must have been flattered and thrilled when, within months of its foundation, the orchestra received an invitation to play two concerts in Paris's magnificent Théâtre du Châtelet in January 1906. This was one of those unusual historical moments when the English and the French, both alarmed by the rising might of Germany, were putting on one of their strained but entertaining displays of *entente cordiale*. Indeed, the very phrase stems from a treaty that had been made two years earlier. Edward VII had just visited France (wittily signing himself 'Edouard' whilst on Gallic soil), and the British Parliament was at that very moment contemplating an even closer link between the two nations, debating a Bill that would enable a tunnel to be built under the English Channel. (It was subsequently rejected by MPs who thought it an absurd notion.)

The LSO's Paris jaunt was very much part of this overt display of Francophilia. In some ways it went well: not only did a hundred players make the Channel crossing, they were also accompanied by three hundred sturdy voices from the Leeds Chorus, as well as a roster of conductors (Colonne, Stanford and the composer André Messager) cannily selected from both sides of the Channel.

But if you wanted to construct a series of programmes specifically designed to repel French audiences from British music, you could probably do no better than to replicate the stodgy programmes of insipid Cowen, worthy Stanford, dull Parry and mediocre Mackenzie that the LSO laid before the Châtelet crowd – comprising music-lovers, remember, who were used to the subtleties of Debussy, Chausson and Fauré. The programme bore every mark of being concocted by a Foreign Office committee rather than the orchestra – and it probably was. Even Elgar was represented only by his immature cantata *King Olaf*.

The *Daily Telegraph*'s correspondent loyally reported that 'the entente cordiale has in the artistic world produced no event comparable in importance with the demonstration – I may say the revelation – offered this afternoon to the Parisian public of English musical art'. But one French critic – a noted Anglophile in his sympathies – commented that the choice of repertoire put the cause of English music in his country back by fifty years.

This, however, was not the chief cause of the players' dismay. To add financial injury to aesthetic discomfort, the trip had left most of them out of pocket to the tune of a hefty five guineas – since they had to pay for deputies to cover the engagements they had missed in London. The LSO board thought this entirely acceptable, 'the splendid advertisement obtained compensating for the financial loss sustained'. Many players didn't agree. At the AGM that year an amendment was passed forbidding the directors from entering into other such 'speculations' without consulting the membership. It was a sharp rap over the knuckles to the LSO's leading lights: a reminder that this was one orchestra where the 'humble' rank and file couldn't be ignored. Fifty years later, a similar trial of strength would trigger something closer to a civil war than a gentlemanly dispute. And only in the late 1980s, with the advent of Clive Gillinson's era as managing director, did the bulk of the LSO players finally agree that the long-term artistic health of the orchestra should invariably be put before short-term financial gain of the players.

*

The lifeline that kept the orchestra afloat, even mildly prosperous, in those pre-1914 seasons was not its own concert series, but the plentiful supply of choral societies, festivals and regional promoters queuing up to hire it. Yet how could this be possible? Wasn't turn-of-the-century Britain famously 'the land without music'? (*Das Land ohne Musik* was the title of a collection of essays about British life published in 1920 by the German historian Oscar Schmitz, but the insulting epithet seems to have been in circulation for decades before that.)

The answer is that Victorian and Edwardian Britain was indeed bereft of the formalised and extensive network of professional musical activities so well advanced in Germany, with its municipal or court opera houses, its securely constituted and funded orchestras, and its long-established tradition of musical scholarship in universities. What's more, such professional music-making as did exist was very much a foreign-led affair. Britain had (and still has) a long tradition of adopting distinguished overseas musicians as its own, from Handel in the eighteenth century and Hallé in the nineteenth to Brendel and Solti in the twentieth. In the days of the Empire they came because London paid best. Later, when Britain became poor, they came because Britain's politics and way of life remained, on the whole, easy-going, congenial and libertarian – at least when compared with the totalitarian horrors of the countries from which many of them had fled. Though it is probably wrong to blame the woeful shortcomings of home-grown Georgian and Victorian talent on this influx of brilliant immigrants, the ubiquitous abundance of foreigners in British musical life probably made the problem of native mediocrity seem less pressing than it was.

Yet the very amateurishness of the indigenous British musical scene was also the source of its unique strength. A genuine grassroots enthusiasm for music was nurtured in the brass bands of the northern collieries and mills, and (much aided by Vincent Novello's cheap paperback vocal scores) in the mighty choral societies and burgeoning church choirs of provincial Victorian England. The annual festivals mounted in prosperous industrial towns such as Leeds and Birmingham – as well as the more venerable jamborees arranged in the ancient cathedral cities (the oldest being the Three Choirs Festival, which had been hosted by Worcester, Gloucester and Hereford in turn since the eighteenth century) – gave this mass musical movement a thrilling focus. They also offered the biggest commissioning fees, which perhaps explains why the leading British composers, even in the early twentieth century, wrote huge choral works (*The Dream of Gerontius*, *A Sea Symphony*, *Belshazzar's Feast*) long before they could think of writing operas.

For the hundreds of amateur singers who took part, the biggest thrill of these festivals was the chance they offered to work, for a day or perhaps a week, with the professionals – the famous soloists, the charismatic maestro, and particularly the big orchestra 'up from London'. (Even when times got hard, in the early 1920s, the provincial festivals were still engaging orchestras of up to 114 players.) It was this market that the new LSO comprehensively cornered.

How was it so successful at freezing its rivals out of the picture? One answer is surely that players such as John Solomon or Arthur Payne had cultivated festival and choral contacts stretching from Eastbourne to Edinburgh over many years. When they defected to the new band they simply took their contacts with them, rather as a leading lawyer might encourage his clients to follow him if he joined a rival law firm. And because the LSO was self-promoting, it could easily match, if not undercut, the rates quoted by fixers who added their own ten per cent to the bill of the orchestras they supplied.

Another answer, however, might be that the LSO simply outshone the opposition. 'I had been brought up symphonically on the Hallé – a very solid orchestra playing under the even solider Hans Richter – and the solidest German masterworks,' recalled the great English writer J. B. Priestley (casting his mind back to events that had happened in his native Bradford fifty years earlier). 'Then one night some strangers arrived and at once changed the whole atmosphere of St George's Hall . . . charging it with electricity and apparently filling it with colour from the palest purest blue to menacing clouds of indigo and violet sheets of lightning. These sorcerers from the South, for whom nobody had prepared me, were the LSO conducted by Nikisch.'

These regional engagements became meat and drink to the nascent LSO – sometimes literally so. An engagement to play for the mighty choral society in Huddersfield was undertaken in return for '£125, and a substantial meat tea'. Admittedly, the orchestra was sometimes worked ferociously hard for its ham sandwiches (or was it lamb stew?). One incredible festival at Bristol in 1912 included, in just four days, all of Wagner's *Ring* cycle (its first British concert performances), plus four full-scale symphonic concerts. Imagine performing *Götterdämmerung* from noon till six p.m., and then returning at eight to play Schubert's 'Unfinished' Symphony, Mendelssohn's opera *Loreley*, the *1812* overture and 'various vocal solos'. One suspects that the players sought out something rather stronger than a 'meat tea', substantial or otherwise.

The regional festivals were not the only people queuing up to book the new orchestra. Dame Clara Butt hired the LSO for one of her much-admired stentorian displays of lung power. A Belgian promoter paid the orchestra £220 to travel to Antwerp for a single concert (though the LSO, stung by its Crystal Palace misadventure, demanded the cash seven days in advance).

And in January 1907 the orchestra was hired under its own name, for the first and last time, by Covent Garden (where many of its members played anyway) for a month-long season of German opera whose contents rivalled the Bristol marathon for posterior-numbing duration and intensity. In four weeks, under a roster of conductors that included Nikisch and the Vienna Opera maestro Franz Schalk, the orchestra was expected to plough through six performances of *Lohengrin*, five of *Meistersinger*, four of *Walküre*, four of *Flying Dutchman*, three each of *Tristan*, *Fidelio* and *Der Freischütz*, two of *Tannhäuser* and (for light relief, presumably) one of Nicolai's *Merry Wives of Windsor*. For this the LSO principals received a comparatively princely £8 8s. a week.

To nobody's great surprise (except the promoter's, presumably) London's taste for such heavy-duty Teutonic fare proved limited, and the season closed a week early. Then tragedy struck. The SS *Berlin*, carrying most of the singers back to Germany, hit a sandbank in fog, and many performers died when the ship sank.

Far more significant for the orchestra in the long term were the regional tours organised by a slightly devious but inventive impresario called Percy Harrison. They started in 1905 and continued right through to the First

World War, at which point Harrison announced that, as a contribution to the war effort, he would expect the LSO to tour for only half its pre-war fee. The LSO retorted that, if this were the case, it would of course send Harrison only half the usual number of players. The relationship appears to have cooled shortly after that.

The 1905 tour, however, was a wonderful showcase for the new orchestra. In eight days, courtesy of the utterly reliable railway network built by the Victorians and slowly ruined by every subsequent generation, the LSO gave concerts in Birmingham, Liverpool, Manchester, Sheffield, Glasgow, Edinburgh, Newcastle and Bradford. Its conductor was a forty-six-year-old composer who, although by then hailed as the finest that England had produced for two centuries, was still sufficiently hard up to jump at Mr Harrison's fee: twenty-six guineas a day, plus full railway expenses. His name was Edward Elgar. For the next three decades his story would be inextricably intertwined with that of the LSO.

*

Elgar, even at the height of his fame in 1905, was complex, chippy, insecure, brittle and prone to frightening mood swings. He was also an outsider, three times over: he was not a Londoner, he was a tradesman's son who left school at fifteen, and he was a Catholic. All this at a time when the British Establishment was overwhelmingly metropolitan, aristocratic and Protestant. What's more, fame (and a certain amount of fortune) had come too late in his life to change what was embedded deep in his psyche.

He was already forty in 1899 when the assurance and mystery of his first true masterpiece, the *Enigma Variations*, gripped all of musical London. Later in life, it's true, he learnt to play the Edwardian-squire role to gruff perfection. But that was all it was – an act. Though he lived for a while in Hampstead, he was never comfortable dealing with the clubbable, complacent and generally philistine cliques of upper-crust London society. Utterly unlike Benjamin Britten in many other respects, he resembled England's other truly great twentieth-century composer in that one crucial matter: both felt themselves to be, in some significant way, forever on the wrong side of the tracks. (This perhaps explains many of the unresolved tensions to be found in both composers' music. Significantly, Britten – who never claimed to be an ardent Elgarian – conducted the LSO in surely the most revelatory recording of *The Dream of Gerontius* ever made.)

All of this insecurity must have entered into Elgar's dealings with the LSO, the most metropolitan and 'aristocratic' of orchestras – in the sense that its players all thought themselves a cut above the rest of musical humanity. Nor did Elgar, unlike Beecham or the many 'society conductors' who inflicted themselves on the LSO in those early years, ever have the income to subsidise his own career either as conductor or composer. On the contrary; he depended on the orchestra much more than it did on him, as the players were aware.

Against that must be set one small but significant word. Genius. English music hadn't seen anything like Elgar since the days of Henry Purcell, and he had died two hundred and ten years earlier. The LSO players must have sensed the potential of the young man from Worcester before almost anyone else. Some of them would have played his early choral and orchestral music at the Three Choirs Festival, where it was regularly programmed from 1890 onwards. (Elgar himself was to be found among the back-desk violins in the Three Choirs orchestra in the 1880s – playing under Dvořák's direction on one occasion.) And many of them would have been in the orchestra at the St James's Hall in 1899 on that momentous night when Richter premièred the *Enigma Variations*.

They would immediately have noted Elgar's masterly use of instruments, his instinctive gift for memorable melody and ripe, richly chromatic harmony. Most of all, they would have appreciated his ability (hitherto unprecedented in British music) to build large-scale musical arguments that gripped the ear, satisfied the intellect and touched the heart from first moment to last. Had they not been so struck, the *Enigma Variations* would never have been given such prominence in the LSO's opening concert. Nor would they have invited the composer to conduct a concert in their first season, nor their first regional tour.

In fact it is hard to think of another relationship between a great composer and an orchestra that lasted as long, or went as deep, as Elgar's with the LSO. Mahler had an intense, not to say torrid, love–hate affair with the Vienna Philharmonic, but virtually all of it was in the form of a *ménage à trois*, conducted through other men's music. The same applies to the New York Philharmonic and Leonard Bernstein, with the added complication that Lenny was as promiscuous with his orchestras as he was with his lovers. True, the Leningrad Philharmonic became Shostakovich's symphonic mouthpiece, but Mravinsky was the man on the podium, not Shostakovich. And so on. Elgar's thirty-year association with the LSO, which lasted until the composer was literally on his deathbed, can justifiably be called unique.

Yet it was never entirely easy. The first problem was that the orchestra clearly had trouble getting to grips with the Elgar pieces with which the individual players were not already familiar. That may seem surprising; after all, the music is brilliantly orchestrated and hardly avant-garde in style, even by the standards of 1904. Yet Elgar's compositions, more than most, live or die according to how much their interpreters understand the music's idiom – the ebb and flow of rubato, the restraint, the wistfulness, the nobility. Today, English orchestras can turn on 'Elgarian style' at the drop of a baton. But that wasn't the case when the music was new – especially given the early LSO's penchant for doing concerts on a wing and a prayer. Elgar was clearly unhappy, for instance, with how the LSO tackled his majestic but fiendishly demanding *Introduction and Allegro* for strings when he conducted it in London in March 1905; only when the piece was constantly repeated on the Harrison tour did the composer confide to Mrs Dora Powell ('Dorabella' of *Enigma* fame) that he had 'at last' got the *Introduction and Allegro* played as he wished.

The lack of rehearsal was, by all accounts, even more detrimental to the LSO's première of the Cello Concerto (with Felix Salmond the soloist), some fourteen years later. Insufficient preparation apparently turned this superb but muted masterpiece, which was always going to be difficult for its first audience, into a well-nigh inscrutable non-event. Here, however, the fault seems to have lain with the man conducting the rest of the programme that night – the boundlessly energetic but disorganised Albert Coates. Desperate to impress in his first concert as the LSO's principal conductor, he spent most of the available time rehearsing his pet Russian composers, Skryabin and Borodin, leaving little time for the tragic new English masterpiece to be rehearsed.

The second problem about Elgar, for the LSO directors, was that, at the very moment when they chose to hitch their wagon to the composer's star by making him their principal conductor, they badly misjudged his pulling power at the box office – an error that could have been fatal for an orchestra which lived or died by its income from tickets. It was, admittedly, an easy mistake to have made. When the orchestra gave the first London performance of Elgar's First Symphony, on 7 December 1908 (a few days after Richter and the Hallé had premièred it in Manchester), the event had been a triumph. Richter had set the tone, prefacing the orchestra's first rehearsal with the words: 'Gentlemen, let us now rehearse the greatest symphony of modern times, written by the greatest modern composer, and not only in this country' – an incredible endorsement, coming from a German in an age of ever-growing nationalistic rivalry. But the reaction of the London public, which had flocked to the Queen's Hall to hear the new symphony (giving the orchestra the biggest payday of its four-year existence) was no less rapturous. The symphony went on to be performed a hundred times in its first year.

The public mood had changed, however, by the time the LSO appointed Elgar as its principal conductor, after Richter retired in 1911. Edward VII was dead, and with him had died much of the swagger, the blithe assurance, the jingoism, the pomp and the circumstance of the era that bears his name. It was of course monstrously unfair that Elgar, the most sensitive and subtle of musicians, had become irredeemably associated with that era. But there was no doubting the fact that for younger listeners, in particular, his music suddenly seemed to have 'an almost intolerable air of smugness, self-assurance and autocratic benevolence' (as Constant Lambert was later to put it). There was still interest in his new pieces, but his music no longer quite chimed with the times.

That was implicitly acknowledged by Elgar himself at the première of his Second Symphony. As he accepted the polite but scarcely ecstatic applause, he reputedly turned to Reed and muttered: 'What's wrong with them, Billy? They're sitting like stuffed pigs.'

The LSO's reaction to Elgar's declining pulling power at the box office (and also, perhaps, to critical reviews in the London press of his conducting – particularly of other men's music) was brutal, but probably necessary in commercial terms. He appeared just six times as principal conductor, and was then unceremoniously dumped in favour of names more likely to attract audiences. Undoubtedly, the composer was wounded by this treatment, and perhaps even more so the following year when the orchestra – bowing to pressure from American sponsors and promoters – dropped plans to programme any of his music for its historic trip to the United States.

Yet curiously, in the late 1920s, when Elgar's music was about as far out of fashion as it was ever to go, the composer's relationship with the LSO blossomed as never before. The catalyst was Fred Gaisberg, the visionary and highly influential figure who controlled HMV's recording output almost from the beginning. He persuaded Elgar to record virtually his entire compositional output with several orchestras, but particularly with the LSO. Thus was born the famous sequence of recordings that remain as a superlative testament of how Elgar wanted his music to sound (which was, usually, a lot less indulgent than most modern conductors make it). Most notably they include the First and Second Symphonies, the Violin Concerto (the unforgettable performance with the seventeen-year-old Yehudi Menuhin) and *Falstaff* – recorded on the first day that the new Abbey Road studios in St John's Wood were open for business.

But the most poignant recording is the one that Elgar didn't conduct, but supervised from his bedroom in Malvern. In early 1934 it became clear that the composer was fading fast, so Gaisberg set up a land-line linking the composer's bedroom with Abbey Road, where the LSO was preparing to record the Triumphal March and Woodland Interlude from *Caractacus* under Lawrence Collingwood's direction. The playing could be relayed directly to the composer, and his comments relayed back to the orchestra. Reed, who was as close to Elgar as any musician ever was, recalled this final, touching (if slightly bizarre) encounter between composer and orchestra in his memoir, *Elgar as I Knew Him*:

Sir Edward's voice was heard, welcoming the players, the conductor, and the others assembled. He said: 'I am afraid my voice is rather like an old crow, but I hope you can all hear what I have to say.' Then he asked us to play over what we had been rehearsing and when this was done he criticised it from his bed – too fast here – the clarinet must come out more there – the flute – the oboe – the strings: he had some little hint to give about all these matters. He listened to the actual recording after the trials had been made, and expressed himself well satisfied with the afternoon's work, just as if he had been at the studio in person.

The date was 22 January 1934. Thirty-two days later, Elgar was dead. The entire LSO played at his memorial service in Worcester Cathedral.

*

Without doubt the high-water mark of the LSO's first decade was its North American tour, undertaken in April 1912 under Artur Nikisch's direction. No European orchestra had ever crossed the Atlantic before, and it could not have taken the LSO players very long to work out why. Even in the twenty-first century, to take an orchestra on tour is a fraught and expensive process. 'You cannot say you have known the full terror of being in the music business,' one London orchestral manager once wryly observed, 'until you have glanced out of the window of the plane in which your orchestra is taking off, and seen your timpani still standing on the tarmac.' No wonder that orchestral folklore the world over is saturated with 'tour' stories, usually involving brass players, language misunderstandings, alcohol, the uncanny propensity of all foreign hotels to look alike at four in the morning, and the local police.

But today there are planes and high-quality hotels, at least in those parts of the world likely to welcome a Western orchestra. In 1912 they slept on boats and trains, snatched their meals at station buffets, and were shackled to a schedule that might just have worked if each day had twenty-six hours rather than the customary twenty-four, but which guaranteed that virtually every concert began late – and that some finished on the day after they started. Not that the American audiences encountered by the LSO that year seemed in the least bit perturbed. 'Oh, we often wait until midnight for a concert to start – the trains are so frequently late,' one Boston lady told an LSO player.

The players gave an astonishing twenty-eight concerts in twenty-one days – starting and ending in Carnegie Hall, New York, and then venturing as far west as Wichita, Kansas, and as far north as Toronto and Montreal. They slept, thirty-two to a coach, in a specially chartered Pullman train that was supposed to arrive at its next destination early each morning so that the players could breakfast and wash in a hotel. Sometimes, however, the train was so late that breakfast had to be grabbed, literally, on the run. The violinist Wynn Reeves recalled:

We arrived at a small station. As soon as the train stopped, I streaked across to the buffet, seizing all I could see, removing glass covers in ten seconds, by which time the buffet was being mobbed. The proprietor, brandishing a revolver, came dashing out from behind the counter, and shouted: 'I refuse to serve another thing until I know who is paying for this.' We looked at the counter which, by this time, was as stripped as if it had been attacked by a swarm of locusts. We assured the proprietor that Mr Fales would pay [Warren Fales was the Rhode Island millionaire and ardent Nikisch fan who was bankrolling the tour] and returned to the train.'

This invigorating scramble round North America was the doing of one Howard Pew, a New York impresario who had spent the best part of two years negotiating with the orchestra and arranging the itinerary. The discussions had not gone entirely smoothly. Pew's main interest was in touring Nikisch, who had made a huge impression on American music-lovers twenty years earlier when he was conductor of the Boston Symphony Orchestra. The question of whether the orchestra accompanying him should be British, German or peopled by little green men from Mars was very much incidental to his main preoccupation.

But Nikisch's association with the LSO went right back to its opening season. And one can imagine the buccaneering entrepreneurs of the London orchestra recognising this unique opportunity to establish a foothold in the prosperous American music market much more quickly than, say, their counterparts at the Berlin Philharmonic or the Leipzig Gewandhaus (the two great German orchestras that Nikisch directed, simultaneously, between 1895 and 1922).

For whatever reason, the LSO was chosen. But then came a squabble about repertoire. The LSO wanted to fly the flag by playing lots of Elgar. Nikisch – not quite such a fan of all things English as Richter was – finally agreed to conduct the *Enigma Variations* and the First Symphony. But back in New York a meddlesome and self-important journalist called Blumenberg – editor of the influential American journal, the *Musical Courier* – told Pew that his periodical wouldn't support the tour if all this nasty new British music was included. His prejudice mattered, apparently. So Pew forced the LSO to drop the Elgar in favour of more Wagner, Tchaikovsky and Beethoven. As a result, not a note of British music was played during the first American tour by a British orchestra.

However, the LSO had reason to thank Pew for one thing. Because he wanted to reschedule the dates of some concerts, the tour started a week earlier than had been originally planned. That meant a last-minute change of travel arrangements. The hundred LSO players, librarian and porter were now to travel from Euston to Liverpool on 28 March and board the White Star liner, the SS *Baltic*. One may imagine the grumbles as the players hastily rearranged their own timetables of playing and teaching. But St Cecilia – or whoever watches over the fortunes of musicians – must have smiled on the LSO that year. For until Pew's change of plan, the orchestra had been booked to travel on the maiden journey of a much-discussed 'unsinkable' new liner – the SS *Titanic*.

Despite all the hardships, the tour was ultimately a triumph. In 1912, Nikisch's alchemy was at its most powerful – he was a mesmerising, brilliant figure, the very antithesis of the stately and solid Richter. ('I am a Hungarian-Hungarian; he is a German-Hungarian,' he quipped.) Known as 'der Magier', he invariably conducted from memory, and never played the same piece the same way twice. 'You should make every performance a complete improvisation,' he told Henry Wood. Yet he exercised complete authority over the players, conveyed via an exquisite repertoire of hand movements and facial expressions. It is said that he started Weber's *Oberon* overture just by raising an eyebrow. 'He doesn't seem to conduct, but rather exercises some mysterious spell,' Tchaikovsky once commented.

The LSO tour clearly found Nikisch in top form, and the LSO – already fired up by the excitement of crossing the Atlantic – ready to be galvanised. To Edgar Wilby, in the second violins, the first sounds of the orchestra in the Carnegie Hall came like 'an electric shock'. 'It made one feel proud of oneself,' he wrote.

The concerts made just as startling an impact on the critics. Before the tour had begun the American newspapers had treated the alleged merits of this new British band with a healthy dose of scepticism. That isn't surprising, for Pew had bombarded them with a level of hype that might make a modern-day Hollywood publicist blush. His posters blithely declared that the orchestra was 'stated by Dr Richter to be the finest in the world', and he yanked ticket prices upwards accordingly. Such tactics are guaranteed to bring out the beast in journalists.

Yet once the critics heard for themselves, they cast cynicism and chauvinism aside, and simply raved. 'The great English band,' wrote the *New York Press* critic, 'played with a vigor, force and temperamental impetuousness that almost lifted the listener out of his seat.' 'It is difficult to refrain from superlatives in attempts to do it justice,' the *New York Herald* chimed in. And even the *New York Times*, in a review stretching to fifteen column inches, could scarce forbear to cheer: 'The orchestra is highly thought of by the Londoners, and deservedly so. The strings have fine solidarity and power. The woodwinds are uncommonly good: first oboe and first clarinet are of unusual delicacy and finish of playing. The brass players are excellent.'

The reviews were similarly enthusiastic everywhere. Yet perhaps the most extraordinary accolade came in the capital. Shortly before they gave a concert that the *Washington Post* declared to be 'the most inspiring heard in Washington in many years', the LSO players were whisked off to the White House, where President Taft shook hands with all one hundred of them – something it is difficult to imagine a Bush or Clinton doing.

The tour had its oddities. Eighteen LSO players, who were also members of the 'King's Private Band', were required to wear their royal medals throughout the trip, presumably so that citizens of His Majesty's former colonies would be suitably awed. One wonders how this hilarious display of stuffy British protocol went down in Wichita, Kansas. In Ohio, meanwhile, a concert was given entirely to students of a women-only university, who afterwards threw themselves enthusiastically at the all-male orchestra.

There were sadder moments, too. One LSO cellist never got to play a note all tour: he broke his leg on the voyage over, and spent three weeks in a New York hospital before rejoining the orchestra for the voyage home. Another player, the second violinist Wallace Sutcliffe, suffered a fatal heart attack in Ottawa, and was buried there.

Nevertheless, the tour came as manna from heaven to the fledgling LSO. It sent out an indisputable message that the band, not yet eight years old, had arrived – not just as the dominant force in British music-making, but as a formidable player on the international stage. In the century to come, the LSO would tour America dozens of times, circumnavigate the globe, and make innumerable excursions into Europe. All stemmed from that audaciously conceived and brilliantly executed transatlantic expedition in 1912.

Yet how arbitrary is the fate that marks some enterprises for glory and others for tragedy and sudden extinction. When the orchestra returned to London, it was immediately engaged to play at a memorial concert in the Albert Hall for victims of the *Titanic* disaster – one of seven orchestras recruited to form what must have been a gargantuan ensemble. But for a tiny quirk of circumstance there would have been only six orchestras playing that evening, and I would not now be writing this book.

*

How did the orchestra sound on that tour? Yes, we know it played with gut strings, wooden flutes, and brass instruments of much smaller bore than the bombastic giants universally favoured today. To modern ears the instrumental timbres would perhaps have seemed sinuous, even wiry. Vibrato was much less liberally applied, portamento (the string player's technique of sliding between notes) much more so. But all this only suggests the available colours on the orchestra's palette. What was the whole picture?

Oddly enough, we know – or at least we have a clue. Shortly after the players returned to England, the board had a discussion about 'the orchestra playing at [sic] a Gramophone Company, the argument being a question of terms'. The terms must have been negotiated satisfactorily, because the orchestra and Nikisch proceeded to record a number of items from the tour repertoire.

The Gramophone Company had been founded in Hayes, Middlesex, fourteen years earlier. It was not the first in the field, but it was among the more progressive, and quickly moved from recording on cumbersome cylinders to discs. By this time, too, it had adopted the trademark that was to become familiar the world over: that of a dog ('Nipper') staring moodily into the gramophone, apparently hypnotised by 'His Master's Voice'. Now, under the visionary leadership of Fred Gaisberg (described at that time, rather grandly, as 'Chief Recorder'), the company was eager to compete with its American rivals by luring the top European musicians into its tiny City Road studio.

Of course, the new-fangled gramophone, with its huge, Sousaphone-style loudspeaker, was still regarded with a mixture of amusement, derision or hostility by many musicians and non-musicians alike. 'Sir, I have tested your machine,' the actor-manager Herbert Beerbohm Tree wrote, to a company soliciting a testimonial. 'It adds a new terror to life and makes death a long-felt want.' But the tide was beginning to turn. Within eight years of its début recording, the LSO would sign its first long-term recording contract, with the Gramophone Company's great rival, Columbia. Of course, that didn't stop the LSO players – in accordance with the time-honoured free-trade traditions of the orchestra – from moonlighting profitably for the Gramophone Company at the same time, under the scarcely impenetrable disguise of 'The Symphony Orchestra, London'.

Those 1912 recordings with Nikisch opened a vital new chapter in the orchestra's life – one that would lead the modern LSO to claim, not without good cause, that it is the world's most recorded orchestra. The hiatus caused by the First World War slowed down the recording industry's growth for a while, but by 1925, when electrical recording replaced the old acoustical method, the orchestra was in the studio at least a dozen times a year. It was in the 1920s that the LSO made the first recording of *The Planets* under Holst himself, and of Strauss's tone poems under the composer's baton. Bruno Walter and Felix Weingartner made classic recordings of the Austro-Germanic symphonic repertoire with the orchestra, and Albert Coates dashed through everything from Wagner to Glinka.

At that time the fee for use of the orchestra's title was £24 15s. a recording – not exactly a princely reward. But by then even the Luddites in the LSO's ranks must have recognised the huge potential of the new medium. Indeed by 1928 (the year that Albert Coates conducted the orchestra's recording of Act III of *Tristan und Isolde* with Göta Ljungberg and Walter Widdop for HMV), some conductors were already demanding 'tied' recording sessions before they would commit themselves to concert engagements, and record companies were increasingly influencing what was heard in concert halls.

The Schubert centenary celebrations of that year, for instance, were dominated by two competitions organised by Columbia – one to 'finish the "Unfinished" Symphony' and the other to write a whole new symphony in honour of Schubert. They were won, respectively, by the composers Frank Merrick and Kurt Atterberg, and the LSO premièred both pieces; neither was strong enough to enter the regular repertoire. The recording industry's prominent part in organising the Schubert centenary proved to be portentous. In the decades to come its priorities would, for better or worse, exert more and more of a grip on the LSO's plans and its members' lives.

Gaisberg later wrote that the pre-1914 LSO which he encountered in those very early recordings produced 'virtuoso playing which was unique at that time'. It is a little hard to ascertain the truth of that now. As one listens to them, through the inevitable fog of decay and distortion, the overwhelming impression is that the players were all crammed inside a cardboard box. That was not far from the truth, as Wynn Reeves recalled:

I remember a series we undertook in midsummer one year. The strings were reduced to two firsts, two seconds, one viola, one cello, one bass, with the minimum of woodwind, brass and percussion. Billy Reed and I were playing into No. 1 bell [the acoustic recording machine], our bows being not more than two inches from the rim. The music being away back under the bell necessitated stooping down to see what we had to play; woe betide me if the music rustled or if my bow touched the bell. Standing behind us with their music-stands leaning on our shoulders were the woodwind blowing in our ears as loudly as possible; behind them again were the brass. High up was an electric fan perched on a block of ice, but perfectly useless as the temperature registered 95 degrees Fahrenheit.

The wonder is that the 1912 Nikisch recordings were made at all, given these circumstances. The playing certainly doesn't strike the modern listener as virtuosic. It is, however, highly dramatic, almost melodramatic, tense, very rhythmic and with a tremendous sense of propulsion after the first few tremulous notes. Of course, technical considerations – primarily the necessity of fitting coherent segments of music onto discs of very limited duration – may account for much of that vim and velocity. Even so, through the barrage of hiss and crackle, it is just about possible to perceive something of the tremendous verve which hit American audiences like an electric shock when they first encountered the LSO.

*

The American tour was the apotheosis of the Edwardian LSO. The Great War with Germany that erupted in August 1914 would, in time, hit the orchestra hard – though in the jingoistic euphoria of the first few weeks that was not immediately apparent. Several players signed up for military service immediately. The LSO board patriotically exempted them from paying deputies for the duration – only to discover that one of those supposedly enlisted was playing nightly in the pit at the Savoy Theatre.

The orchestra as a whole also did its patriotic duty by performing heroic war pieces. Some of them were outstanding. In December 1914 Elgar conducted the première of his recent composition, *Carillon*, a 'recitation with music' that set stirring patriotic words by the Belgian poet Emile Cammaerts with controlled fury. 'Its effect was like the brandishing of a sword,' recalled Elgar's biographer, Basil Milne. 'Nothing else in English art had so truly caught the horror with which the news of Germany's invasion of Poland was received.' Later in the war the LSO was also involved in the premières of Elgar's most touching war music: the noble and haunting settings of Laurence Binyon's poems 'To Women' and 'For the Fallen' (later to become part of *The Spirit of England*). These were performed as preludes to six Queen's Hall performances of *The Dream of Gerontius* which Elgar conducted on consecutive nights in May 1916, in a series organised by Clara Butt to aid the Red Cross. The formidable contralto herself sang the role of the Angel.

Some of the other war premières, by contrast, were clearly very mediocre. In May 1915 the LSO played the first (and possibly last) performance of a *Heroic Overture* by one Montague Phillips. Mr Phillips had originally wanted to call it *Victory Overture*, but the LSO wisely decided that the title was 'somewhat premature' and told the composer to change it. Even the word 'heroic' would have been considered bland and inapt a year later, as news of the dreadful and senseless carnage in Flanders began to filter back to Britain.

What is clear, however, is that the LSO felt under pressure to 'wave the flag' in its choice of music. Despite its shabby expulsion of the 'alien' Borsdorf, the orchestra had come under attack from the nationalistic *Pall Mall Gazette* for programming 'too much German music' in its own concert series. The magazine even accused the players of lacking patriotism, a charge that prompted the LSO board to consult its solicitors (the lawyers wisely advised against suing over such a subjective matter in the tense and volatile atmosphere of wartime England).

But the chief worry for the LSO in those war years was not being libelled but being bankrupted. The great regional music festivals – Birmingham, Cardiff, Norwich, Sheffield, the Three Choirs, Leeds – closed for the duration. And when they returned (if they returned) they were often shadows of their former selves. The era when London orchestral players could confidently rely on ten or more weeks of provincial festival bookings each year was gone for ever.

The effect of the closure of the festivals was compounded by the disastrous drop in subscriptions for the orchestra's own London concert season – a falling off partly caused by the unexpected (and most unwelcome) new phenomenon of air raids. In their financial desperation, the orchestra turned to a man who, over the next thirty years, was to have an extraordinary influence, positive and negative, on the LSO's fortunes.

*

In 1915, Thomas Beecham was thirty-six. Born in St Helens, Lancashire, he was the scion of a wealthy family that had made its fortune from patent medicines (Beecham's Pills and Powders). His conducting talents had come to light when Joseph Beecham, his father, became Mayor of St Helens and engaged the Hallé and Richter to celebrate the great event with a concert in the Town Hall. Richter withdrew at the last minute, and the twenty-year-old Tommy, who would never be accused of lacking chutzpah or confidence, dashed on in his place to conduct Beethoven's Fifth Symphony and Tchaikovsky's Sixth – without either score or rehearsal.

Shortly after that he fell out with his father, travelled widely, and then landed up in London, where his mother's income (a tolerable £4,500 a year; equivalent to about £4 million at today's prices) proved very handy for financing his burgeoning musical ambitions. At first these were orchestral in nature. As Boult noted: 'Sir Thomas, expedient like Lloyd George, formed orchestras for the whim of the moment.' If he didn't actually launch the New Symphony Orchestra (a direct rival and imitator of the LSO in the early days) he certainly financed and controlled it from 1905. Then in 1908 he recruited some of the finest young players in London, including Albert Sammons as leader and a viola section led by Lionel Tertis and Eric Coates, and started the modestly named Beecham Symphony Orchestra.

It would be the first of three indisputably superb orchestras that Beecham would recruit and bankroll. But in 1910 the restless enthusiasms of the young TB swiftly turned away from concerts and towards opera. Reconciliation with his father brought access to much greater riches, and in less than a decade he poured an estimated £300,000 of 'pill money' – a fortune of Aga Khan dimensions – into the production of nearly ninety operas, mostly at Covent Garden, where his father, conveniently, was landlord.

It was a glorious extravagance, and it couldn't last. Beecham senior died; the money ran out; and Tommy spent the rest of his life scurrying between bankruptcy courts, orchestras, opera houses, and a circle of rich friends on whom he came increasingly to depend for the bottomless pits of money he needed to fulfil his musical dreams. He could never quite understand – or at least, he pretended he could never understand – why those wealthy chums were never given the tax breaks in Britain to which their musical patronage would have entitled them in America. 'The Inland Revenue Commission sees only larcenists and Artful Dodgers,' he complained, 'where I see philanthropists and angels.' It is a moan that British millionaires – and those in the arts who desperately solicit some of their spare cash – have been echoing ever since.

Beecham's own brand of musical patronage – his impetuous distribution of vast handouts during the First World War, for instance, which kept not only the LSO in business, but the Hallé and the Royal Philharmonic Society as well – was equally incomprehensible to many of his social peers. Then as now, a large segment of the British Establishment flaunted its philistine instincts fairly brazenly. Beecham's bankruptcy case in 1919 hilariously exposed that. His lawyer, Frederick Maugham, tried to argue in his client's defence that Beecham had not frittered away his vast fortune, but spent it advancing the cause of music. 'And what good does that do anybody?' the judge, Mr Justice Eve, asked. 'That is a question on which opinions may differ,' Maugham gamely replied. 'They do,' the judge responded acidly.

The London musical world was undoubtedly a livelier place for Beecham's fifty-five years of incessant plotting, poaching and scheming – to say nothing of his celebrated quips, which have been ceremoniously collected, polished and published several times by his devoted acolytes. But his very ubiquity made him a source of intense irritation to his colleagues and competitors. When Henry Wood published his autobiography, *My Life in Music*, he gleefully told friends that it contained 'four hundred and ninety-five pages, and not a single reference to Beecham.'

And the question of whether Tommy's multifarious meddlings made London a better place for musicians or audiences has always been a matter of intense dispute. The LSO would certainly have had a smoother ride through the twentieth century if Beecham had not been around to complicate matters by continually upturning the orchestral apple-cart, just when everybody was starting to get comfortable. On the other hand, one might easily argue that by forming new orchestras that were usually markedly superior to the ones which already existed, Beecham was largely responsible for lifting orchestral standards in London over the first half of the twentieth century.

What is indisputable is that without him the LSO's story would be a lot duller.

*

In 1915, the young Beecham must have seemed highly useful – indeed crucial – to the survival of the orchestra. After two successful concerts that season he was invited to become, in effect (though curiously, not in name), the LSO's principal conductor. Not only did he conduct with infectious glee, he also picked fresh and interesting repertoire at a time when everyone else was playing safe – such rarely heard pieces as Berlioz's *Roméo et Juliette*, scenes from Mussorgsky's *Boris Godunov* and, even more esoterically, Granville

Bantock's *Omar Khayyám*. And from the LSO's point of view, not least among his qualities was the small matter of him picking up the tab for the orchestra's fee (or most of it) afterwards.

It was good while it lasted, but nothing in Beecham's life lasted long. As the complications of dealing with his father's estate and his own long list of creditors closed in on him like demons in a nightmare, Beecham temporarily disappeared from the LSO's life. By early 1917 the orchestra was back in the doldrums. With thirty-three members on active service (and one, Sydney Moxon, killed in action), its ranks were being filled by deputies who tended to be either doddery veterans or callow youths (including a precocious teenage cellist called John Barbirolli). More worryingly, audiences for serious symphonic programmes had mostly dried up. The players were reduced to playing Sunday afternoon concerts of 'light classics' at the Palladium and touring suburban halls for rock-bottom rates with programmes of music that were, if possible, even 'lighter' in tone. The board wisely instructed that the LSO's name 'be entirely left out' of the publicity for the latter.

All these efforts were to no avail. The psychology of a nation at war is complex and unpredictable. During the early years of the Second World War, when Britain was under imminent threat of invasion and the British way of life seemed likely to be destroyed for ever, the appetite for music blossomed as never before. The mood in 1916 and 1917 was very different. Devastating news of the mass slaughter in Flanders must have made the very notion of enjoying a good night out seem inappropriate, perhaps even obscene. In one horrendously futile four-month attack on the Somme, four hundred and twenty thousand British men were killed for a net advance of just two miles. Virtually every family in London had someone to grieve. The capital had been bombed; one hundred had died. Food was rationed throughout Britain; restaurants were ordered to go meatless twice a week. The atmosphere was close to despair – 'each slow dusk a drawing down of blinds' – as Wilfred Owen put it.

In certain terrible circumstances, music can comfort the bereaved and inspire the oppressed. That was certainly true of the extraordinarily brave musicians who wrote and performed operas in the Theresienstadt concentration camp during the Second World War. But those circumstances did not exist in Britain in 1916. The war had shattered all certainty, torn apart social conventions, smashed for ever the imperial notion of 'Pax Britannica', and destroyed many people's faith and ideals. Confronted with such widespread public numbness and nihilism, even a Beethoven symphony may seem frivolous.

The LSO struggled on, but by the summer of 1917 its position had become unsustainable. Many of the older veterans of 1904 were exhausted and demoralised by the traumas of the war. Audience figures were, the board noted, 'deplorable'. On 26 September the LSO's directors unanimously resolved that 'no further symphony concerts be given until the termination of the war'.

What they actually meant was no more of their own promotions. The orchestra could still be hired by other promoters, and frequently was. But after surviving thirteen years as an independent concert-giving organisation, the old Edwardian LSO, jaunty, cavalier and blissfully self-confident, was now reduced to no more than a fading memory – rather like the Edwardian era itself.

*

British professional musicians, on the whole, are neither optimists nor pessimists, but imperturbable pragmatists. They deal with the problems that are imminent. Tomorrow may bring glory or disaster, but what chiefly matters is getting a performance together for that evening. You could call this attitude 'short-sighted', but that would be uncharitable. Given the extraordinarily insecure and unpredictable circumstances in which most British musicians work, a policy of concentrating on the work in hand is sometimes the only means of ensuring survival and preserving sanity.

It's likely that the LSO's musicians spent most of 1919 in that frame of mind. Few would have been dazzled by Lloyd George's airy talk of building 'a land fit for heroes'; fewer still by the rose-tinted notion circulating in the musical world that business would soon be 'back to normal'. The reality was very different. Neither in Britain nor anywhere else would the music business recover the grandeur or scope of the palmy pre-1914 era. This fact affected everything. Before the war, a composer like Stravinsky was able to write colossal scores for the largest orchestras ever assembled in theatre pits. In 1918 he thought it expedient to score his new music-theatre work, *The Soldier's Tale*, for just seven instrumentalists.

Britain in 1919 was hit not just by the vicious world recession, but by soaring inflation, a spate of strikes in many of the heavy industries – thirty million working days were lost – and a 'Spanish flu' epidemic that killed 150,000 people. (Around the world the same epidemic killed more people than had died in the Great War.) For an orchestra trying to establish 'business as normal' the circumstances could hardly have been less propitious. Widespread panic about the flu meant that people shunned large public gatherings, especially in airless concert halls. In any case, money was scarce. The old music halls had been killed off by the new craze for cinema; indeed, live entertainment everywhere was under threat. And the rocketing cost of food and accommodation meant that the orchestra had to raise its hire fee at exactly the moment when promoters could least afford to pay it.

The negotiations between the LSO and the Three Choirs Festival early in 1920 must have been typical of the constant haggling throughout the music business at that time. In Worcester Ivor Atkins, the cathedral organist and close friend of Elgar, was desperately trying to re-establish the Three Choirs Festival as the mighty choral and orchestral jamboree that it had been in pre-war days. He wrote to the LSO asking what it would charge to resume its pre-1914 role as the festival's resident orchestra. When the LSO quoted its terms, he was genuinely shocked. He wrote back asking for a reduction, 'as otherwise the festival could not be held'.

Doubtless spurred by W. H. Reed, the LSO leader – who had a close relationship with the festival and with Elgar – the orchestra responded by quoting a lower figure, though even this was still fifty per cent above the 1914 fee. But that immediately brought the LSO board into conflict with the Orchestral Union (forerunner of the modern Musicians Union), which called the figure 'totally inadequate', especially as the players had to pay for their own rail travel out of their fees. So the arguments went on, back and forth. Eventually a deal was struck whereby the LSO's own endowment fund (a legacy of happier and more profitable days) purchased the rail tickets on the players' behalf. But because rail fares were rising almost monthly, the Three Choirs agreed to pay the difference between the price of tickets at the time when the contract was signed and the eventual bill paid by the orchestra.

On that complicated basis the LSO played at the Three Choirs in 1920, and for many years afterwards. But other festivals simply folded or faded from the scene. In many towns the tradition of the annual amateur–professional musical collaboration was allowed to die, simply because temporary economic problems had greatly reduced the means of the private patrons who kept such festivals going. The obvious remedy (obvious to us today, anyway) would have been for local or central government to have stepped in with a loan, a guarantee against loss, or even a full-blown subsidy – for once these events had disappeared from the annual calendar they were seldom restored. But state subsidy of the arts in Britain was still twenty years in the future. In 1920 the notion of musicians receiving a 'handout' from the taxpayer would have struck most people as either peculiar or outrageous.

*

Not least among the LSO's many difficulties at the end of the war was finding a conductor good enough to rebuild its musical qualities, charismatic enough to attract an audience, available enough to supervise most of its self-promoted concerts, and cheap enough not to wipe out the orchestra's slender financial resources. In addition, it was thought advisable that he should not be German; feelings still ran high on that matter. But where was this paragon to be found? Beecham was too busy in the law courts, and many of the orchestra's pre-war stable of podium regulars were dead or decrepit.

Into this void stepped the vast, ebullient figure of Albert Coates. Rarely can so plain a name have announced such a whirlwind of a personality. British by birth, but Russian by temperament, Hungarian by training (Nikisch had taught him conducting) and German by association (he had worked his way up through a handful of small German opera houses), Coates was to drift in and out of London's musical life for the next thirty years, while maintaining a frenetic schedule of conducting in half the opera houses and orchestras of Europe, North America and (in his final years) South Africa. He was only in Britain in 1919 because St Petersburg, where he had conducted at the Mariinsky Theatre for the previous eight years, had become a rather complicated place in which to survive, particularly as a foreign maestro, after the Revolution.

So he came to London, conducted at Covent Garden, and then wrote to the LSO magnanimously offering to 'throw in his lot' with the orchestra if he was made principal conductor. Perhaps because he was a Nikisch pupil, but more likely because he offered to conduct the entire season without a fee, the LSO took him on. His great passion was for Russian music, and in the interpretation of everything from Glinka through to Skryabin, Rachmaninov and even Stravinsky (the LSO played *The Firebird* for the first time under his direction) he was unrivalled. But with the LSO he also conducted (and recorded) the first complete performance of Holst's *The Planets* and a great deal of Wagner, albeit in 'bleeding chunks' rather than complete.

Coates had one other useful ability: he was what would be called today an 'adroit operator' in society circles. And it was initially through him that the LSO cultivated links with a circle of wealthy music-lovers who were to keep the orchestra financially afloat through those difficult years. But just as there is no such thing as a free lunch in politics or journalism, there is very rarely any such thing as a 'disinterested sponsor' in the arts. Three of those wealthy patrons – the eccentric Lord Berners, the Swiss-German merchant banker Baron Frederic d'Erlanger, and a pompous Welshman called

Cyril Jenkins – were also budding composers, of greater or lesser distinction. They expected their music to be played by the orchestra they were
sponsoring. Mostly this was conveyed by 'gentleman's agreement', but
Jenkins and another rich backer, Lord Howard de Walden, actually specified in writing in December 1920 that their money was given on condition
that the LSO perform certain pieces by Bantock, Elgar and a certain Cyril
Jenkins later that season. What's more, they demanded that, in future,
British works should 'receive preference over all foreign works at
rehearsal'.

The insertion of that last condition must have been largely an outraged
reaction to Coates's shoddy treatment of Elgar's Cello Concerto earlier that
year: he had jeopardised its première by devoting too much rehearsal time to
Skryabin's *Poem of Ecstasy* and a Borodin symphony. But the two pushy
sponsors also wanted a public apology from the maestro for another perceived slight. They claimed that he had insulted them at an LSO rehearsal.

One may well imagine that the tempestuous conductor, faced with interference from two amateurs in his own rehearsal, might have uttered a few
choice selections of undiplomatic language. It's hard to think of any conductor, alive or dead, who would not have done the same. But an orchestra that
has its chief conductor and chief sponsors at loggerheads is never going to be
a stable organisation.

In the end, Jenkins disappeared from the scene – though not before the
LSO had been forced to give the first (and, as far as one can tell, the last) performance of his epic tone poem, *The Magic Cauldron*. But Coates himself
lasted only two seasons as the orchestra's principal conductor. He would
continue to be an important influence on the LSO in the recording studio,
but he would not play a central role in the orchestra's life again until the mid-
1930s – when he would once again become involved in behind-the-scenes
shenanigans with wealthy patrons brandishing fistfuls of ulterior motives.

*

Coates deserves credit for breathing life and energy into the orchestra at a
time when the demoralised band could easily have slipped into a fatal
malaise. After his departure, however, the players reverted to their guest-
conductor tradition. And for several years, their old policy of not restricting
themselves to one maestro seemed to pay off. In the early 1920s the LSO
really did look as if it could achieve the impossible, and restore its prestige
and fortunes to pre-war levels. The 1922–3 season was especially bold: it
contained not only the first performance of the First Symphony by the

incurably romantic Arnold Bax, but also the British première of some strange piano pieces by Mussorgsky, in a new orchestration commissioned from Maurice Ravel by Serge Koussevitzky, who conducted it. The critics that night didn't know what to make of *The Paintings from the Picture Show*, as the LSO programme quaintly translated it. They have had plenty of opportunities to make up their minds in the eighty years since. Now called *Pictures at an Exhibition*, this dazzling showstopper must have been played hundreds of times by successive generations of LSO players. Also in London that season, for the first and last time, was Carl Nielsen, who conducted the LSO in his own Fourth Symphony and Violin Concerto. Having mugged up for the occasion with a language course called *English in a Hundred Hours*, the great Dane felt sufficiently confident to begin the first rehearsal with a joke: 'Gentlemen, I am glad to see you. I hope I also am glad to hear you.' The LSO players are said to have responded with a polite laugh.

Nielsen was just one of a host of great names that appeared with the orchestra in the 1920s. Felix Weingartner, Wilhelm Furtwängler, Otto Klemperer and Bruno Walter all conducted. Rachmaninov performed his own Fourth Piano Concerto, while Artur Schnabel played no fewer than three concertos in one evening. Fritz Busch conducted the orchestra for the first time in 1929, in the concert when a twelve-year-old American prodigy called Yehudi Menuhin astonished everyone with a sensational performance of Brahms's Violin Concerto.

Beecham returned, more pompous and yet more popular than ever. And in 1927, when the great man was taken ill, a budding twenty-eight-year-old conductor who had once played cello in the LSO's ranks stepped in at short notice and acquitted himself brilliantly in a programme that included Elgar's Second Symphony and Haydn's D major Cello Concerto, with Pablo Casals as soloist. 'It is probable a lot more will be heard of this gentleman,' wrote one critic. The conductor's name was John Barbirolli. Nine years later he was in charge of the New York Philharmonic.

The growing roster of starry names who worked with the LSO in those years pulled in big crowds, and went a long way towards restoring the orchestra's financial health. By the time the orchestra celebrated its twenty-first birthday, on 9 June 1925, its cash reserves had grown to more than £2,000, and it was regularly distributing handsome dividends to its 'shareholders' (the players themselves, of course).

No wonder there was an atmosphere of euphoria at the birthday celebration that night. First, in the Queen's Hall, the orchestra performed the same programme that it had given on 9 June 1904. Elgar, who had been appointed Master of the King's Musick the previous year, conducted the *Enigma Variations*; Koussevitzky directed the rest. Then, at the Hotel Cecil on the Embankment, Beecham hosted probably the most sumptuous dinner in British orchestral history. Eight courses, each with 'appropriate wines', were served to a hundred and fifty LSO members, their wives, and a list of musical luminaries that included practically every distinguished composer and conductor in the land, and quite a few undistinguished ones as well.

It was a great moment. The LSO players had many reasons for feeling smug. Those that had been there from the start had survived initial hostility, the Great War, and a debilitating recession that had killed off several much older musical institutions, and were now giving concerts with the finest conductors and soloists in the world. True, there had lately been some ill-mannered sniping in the press about the shoddy quality of many performances. But wasn't the tradition of putting on a concert with almost no rehearsal almost part of the orchestra's constitution? In any case, the orchestra had very little serious competition in London, and it was making a great deal of money for its members. What could possibly go wrong?

The answer, as it turned out, was practically everything.

4 Rivals and survival
1925–39

Prögramme cover from the LSO's 21st Anniversary Concert at the Queen's Hall
on 9 June 1925, conducted by Sir Edward Elgar and Serge Koussevitzky

previous page Beecham greets Mengelberg, 1930

Most of life's vicissitudes can be pithily summarised by quoting something or other from *Hamlet*. And as the LSO members surveyed the wreckage of their dreams in the early 1930s, after having achieved such a golden era of prosperity in the mid-1920s, someone must have observed that 'when sorrows come, they come not as single spies, but in battalions.'

The battalions included the Wall Street Crash of 1929 and the Great Depression. The British economy went into an Ice Age, and the market for live music was one of the first to freeze. To make matters worse, the new-fangled British Broadcasting Company (as it was called when it was founded in 1922) was intervening more and more in the concert world. By the end of the decade it had become clear that nothing short of a full 'in-house' symphony orchestra would satisfy the musical ambitions of those running what by then had become an extremely wealthy and powerful organisation.

One well-funded competitor, intent on cherry-picking the top talent from other bands, would have been bad enough news. Yet a couple of years later, Beecham founded the London Philharmonic, and the poaching – of players, of audiences and, not least, of wealthy patrons – started all over again. The 1930s were a dangerous period for the LSO. The players scraped and scrimped, fought ferociously hard for every booking, every tour, every festival engagement, and mobilised whatever high-placed supporters they could find to complain at what they saw as unfair competition from the publicly subsidised BBC. In the end, the orchestra survived – but from being the aristocrats of the London musical world, they sank to the status of underdogs and also-rans: a band for hire, rather than a proud co-operative of virtuoso musicians. And this sense of 'How are the mighty fallen' was not completely shaken off until well after the Second World War.

Of course, the orchestra's plight was not chiefly of its own making. The plunging stock market, the naked ambition of a nascent broadcasting giant, the irrepressible urge of Beecham to create a new toy band for himself every decade or so: none of this could be controlled, or even countered, for the most part, by the LSO. In one respect, however, the LSO's players undoubtedly made problems for themselves. A fatal complacency seems to have crept into their playing in the mid-1920s, when there was little competition to spur the highest standards. Consequently, they forfeited the affection of discerning music-lovers, and especially the critics. That didn't matter when the LSO was effectively the only quality orchestral show in town. It mattered a great deal when it wasn't.

*

Even in the palmy days of the mid-1920s, the orchestra's standards were variable. In his autobiography, *First Flute*, Gerald Jackson sourly recalled the LSO of that era as being a clique-ridden bunch of what we would now call jobsworths. Of course, this blunt Yorkshireman was not an entirely unbiased authority. By the time he came to write his entertaining memoirs he had served successively as principal flute in two of the LSO's rivals (the BBC Symphony and then Beecham's original RPO). Nevertheless, the picture he paints of a parochial and unsophisticated playing style at the LSO in the mid-1920s is too detailed to be ignored. For instance, he contends that 'few, if any, of the players seemed to have heard of the word vibrato.'

He was clearly not alone in his judgement. One critic, writing in 1929, branded the orchestra 'a national disgrace'. But the most serious assault came from W. J. Turner, the critic of the *New Statesman*. He argued, more subtly, that the LSO's standards hadn't really dropped over the years; they had simply failed to keep pace with the huge leaps in technique apparent in the best orchestras on the Continent and in America. (Which would explain Jackson's comment about vibrato: a trait pioneered, at least in woodwind circles, by French virtuosi.)

Turner had particularly harsh things to say about the LSO's apparent lack of cohesion in performance. The ensemble, he wrote, 'always reminds me of what happens when you disturb an ants' nest with a stick'. Those words hurt, but not as much as what followed as Turner warmed to his theme. How could any orchestra play cohesively, he argued, when its personnel changed as often as the LSO's did? Once again, the old deputy system was weighed in the balance and found wanting. 'As each member has the right to send a proxy, should he have another engagement,' Turner wrote, 'and as the proxies themselves send proxies even to the third and fourth degree, it is evident that the LSO is not a single homogeneous body at all.'

Unease at London's orchestral standards, over the vexed question of deputies, and about the amount of rehearsal time considered adequate, was not confined to the LSO and its critics. Indeed, it was a Royal Philharmonic Society concert in January 1930 that brought the simmering unease within the profession out into the open. The great pianist Artur Schnabel complained that, although he had paid for extra rehearsals out of his own pocket, a performance of a Mozart concerto had been marred by late substitutions in the orchestra's ranks. In a subsequent letter to *The Times* he trenchantly outlined his general objection to London's way of making orchestral music:

Long experience has formed in me a profound conviction that it is an artist's duty to decline to take part in any musical activity which has not been approached in the right spirit from the beginning. Insufficient rehearsal may end in a successful performance, but as a matter of principle that fact is irrelevant. Time, concentration and enthusiasm are essential in every phase of musical activity, and when these are absent, or only occasionally present, nothing of permanent value can be achieved.

If London's critics or audiences had been given nothing against which to measure the worth of their own musicians, the debate about standards might have petered out. Unfortunately for the LSO, however, London in the late 1920s was becoming an increasingly popular destination for very fine foreign orchestras. Wilhelm Furtwängler brought the Berlin Philharmonic in 1927, and Ernst von Dohnányi came with the Budapest Philharmonic the following year. Both made a hugely favourable impression. Frank Howes, the music critic of *The Times*, recalled that 'the British public was electrified when it heard the disciplined precision . . . This was apparently how an orchestra could, and, therefore, ought to sound.'

But it was in 1930, when a succession of magnificent foreign bands blazed a trail through London, that the critics' passions were really stirred. Willem Mengelberg brought the Concertgebouw from Amsterdam – an orchestra he had been lovingly and painstakingly moulding for the past thirty-five years. Paris's finest ensemble, the Colonne Orchestra, appeared under the conductor, composer and Debussy champion, Gabriel Pierné. Furtwängler returned with his 'other' orchestra – the Vienna Philharmonic. And then, to make even this illustrious parade sound a touch pedestrian, the magisterial Arturo Toscanini appeared with the band then known by the cumbersome name of the New York Philharmonic Symphony Orchestra. The critics were enthusiastic, the public was dazzled – and London's musicians sulked.

The LSO's first reaction to the increasingly unflattering comparisons in the press was to shoot the messenger, by cancelling its press cuttings service, and then, in an astonishing move, to arrange a meeting with Lord Beaverbrook, proprietor of the then all-powerful *Daily Express*. One wonders what the delegation from the orchestra hoped to achieve. The era of 'reader offers' and newspaper 'cross-promotions' had not yet dawned. Was the staunchly pro-Empire newspaper tycoon expected to support the British orchestra by muting or stifling his critics' praise of continental and American ensembles?

We will never know what was said, but the meeting evidently led nowhere. It eventually occurred to the LSO directors that the best way to silence a hostile press was to give the critics nothing to criticise, by making the orchestra as well-drilled and technically proficient as the best overseas bands. Who was willing and able to undertake such a task? The obvious answer was Willem Mengelberg. Not only was he renowned as a conscientious and inspiring trainer of orchestras, he had also just demonstrated his prowess to London with his exemplary Concertgebouw concerts. What's more, he had had a long, if somewhat on-off, relationship with the LSO, stretching back to before the First World War.

The LSO board approached the autocratic Dutchman, then near his sixtieth birthday. Would he be prepared to spend the best part of a season in London, instilling the discipline and ensemble skills that the LSO lacked? Mengelberg said yes, on only one condition: the deputy system had to go. If the LSO truly wanted to improve, Mengelberg argued, he had to work with the same players all the time.

It was Henry Wood in 1904 all over again, except that this time the LSO had little choice but to agree. The principal players were cajoled into committing themselves to the LSO, at least for all of Mengelberg's concerts. And Mengelberg kept his side of the bargain: he worked his painstaking magic, he took the orchestra apart, section by section, bar by bar, he cleaned it up, finetuned every note, and put it back together again – rather like a master mechanic working on a vintage Rolls that needs a complete overhaul.

No nonsense was tolerated. 'The very first concerts I did with the LSO were with Mengelberg,' recalls the violinist Lionel Bentley, who went on to lead the orchestra. 'He frightened the life out of me. I had never known anyone so strict.' Mengelberg spent the entire first hour of his first rehearsal perfecting the tuning of four chords: the opening to Mendelssohn's *A Midsummer Night's Dream* overture. He made the revolutionary suggestion that the woodwind listen to each other, tune together in the band room beforehand, adjust their intonation according to the harmonic flavour and instrumentation of each chord – in short, play as a team, not as a line of self-regarding individuals who happened to sit next to each other. Then he started on the strings. Everyone, he said, should be playing with the same part of the bow at the same time. This apparently struck some of the older players as little short of heresy: they had only recently recovered from the shock of having to co-ordinate up-bows and down-bows with their colleagues.

Mengelberg is regarded today as one of the very greatest conductors of the twentieth century, though he was fated to spend his final years in ignominious exile, after having allegedly collaborated with the Nazis during the occupation of the Netherlands. He was precision personified, the ultimate perfectionist: it is said that he once cut a concert interval to five minutes because 'the orchestra is so splendidly in tune tonight' and he didn't want the players' concentration to break.

In other moods, in other eras, the LSO would have rebelled, and there were mutterings even in 1930. 'The older members of the orchestra did take rather a resentful attitude at first,' Bentley recalls. In their hearts, though, the players must have known that the hard work on basics had to be done.

Critics started to notice the difference. 'Even after the first concert with Mengelberg,' Bentley recalls, 'there was a newspaper review which said that the LSO sounded as if it had been "taken off the shelf and dusted". So it did too. It was a wonderful transformation. He made them play as they hadn't done for a very long time.' So proud were the LSO players of their progress under Mengelberg's direction that they even drew attention to it in the printed concert programmes during the autumn 1930 season. 'Throughout his career,' the programmes noted, 'Dr Mengelberg has imbued orchestras with that mysterious quality of coherence which makes them as sentient as a single musician . . . The despondency concerning our orchestral position which was so prevalent in the spring has vanished at the coming of a leader . . . The result has been remarkable, electrifying.'

They might have added 'if we say so ourselves', though the tone of the announcement strikes one as being less boastful than relieved. The LSO players clearly felt that they had emerged from a long, dark tunnel. But the transformation unfortunately came too late to stave off the greatest threat that the LSO had yet faced – competition from the BBC.

*

'All the London orchestras tended to start as the top dog,' Colin Davis observes. 'It's what happened to them afterwards which is so interesting.' Because the LSO has the longest continuous history of any surviving orchestra in London, one tends to forget that it had rivals from its earliest days. At first it competed for audiences with the Queen's Hall Orchestra, which Wood quickly restocked, and the orchestra of the Philharmonic Society (though in practice many LSO players seamlessly transmuted into members of the latter body, since engagements rarely clashed).

Then came a much more serious rival: the New Symphony Orchestra, conducted first by Beecham, then by the opportunistic Landon Ronald, who boasted that it had 'a set of principal players such as I had never dreamed of'. Beecham, meanwhile, went off and formed the Beecham Symphony Orchestra, which at least had the merit of proclaiming its allegiance, its style of music-making and its chief source of revenue, all in one title.

All those bands were jostling for the same London audience, the same wealthy patrons, the same summer festival engagements. Clearly, one should not underestimate the competition in the pre-1914 London orchestral world, nor the LSO's achievement in emerging as top dog by the outbreak of war. But at least the playing field was level for those Edwardian bands: none was subsidised, none had security, all had the same pool of talent from which to fill their ranks, and all struggled to establish a corporate identity in the rather anarchic free-for-all of London musical life.

The BBC, when it chose to enter the orchestral game, was in a different league altogether. It had been founded in accordance with the highest cultural and ethical ideals. As John Reith, its first manager (and later its first director-general) put it, in a characteristically majestic sweep of rhetoric: 'To have exploited so great a scientific invention [as broadcasting] for the purpose or pursuit of 'entertainment' alone would have been a prostitution of its powers and an insult to the character and intelligence of its people.' Reith had a paternalistic vision of broadcasting as a tool of national education and enlightenment. Naturally, music – or at least, the most 'improving' branches of it – would have a part to play in this noble mission.

At first this bizarre invention called 'the wireless' was treated by the music profession with indifference, disdain, amusement or outright scepticism. People listening to concerts taking place hundreds of miles away? Absurd! It would never catch on. All that changed in 1923 when the BBC not only started broadcasting regular concerts, but advertising them nationally in a popular new publication called Radio Times. Suddenly, even the most unworldly musicians realised the importance of the new medium. As the Musical Times succinctly put it: 'The invention which seemed a year ago like a futile toy is about to create something like revolution in the musical world.'

Some musicians felt, or pretended to feel, that broadcasting was a monstrous threat to their livelihoods, to the British way of life, to civilisation itself. 'If the wireless authorities are permitted to carry on their devilish work, in two years' time the concert halls will be deserted,' Beecham declared. The wireless, he went on, was 'the most abominable row that ever stunned and cursed the human ear, a horrible gibbering, chortling and shrieking of devils and goblins.' But the wily Beecham was being disingenuous. As was soon to be revealed, he had plans to become a major part of this 'devilish work' himself.

The LSO board took the more sanguine view that 'broadcasting would create a keener desire on the part of the public to hear the music at first hand'. Oddly, that view was also mistaken. Moreover, the LSO's directors crucially failed at first to recognise the real danger to themselves: that the new-born but intensely ambitious BBC would not be content simply to be a conduit for the wider dissemination of music, but would soon want to control and employ musicians itself.

At first, however, the LSO's optimism about broadcasting seemed justified. The orchestra was featured on the wireless as early as February 1924, playing Vaughan Williams's *Pastoral Symphony* in Southwark Cathedral. Six weeks later, in Westminster Hall, it was broadcast again – in the first series of concerts directly organised by the BBC – playing Stravinsky's *Firebird* under Eugene Goossens. Astonishingly, the broadcast was held up because a percussion player had gone missing – clearly unaware of, or indifferent to, the unseen thousands crouching by their receivers. He was fined one guinea for 'keeping the wireless waiting'.

Within four years the extent of the BBC's true orchestral ambitions began to be revealed. The Corporation (as it had become in 1927) announced its intention to recruit players from a range of orchestras for a series of public concerts. The LSO board was in a dilemma. First it tried to prohibit all LSO players from playing in the BBC's new 'all stars' band (billed as the British Symphony Orchestra). That didn't work. One player immediately offered his resignation, on the grounds that 'he was not prepared to be dictated to by the board as to what engagements he should accept'. He was supported by twenty-three other players, who called an extraordinary general meeting and forced the board to back down. It was the old issue of the LSO's best players disappearing to do better-paid work elsewhere – a 'right' which was at the heart of the LSO's *raison d'être*. The arguments about this prerogative would recur, with increasingly bitter repercussions, for decades to come.

The LSO board was not alone in its hostility to the BBC's musical plans. Elsewhere in the music world there was fury as the scope of the Corporation's ambitions became apparent. As promoters and managers quickly realised, the BBC had access to huge funds. By 1926, more than two million households had bought the new ten-shilling wireless licence, and the figure leapt by half a million each year. The licence fee was a gold-mine that enabled the BBC easily to outbid everyone else for the top musicians, frequently paying twice the rates offered elsewhere. But this enormous subsidy also allowed the BBC to undercut the ticket prices of commercial promoters, and still mount adventurous, well-rehearsed programmes that were too uneconomic for the private sector to contemplate. (In essence, this is exactly what the BBC Symphony Orchestra and the BBC Proms do to this day.) That reality was spectacularly underlined in 1928, when the BBC mounted a performance and broadcast of Schoenberg's massive *Gurrelieder*, conducted by the composer, in the Queen's Hall.

By then, the lure of lucrative BBC work was badly eroding the LSO's view of itself as a unified and independent orchestral entity. Indeed, so frequently did the top LSO talent disappear to fulfil BBC engagements that the orchestra had to create paradoxical creatures called 'permanent deputies' to flesh out its depleted ranks. But the tactic misfired, as the LSO board discovered that it had caused 'a great deal of dissatisfaction' among those in the orchestra (usually the rank and file, of course) who had remained faithful.

Into this volatile situation stepped Beecham. The great patrician-maestro was at a low ebb in his career. His own money had gone. He had not been able to operate his own orchestra or opera company for the best part of a decade. He was angry, frustrated and ill a lot of the time. His wit turned sour, his plans became increasingly unhinged. In the back of his mind, clearly, was the thought that if a permanent, fully contracted orchestra was going to be created in London – by the BBC or anyone else – he should be at its helm.

Throughout the spring of 1928 he flirted variously with the BBC, the Royal Philharmonic Society and the Columbia recording company – peddling the notion of a 'first-rate permanent orchestra' created with money partly supplied by his (suspiciously anonymous) guarantors. And the name of this super-band? Beecham hinted at first that it would be the 'London Philharmonic'. Clearly other names were in the air, though, since in January 1929 he felt it necessary to tell the gossip columnist of the *Daily Mail*, his usual confessor, that 'As for the title, I can tell you that it will not be "the BBC Orchestra".' Back to the London Philharmonic, then? Not a bit of it. 'Probably it will be the Royal Philharmonic,' Beecham declared, thus anticipating the orchestra he would form eighteen years and one world war later! In the same interview he also floated the idea for a brand-new London concert hall which, he said, his 'backers' would finance and run.

The interview was, it transpired, largely hot air and mischief-making. Beecham's increasingly contradictory public declarations infuriated the BBC and Reith, who imagined that they had been conducting a private negotiation. But the Royal Philharmonic Society was also incensed. Beecham, it turned out, had been promising different schemes to different parties – which explains why he was so keen that the BBC and the RPS never met face to face. Eventually, the BBC decided that Beecham must, in modern parlance, 'put up or shut up'. To nobody's great surprise, his backers never materialised, and early in 1929 the BBC broke off negotiations with him.

Beecham reverted to a scheme which his agent, the wily Lionel Power, had been quietly cooking up in the background. The conductor approached the LSO. First he suggested a closer association with himself. The advantage for the orchestra was that Beecham offered to pay for, as well as conduct, two extra concerts each season. Then he went a step further, proposing the creation of an entirely new sort of LSO – one which eschewed the hallowed principle of deputies.

The players rejected that as unacceptable, but they must have recognised the threat posed by Beecham, if they spurned his advances, as well as the BBC. They needed some sort of security, some guarantee of well-paid work – and quickly. The LSO board opened negotiations with the Gramophone Company and with Covent Garden. A tripartite deal was concocted, whereby the orchestra (or rather, seventy-five hand-picked players from it) would present international seasons of opera at Covent Garden, and also make a guaranteed number of recordings each year for the HMV label.

Once again the LSO board seems to have misjudged the mood of its own players. The proposal caused immense unrest in the ranks, mostly because it was so divisive. The LSO had a hundred shareholding members, but this guaranteed work for just seventy-five of them. Who would choose the lucky players? And on what legal basis was this to be secured, since each full member was entitled to a share in whatever work or profits the orchestra generated?

The board's response was to go back to the Gramophone Company and Covent Garden, and suggest that the work for the seventy-five players be shared around the orchestra. That was rejected by the other parties, not surprisingly. This, remember, was 1929. The LSO had not yet been through its rejuvenation under Mengelberg – and the general perception in the music business was that if the orchestra was once more to shine, it needed ruthlessly to prune its 'dead wood'. That was why the 'seventy-five players only' clause had been introduced in the first place – as the LSO board had presumably known all along. In any case, in collaboration with the men from the record company and Covent Garden, the LSO directors proceeded to compile the divisive list of chosen players.

The bitterness in the ranks erupted at an extraordinary general meeting in July 1929. Player after player stood up and aired his grievances. At first the orchestra's chairman, Henri van der Meerschen (one of the LSO's founders, of course), tried to pour oil on troubled waters by saying that the selection of the seventy-five had been 'a very painful business' for him and his colleagues. 'Not as painful as for us,' someone at the back muttered. But then the gloves came off. The LSO directors, the chairman continued, had been 'aware of certain weaknesses in the orchestra for some considerable time' but had 'acted in the spirit of leniency'. However, Beecham's plan to create a permanent orchestra had 'brought matters to a crisis'.

The meeting ended in disarray. The board demanded the resignations of certain players, since it had no legal right to sack shareholders. The rank and file in turn castigated the board for not representing their interests. The deal went through – but almost exactly twenty-five years after its first public appearance, the LSO seemed to be shaking itself apart.

Worse followed after the summer. The BBC's intention to form its own permanent, salaried symphony orchestra under the direction of Adrian Boult (less exciting but more dependable than Beecham) was now an open secret. At first, it seems, the LSO's deal with the Gramophone Company and Covent Garden caused the BBC hierarchy to hesitate over implementing its own plan. 'I cannot conceive,' Reith wrote in an internal memo on 18 March, 'that there is room for two permanent orchestras in London.' But Reith was quickly – and correctly – persuaded by his music department that the LSO was certainly not planning a 'permanent salaried orchestra', so the BBC pressed ahead.

Viewed from a twenty-first-century perspective, the BBC's ambition seems quaint, even perverse. Why on earth would a broadcasting organisation want its own orchestra? It is certainly hard to imagine the ratings-orientated BBC of the John Birt or Greg Dyke era dreaming up the notion of running an orchestra (or five!), had it not been lumbered with the musical legacy of earlier managements. But Reith's BBC of the 1920s was a very different animal, imbued with an almost religious zeal for 'enlightening' the public through the magical medium of the wireless. An orchestra, and particularly one that was unencumbered by commercial constraints and thus free to deliver the highest of highbrow programmes, would fit very well into that idealistic philosophy.

In the autumn of 1929, then, the BBC began recruiting. It was quickly decided that the old Queen's Hall Orchestra would form the basis of the new BBC Orchestra – a logical move, since the BBC had taken over the running of the Proms after Robert Newman had died two years earlier. But some of the LSO's best players – such as the trumpeter Ernest Hall and the double-bass player Eugene Cruft (whose father had been one of the founder members of the viola section, and whose son, John Cruft, would become the LSO's secretary in the 1950s) were also prime targets for BBC poaching.

Perhaps if the economic climate had been less volatile, and the market for orchestral music more buoyant, the BBC would have encountered much stiffer resistance. But in three days of trading between 24 and 28 October some fifteen billion dollars were wiped off the price of shares traded on the New York Stock Exchange. The Wall Street Crash, as this traumatic event was quickly labelled, sent the entire world spinning into an economic and industrial depression. Suddenly, a permanent job – well paid, secure, and with a pension at the end – seemed a very desirable proposition to many orchestral musicians.

Of course, there were some players – especially younger ones – who didn't want to be tied down, and who calculated that they would be better off with the LSO's less regimented system. One such was the young violinist Lionel Bentley. When he joined the LSO on a rank-and-file contract in the late 1920s, he would have received a concert fee of twenty-seven shillings. (LSO principals were then getting 32s. 6d. per concert.) That, he reckoned, gave him weekly earnings from the LSO of around five pounds, though he admits that the work was 'sporadic'. 'Nevertheless, I thought that this was preferable to the eleven pounds a week that the BBC offered to rank-and-file,' Bentley says. 'They tied you down, whereas you could do all sorts of deputy work if you were in the LSO, and easily make up the difference. By joining the LSO I felt I was on the verge of the magic circle, where people had other sorts of work.'

The BBC Symphony Orchestra finally gave its first concert on 22 October 1930, under the direction of Adrian Boult. 'They said it was the best orchestra in the world,' Bentley recalls. 'Well, it wasn't. It was mostly full of very young players, who had to gain experience. Nevertheless it did have some really outstanding wind players.' Its wind principals included Archie Camden on bassoon, Aubrey Brain (son of A. E. Brain, an LSO founder member, and father of Dennis) on horn, Frederick Thurston on clarinet, and the oboist Terence MacDonagh. For all Bentley's reservations, the youngsters in the BBC orchestra must have learnt fast, for when Toscanini came to

73

conduct his legendary concerts and recordings with the BBCSO, between 1935 and 1939, he famously declared it to be the finest orchestra he had ever directed – better, even, than the symphony orchestra formed especially for him by the American broadcasting giant, NBC.

At the time when the BBC was recruiting players the atmosphere within the LSO must have been poisonous. At first the board tried to prevent LSO members joining the BBC by forcing them to 'honour their contracts' with the LSO. When this was challenged legally – as was bound to happen, since it amounted to a restraint of trade – the board resorted to vilification, declaring that 'members who could act in a manner so disloyal to the true spirit of the orchestra were not worthy to remain members any longer'. Loyalty suddenly became the most emotive word in the London orchestral world.

It is in this context that some of the press vilification of the LSO and its playing standards must be viewed. Perhaps it goes some way towards explaining why the LSO board became so paranoid about the reviews it was receiving. In that highly charged atmosphere of betrayal and jealousy, it must have seemed as if the BBC had not only pinched the LSO's best players, but nobbled the leading newspaper critics as well. Ernest Newman of the *Sunday Times* certainly appeared to some LSO directors to be 'obviously a paid servant of the BBC', so often did he argue in print that the creation of a permanent, salaried orchestra was the only way to improve playing standards in London. (In fact he had attacked the LSO as early as 1925 when he returned from a trip to America and declared, with vicious sarcasm, that the London band was not so bad after all, since it 'compared not unfavourably with the orchestras in some of the New York picture houses'.)

The atmosphere was scarcely improved by rumours in the autumn of 1930 that the BBC had offered financial inducements to the big choral societies outside London to engage its new orchestra rather than the LSO. The orchestra certainly believed that it had lost its annual engagement at the Leeds Festival through a combination of appalling press coverage and BBC pressure.

Even today, there is a lingering resentment in some quarters about the way in which the BBC uses its licence-fee monopoly to compete with, and usually outbid the private sector. Many of the Hallé Orchestra's troubles of the early 1990s, for instance, were blamed by its supporters – rightly or wrongly – on subsidised competition from a resurgent BBC Philharmonic, which was also based in Manchester. And there was resentment in the London freelance world at around the same time when the management of the BBC Concert

Orchestra started to manipulate the 'spare capacity' of that highly subsidised light-music band in order to bid aggressively for commercial engagements.

Against this should be set one indisputable fact: the BBC has funded and promoted a huge amount of serious music-making and composition that would otherwise not have happened. At the same time it has nudged public taste onto more adventurous paths without, in general, resorting to heavy-handed partisanship. Seventy years on, those remain striking achievements.

Back in the early 1930s, however, the BBC's decision to use its vast resources to make itself the most important force in British musical life was something that the LSO, and many other privately run musical organisa-tions, strongly and publicly deplored. Indeed, they jointly organised a letter-writing campaign in the press against the upstart Corporation. The nub of their argument was that the BBC should confine its own music-making to the studio and only broadcast public concerts by outside ensembles.

But the notion that the BBC would back away from the public arena was patently absurd. The Corporation had spent a small fortune recruiting some of the best players in Britain, and was committed to spending a much larger one sustaining and enhancing its orchestral empire. (In 2002 the BBC's annual orchestral budget stood at more than £20 million, of which £6 mil-lion went on the BBC Symphony Orchestra alone). It is understandable that the BBC would not want to confine such highly paid instrumentalists to a dingy studio.

That was graphically demonstrated by one incident in 1931. The Royal Albert Hall was sixty years old. A grand Diamond Jubilee Concert was organised to celebrate 'the nation's village hall' – a venue which, despite its bizarre acoustics (an echo that gave the audience the same performance twice over) was still the only place in London capable of hosting really big shows. For this concert, it was decided, the players of the LSO, New Symphony Orchestra and the BBC Orchestra would be combined into one gargantuan band.

Very comradely – except that the BBC demanded that its own principals occupy the first chair of each section. The idea was as petty as it was high-handed and inflammatory. The LSO resisted, and won its point: in the end the principals' duties were shared between the orchestras. But that was one of the few victories that the LSO did win in those turbulent years. And there was another black cloud looming on its horizon. Its name was the London Philharmonic Orchestra.

*

Utterly unfazed by the LSO's rejection of his 'permanent orchestra scheme' two years earlier, Sir Thomas Beecham, Bt, was back on the orchestra's podium again in 1931. In fact he conducted six out of the ten concerts that the LSO promoted for itself in the 1931–2 season. Artistically, they were highly successful: the hard hours of training under Mengelberg had clearly paid off, and the critics were impressed. The *London Evening Standard* noted, rather condescendingly, that the LSO players' 'progress this season has been astonishing'.

Behind the scenes, though, a financial and management crisis was looming. At the end of 1931 the London concert agent Lionel Power suddenly died at the age of fifty-four. To the horror of the musical world, his operation was found to be all but bankrupt, rendering the contracts he had signed null and void. This was appalling news for the LSO, since Power supplied extensive quantities of work. At first the orchestra tried to take on financial responsibility, not only for the London concerts fixed by Power, but for the provincial ones as well. Faced with dogged competition from the BBC, however, the LSO board floundered hopelessly. After all, the orchestra's directors were players, not impresarios.

Beecham, his fortunes somewhat improved, played the generous benefactor role to perfection. He provided rail tickets out of his own pocket to get the orchestra to its regional engagements. He rallied support for the LSO in high (and well-heeled) quarters. And on 25 January 1932, he even made a rousing speech from the podium, urging the public to come to the aid of the stricken band.

Four days later, support came from an even more influential quarter. In a memorably outspoken editorial, *The Times* (no great ally of the BBC, then or now) also waved the flag for the 'courageous' and 'self-supporting' LSO. Not only did the LSO have to contend with the unforseen ramifications of Power's death, *The Times* said, it was also valiantly trying to survive 'under pressure of competition with what is virtually a State-aided orchestra, that of the BBC'. The article described recent press criticism of the LSO as 'not always completely unbiased', and concluded with a resounding rallying cry: 'The spirited action of an important body of native musicians calls for a response from the public in the combined names of patriotism and artistic interest.'

That powerful editorial, harnessed to Beecham's rhetoric, seemed to work. Beecham's high-society friends were touched by the LSO's plight, and donations flooded in. And the Gramophone Company gave the orchestra a £2,000 guarantee against loss (pretty well inevitable that season) in return for the right to record live concerts – an innovation that prefigures the orchestra's own LSO Live recordings in the 1990s.

More disaster loomed, however. The recession had hit Covent Garden badly, and the annual two-month opera season – for which the LSO had supplied the orchestra under its 1929 agreement – was suddenly scrapped. The LSO board hunted desperately for other work. Beecham hurriedly put together a four-week season of German opera, and engaged the LSO. A two-week run of Coleridge-Taylor's inexplicably popular *Hiawatha* at the Albert Hall provided work for some musicians in the remaining weeks; others toured with a ballet company.

It wasn't an ideal way to keep an orchestra together, but at least the players could eat. In 1931, that was an achievement in itself: sterling had been devalued by twenty-five per cent, there were nearly three million unemployed, a near mutiny over pay in the Royal Navy and riots on the streets over the austerity measures imposed by Ramsay MacDonald's 'Government of National Unity'. They were hand-to-mouth times.

So the players' morale must have been pretty low that autumn when Beecham – their saviour time and again that year – finally revealed his true intentions. He had been asked, he told the LSO board, to form 'an orchestra of the first rank'. Naturally he was hopeful that the LSO could become this orchestra, but would the board be willing to consider personnel changes in the band to make this happen?

The LSO members must have felt a strange sense of déjà vu, but negotiations with Beecham began anyway. It transpired that Beecham wanted twenty-five players, whom he considered inadequate, to be replaced. These he named. In return he offered ninety concerts and ten weeks of opera a year. This work would be 'co-ordinated', he revealed, by an independent committee chaired by the textiles magnate Samuel Courtauld.

The LSO board had every right to be dazzled. Even after the Wall Street Crash, Courtauld was among the five richest men in England. His family, Huguenot in origin, had been in textile manufacturing for centuries, and in the late nineteenth century had made handsome profits from manufacturing widows' weeds – in the Victorian era, mourning was a protracted and intensive affair. Handsome profits turned into stupendous riches when a canny Courtaulds manager acquired the rights to manufacture an artificial silk that came to be known as 'rayon'. The company's share price rose six thousand per cent in little more than a decade.

This was just as well for British culture, because in the 1920s Samuel Courtauld IV and his highly cultured wife, Elizabeth, became a kind of one-family private Arts Council. They ran magnificent salons in their London house, 20 Portman Square. They filled their country seat, Gatcombe Park (later purchased by the Royal Family for Princess Anne) with a sensational collection of Impressionists. And they poured millions into Covent Garden, the National Gallery, the Tate and several other of London's leading arts institutions.

In short, Courtauld was the most powerful and munificent arts philanthropist in Britain between the wars. No wonder that, by dangling the name, Beecham suddenly had the LSO board's full attention. But although the orchestra's pride was battered and bruised by the travails of the past four or five years, it was not so broken that its directors felt obliged to fall in with Beecham's rather peremptory demands for sackings and 'new blood'. Instead, the LSO board responded by offering its own lists of players to be retained or replaced.

Meanwhile, other parties got wind of change in the air, and poked their fingers in the pie. Sir Landon Ronald – the same Ronald who had been snubbed by the LSO twenty-five years earlier – helpfully suggested an amalgamation of the LSO with his own New Symphony Orchestra. Meanwhile, the Columbia record company suggested that if the LSO board found it difficult to decide which of its players were worthy of retention, its own executives would be happy to take on the task.

The LSO board also had to contend with the Machiavellian machinations of the young and competent, but intensely ambitious and much-disliked Malcolm Sargent, whose capacity for exhibiting arrogance towards orchestral players was exceeded only by his ability to flatter rich patrons, especially female ones. In less than a decade 'Flash Harry', as generations of orchestral musicians called him, had risen from conducting concerts with such humble outfits as the Leicester Symphony Orchestra and the band on the end of Llandudno Pier to become Beecham's sidekick at Covent Garden – a role he coveted so much that he endured years as the chief butt of Beecham's jokes.

He had also become a considerable force in London concert life, mainly because of the connection he had assiduously cultivated with the Courtaulds. He had used Mrs Courtauld's money three years earlier to start a 'cheap ticket' concert series, modestly named 'the Courtauld–Sargent Concerts'. Now Mrs Courtauld, who was terminally ill, had helpfully supplied Sargent with a lump sum of £30,000 (with the promise of annual subsidy to follow) so that he could create an orchestra worthy of his talent.

As his mentor Beecham had done on numerous occasions, Sargent began to play mind games with the LSO, dangling the £30,000 as a carrot while never committing himself (or the money) to the orchestra's cause. Perhaps his role was merely to create a smokescreen of confusion in the minds of the LSO directors, while Beecham made his plans elsewhere. In July 1932 Sargent informed two LSO representatives that – whatever they may have surmised from Beecham's earlier approaches – the Courtaulds and their cohorts felt the LSO's board to be entirely superfluous to their project. In other words, they wanted to control the 'new' orchestra completely, irrespective of whether it comprised LSO players or not.

The following week the board received a letter from Harold Holt, the agent acting for this new venture. It was a bombshell, insulting in tone, shattering in content. Since the LSO 'no longer commanded the confidence of the public', it said, the backers did not propose either to negotiate with it or use the orchestra's name. The months of discussions with Beecham and Sargent had, it seemed, been a charade.

Beecham was urgently sought out. Had he been party to this letter? Yes, he cheerfully admitted, actually he had dictated it. But no, it wasn't his decision to renege on his earlier assurances to the LSO. It was purely the wish of his board members. He had no say in the matter. But since it had been raised, would the LSO board be prepared to sell the title 'London Symphony Orchestra' to him?

The request was debated, for about two minutes, by the outraged LSO board. 'I think,' said the doughty flautist Gordon Walker, who later became the orchestra's chairman, 'that we should offer the title to Beecham.' When there was a howl of protest, he added: 'For £100,000.' In the end the LSO did not even deign to give Beecham and his backers a reply. Instead, the players established a 'fighting fund' and voted overwhelmingly to remain what they always were – a fiercely independent orchestra, beholden to no conductor, no matter how wealthy or charismatic.

One month later, in August 1932, Beecham announced the formation of his new London Philharmonic Orchestra, which gave its first concert in October. Sargent, who lost no time in telling influential music-business people that the LSO would 'soon cease to exist', was rewarded for his various dubious plottings by being made Beecham's assistant conductor. 'Always appoint a deputy whose calibre is such that the public is glad to see you back again,' Beecham later quipped.

Again the air was rife with talk of defections to the new band. Seventeen LSO players (including one of the very directors who had been involved in the negotiations on behalf of the orchestra) immediately jumped ship. They, and several others who did not swallow the bait, had received telegrams from Beecham inviting them to join his new enterprise while they were play-ing with the LSO at the Three Choirs Festival. The telegrams were pinned up on the green baize noticeboard in the bandroom for all to see.

Some who expected to receive a telegram didn't. Among them was the LSO's veteran leader, W. H. Reed. Earlier in the year, sharing a train journey with Beecham, he had asked the conductor whether, if the LSO threw in its lot with Beecham, he could expect to be leader. 'My dear Billy, the LSO would be unthinkable without you,' replied Beecham, at his most plummily disingenu-ous. In the event, Paul Beard was lured from the City of Birmingham Symphony Orchestra to lead the LPO. Other stars who joined the new band included Leon Goossens, the oboist brother of the conductor Eugene.

Others, however, contemptuously rejected the offer. Beecham's 'credit rating' with London players was, by that time, not especially high. Besides which, the pressure on players to stay loyal to colleagues and friends by stay-ing (or indeed by joining the new band) must have been intense. Some indi-cation of how high feelings were running can be gauged from the action of Charles Winterbottom, the LSO's veteran principal double bass, who offered to resign if the vacant principal's stool would induce others in his section to stay in the orchestra. He later confided that the worry about losing his close friends in the orchestra to the LPO had made him ill.

The fight wasn't just about retaining the best players. Almost as damag-ingly for the LSO, Beecham had persuaded some of the orchestra's most loyal and generous patrons to support his new venture – men like Lord Howard de Walden who had supported the LSO since its earliest days. Beecham also seemed to have the press on his side. In the *Sunday Times*, Ernest Newman loftily declared that the LPO's first concert showed 'you Londoners . . . what an orchestra ought to be like'. So it should have done, one might have thought, since Beecham had preceded it with an astonishing twelve rehearsals.

Nevertheless, it was a remark pointedly calculated to infuriate LSO mem-bers, who already believed that Newman was unfairly biased against them. There seems to have been no truth in this suspicion, for when the LSO's stan-dards improved again, a season or two later, Newman was quick to write an encouraging and positive notice. What's more likely is that Newman was infuriated, as most music critics were, by the refusal of the 'deputy system' (which the LSO represented) to lie down and die. He once described it – in a phrase that typifies the Olympian detachment of a certain breed of music critics from the realities of day-to-day survival faced by musicians – as a 'wild absurdity and immorality'.

The unarguable truth, however, was that in 1932 the LSO was not at its best, while the new LPO was indeed a first-class orchestra. For the next six years, until it was bankrupted and then abandoned by the whimsical Sir Thomas, it rivalled the BBC Orchestra for quality, and embarked on several high-profile overseas tours. These included, most notoriously, a trip to Berlin in 1936 to play for Hitler, a figure much admired by some in Beecham's circle: Beecham and the orchestra spinelessly agreed to drop Mendelssohn from the proposed programme when the German ambassador, Von Ribbentrop, pointed out that he was Jewish.

Meanwhile, the LSO, though forced to play 'third fiddle' in London for the first time in its history, did not cease to exist, as Sargent had predicted. Instead, it did what London orchestras always do when threatened with extinction. It battened down the hatches, it scrabbled like fury for festival and session dates, and it performed its own London concert series without the players taking fees, in order to keep the orchestra's flag flying in the capital.

Call the tactics bloody-minded, stubborn or indomitable: they have been repeated, by all the London orchestras, many times since. This is why the city still has so many orchestras, in spite of the numerous efforts of tidy-minded bureaucrats to 'rationalise' the situation.

*

Survival wasn't easy in 1933 and 1934. This was the height of the Depression. A worldwide economic slump was exacerbated in Britain by a savage erosion of the very industries – steel, coal, shipbuilding, textiles – on which the mighty prosperity of Victorian Britain was founded. London was not afflicted by the terminal malaise that was beginning to dog the industrial cities of Northern England. In fact by the mid-1930s the capital's population had soared by ten per cent in a decade, to over eight million, and the suburbs of 'Greater London' now stretched into Hertfordshire to the north and Kent to the south. As the country's greatest port, however, London was heavily reliant on world trade: when that slumped, the Pool of London went into a steep and fatal decline.

This, in turn, had a negative effect on the entire economy of the capital. And where money is tight, live entertainment dies. By 1933, three and a half million people were out of work in Britain. There was no artistic or economic reason why a hundred or so orchestral players shouldn't have joined them, especially as this particular bunch of players were widely perceived (after the founding of the BBC Symphony and London Philharmonic Orchestras) to be superfluous to requirements.

Failure in the arts is a vicious circle. If the critics are unkind, people don't come to your concerts. If people don't come, you have to cut costs. If you cut costs, you can't hire the best artists. If you don't hire the best artists the critics are unkind and even fewer people come. And so on.

This was the case for the LSO in the early 1930s. The orchestra's morale, so recently uplifted by the remedial rehearsals with Mengelberg, was now shattered. The players felt betrayed by the two English conductors with whom they had the closest links. (Apart from a benefit concert in 1946, Beecham was never again invited to conduct the LSO. Sargent was also *persona non grata* for a while, but took care to mend his bridges five years later.)

To make matters worse, the economic depression had devastated the festival and choral tradition of provincial England – which had been a source of useful income for so long for the LSO. The great choral societies of the North prided themselves on drawing their singers from working-class as much as middle-class backgrounds. Now, though, there was real hardship among those who worked in the pits and mills. If they couldn't pay their 'subs', the choral society couldn't afford to hire professional musicians – and certainly not players whose return train fares from London also had to be covered.

Within London, too, the outlook was bleak for the LSO. The LPO had snapped up several annual engagements that the LSO had come to regard as its private property. Among them were the Covent Garden opera seasons, the Royal Philharmonic Society concerts, and of course the Courtauld–Sargent series. The BBC Orchestra was also making its weighty presence felt on the London concert scene.

To cap humiliation with absurdity, the LSO players discovered to their horror that the 'traitors' who had defected to the other orchestras could still have a say in managing the affairs of their old band. The twenty-nine former LSO players now gracing the ranks of the LPO and BBC had retained their LSO shares and were, therefore, perfectly entitled to full voting rights at LSO meetings. It would be four years before the LSO's solicitors could successfully tiptoe their way through that legal minefield.

Deprived of Beecham's glamour and Sargent's blithe self-confidence, the orchestra turned to Sir Hamilton Harty. The Irishman, then in his early fifties, was an imaginative and charming conductor who had built the Hallé into a formidable orchestra during the 1920s. Unfortunately he was no great crowd-puller, and consequently the orchestra lost nearly £2,000 on its own promotions in one season.

1 Hans Richter, LSO Principal Conductor, 1904–11

2 LSO with conductor Hans Richter, Richter Farewell Concert, 1911
3 LSO, Handel Festival *Israel in Egypt*, Crystal Palace, 1912

4 Members of the LSO, John Solomon *centre*, 1912
5 Founding Members of the LSO, *l to r*: Jesse Stamp (trombone), E. T. Garvin (trombone), Francis Ash (tuba), R. Evans (trombone); Leeds Festival 1922

6 LSO on board the SS *Potsdam*, LSO American Tour, 1912
7 LSO returning home, LSO American Tour, 1912

8 Commemorative medal from LSO American Tour, 1912
9 Artur Nikisch, LSO Principal Conductor 1912–14
10 First British orchestra to visit USA; Wichita, Kansas, LSO American Tour, 1912

(Part) London. Sympo. Orchestra.
1913. Aug.ᵗ "Bray
Ireland"

Cond.ᵗ Hamilton. Harty.

Back Row.
   E. Atherley. R. Evans. H. Barlow.
      J. Soloman — S. Moxon. F. James.
                                          et.
G. Anderson — F. James. (Bassoon)
     C. Darling.   A. Alexandra.
     Marion. Thimoty. (Harp)
J. Eyers. H. Parker— R. Carrodus—
                 m. Brennan.
       C. Woodhouse.   c. Hayes.
                  C. Newton.

11 LSO, Bray, Ireland, 1913

12 Founding Members of the LSO, *l to r, back row*: E. W. Whitmore (double bass),
H. Barlow (tuba), H. van der Meerschen (horn); *front row*: F. G. James (trumpet),
E. Carrodus (double bass), J. Solomon (trumpet); Three Choirs Festival, Worcester, 1912
13 Members of the LSO, Three Choirs Festival, Worcester, 1914

14 Thomas Busby, Founding Member, First Managing Director, 1904–24

Crowd-pullers, in truth, were rather beyond the LSO's means. A couple of years later, the BBC mustered the wherewithal to hire Toscanini for a whole series of concerts and broadcasts. When the LSO's directors made tentative enquiries as to the tempestuous Italian's availability, they had to beat a swift and embarrassed retreat when he demanded £1,000 and nine rehearsals for a single concert.

Some relief came in 1934. Down in Sussex an eccentric, opera-mad country squire called John Christie had decided to start a summer opera festival at his mansion – an enchanting place called Glyndebourne. In spite of the improbability of the venture, or perhaps because it exactly matched foreign expectations as to what mad English gentlemen did in their spare time, he attracted top-quality collaborators from the Continent – such legendary (or soon to be legendary) figures as the conductor Fritz Busch, the theatre director Carl Ebert and the administrator Rudolf Bing, later the general manager of the Metropolitan Opera in New York. Of course, Christie did have an unwitting ally – Adolf Hitler, whose repressive policies were increasingly driving such liberal-minded geniuses out of their native country.

Glyndebourne came as a lifeline to the LSO players. The orchestra that played for both productions (*Le Nozze di Figaro* and *Così fan tutte*) in that original season, and for several seasons afterwards, was drawn almost entirely from LSO ranks. Quite apart from the work it offered, the engagement must also have acted as an invaluable morale-booster and showcase for the players in that *annus horribilis*. Glyndebourne's patrons, then as now, were among the richest movers and shakers in England.

There was more good news from another unexpected quarter. The BBC, the very organisation that had, wittingly or unwittingly, perpetrated so much distress on the LSO in the previous ten years, now showered the orchestra with largesse. In April 1934 a delegation from the LSO met with Reith, and the great man subsequently ordered that £2,500 worth of work be put in the orchestra's direction by his music producers.

It was not a period when the orchestra could afford to be choosy about its patrons, even when what they demanded in return seemed to cut across the very independence that the LSO had cherished since its first days. In the case of F. J. Nettlefold, the phrase 'he who pays the piper calls the tune' can rarely have been more literally true. Nettlefold was another Courtaulds' contact – the chairman of Courtaulds Ltd, in fact. He also prided himself on his compositions, in a light idiom, and was a substantial patron of the arts in his own right. His support for, and influence on, the LSO had been growing through the mid-1930s.

In 1936 Nettlefold approached the orchestra with an offer that the beleaguered board felt it couldn't refuse. He offered to assume 'full financial responsibility' for the LSO's 1936–7 series. The catch was that he would nominate the soloists and conductors. The board swallowed hard; this clearly went against the LSO's most hallowed principles. In the end, though, Nettlefold's offer was accepted.

The situation quickly became messy. Mrs Nettlefold was an ambitious mezzo-soprano called Vera de Villiers. She had to be included in the plans. But she was having a relationship – supposedly secret, though common knowledge throughout the musical world – with the conductor Albert Coates, the LSO's old friend. Spurred by who knows what mixed-up feelings towards his wife and her lover, Nettlefold recruited Coates to the LSO as 'artistic advisor'. LSO board meetings – at which Nettlefold, his wife, his wife's lover and his wife's lover's agent were sometimes all present – started to resemble Noel Coward plays.

It couldn't go on, and it didn't. The losses on the 1936–7 season were enormous, too much even for Nettlefold's capacious wallet to bear without severe strain. He demanded that the LSO call upon their other guarantors to help meet them. The orchestra's directors pointed out that it was Nettlefold who had suggested running their season and paying for it. Both sides reached for their solicitors. In the end Nettlefold paid the money, but left the LSO for ever. Mrs Nettlefold, meanwhile, became the second Mrs Coates.

*

The LSO had started to fill the gaps left by the players who had transferred to the LPO. Harty had suggested doing to his old orchestra, the Hallé, what the LPO had done to the LSO, and the LSO wasted no time or moral scruples in doing exactly that. As a result, eight Hallé players, including the orchestra's leader, were lured from Manchester. Rather cheekily, too, the LSO managed to woo back George Stratton, who had been pinched by Beecham to be principal second violin of the LPO. Stratton was brought back to replace – tactfully and gradually – the great, but by now rather declining, W. H. Reed as the LSO's leader. The new man's qualifications were not in dispute. Even so, his return caused some dissent within the LSO. Had he not been one of the traitors who had defected only a year earlier?

The appointment proved shrewd. Stocky, irrepressibly cheerful and no-nonsense, Stratton had played in London's cafes and restaurants in his youth, learnt the orchestral trade in Wood's Queen's Hall Orchestra, then joined the LSO in 1925 – all the time keeping his own string quartet going.

After he returned to the orchestra in 1933 he remained as leader until the early 1950s. He was a superbly competent violinist, though his tone was a little strident for the recording and film studio, and he resigned after his solos in a recording of *Swan Lake* were re-recorded by another violinist. He was also a man who revelled in the competitive spirit of London's orchestral life, and that was just as important to the LSO in those somewhat desperate years. 'There was a do-or-die spirit in the orchestra at that time,' he was to recall. 'The result was so magnificent that all the critics were won over (for they had been very hard of late). The LSO was still very much alive.'

The recovery had really started back in 1934. The orchestra had been engaged to give the first performance of the most eagerly awaited new British symphony since Elgar's Second, more than twenty years before. The new piece was by William Walton, a thirty-two-year-old Oldham-born genius who had dazzled everybody four years previously with his exhilarating choral romp *Belshazzar's Feast*, which the LSO and local singers had premièred at the Leeds Festival under Sargent's direction.

Could he be 'the new Elgar'? The burden of expectation weighed heavily on the young composer's shoulders – even on his best days he wasn't the fastest man on manuscript – and the première of the symphony had already been put back a year. As the new date approached the composer confessed that his symphony still lacked a finale. 'There is little doubt,' he wrote, a little pompously, to his friend and fellow composer, Patrick Hadley, 'that I could have pumped out tolerably easily a brilliant, out-of-place pointless and vacuous finale in time for the performance . . . Instead of doing that, egged on by you, I persisted in finding something which I felt to be right and tolerably up to the standard of the previous movements. This involved me in endless trouble and I've burnt about three finales.'

There were frantic negotiations between publisher, promoter and orchestra. Again the première was postponed. 'Harty was very annoyed,' recalled the LSO violinist Lionel Bentley. 'He said: "We'll have to put it off till the next concert." The next concert was a month later, and it still wasn't complete. So Harty said: "Whether it's complete or not, we will play what we've got." So the first performance was only of the first three movements.'

According to Walton, however, Harty himself had 'behaved like a lamb [and] was more or less willing to wait till March, but the LSO committee said that another postponement would be fatal, and that if I agreed, they would do it without the finale. It being pointed out very forcibly, by my friends and advisers, that it was the lesser of two evils, I concurred.'

The performance, under Harty's baton, was received with tremendous enthusiasm – not least because the revitalised LSO tore into this virtuoso music with, according to some reports, ferocious zeal. 'We imagine that further rehearsal might smooth away some of the asperities of this hearing,' wrote *The Times*'s critic, Frank Howes, a trifle tartly. Perhaps he had learnt that only two of the four scheduled rehearsals had been used – composer and conductor apparently deciding that any further preparation was unnecessary.

The première was important for the LSO: it signalled that, far from being a spent force, the orchestra was capable of rising to the challenge of the most demanding contemporary scores. It would be many years before the LSO became 'top dog' in London again, but through their determination to survive and retain their independence, its players had evolved a modus operandi that would see them safely, if unspectacularly, through the uncertain 1930s.

Four more seasons came and went without much incident. The vexatious and whiskery arguments over deputies continued to rumble on, unresolved. One attempt by the board to ensure regular attendance – by issuing players with details of programmes and conductors well in advance – backfired completely: the use of deputies actually increased when players realised what was in store for them! But by May 1939 the LSO's directors clearly felt much more confident about the orchestra's future. They entered into negotiations with a whole raft of great names who might conduct the following year – among them, Bruno Walter, Busch, Kleiber, Szell, Ormandy, Stokowski and even Toscanini. The 1939–40 season could have been unforgettable. And in a way, it was.

5 Years of war and austerity
1939–55

Percussion Section, 1950, *l to r*: James Blades (Principal), Reg Rashleigh
and Alan Taylor

previous page
Wind Section, 1950, Lowry Sanders (2nd flute), John Cruft (oboe)
Harp Section, 1950, John Cockerill and Marie Goossens

September 1939. At first, everyone assumed that London would be pounded by an aerial bombardment from Day One, and all musical and theatrical life was suspended. Then came the eerie calm, the sense of anti-climax and – in the entertainment world – the thankful realisation that people would still want to hear music and see shows, even (or perhaps especially) in the middle of a war.

The LSO took the lead. A fortnight after war had been declared, the orchestra's board resolved that it was 'essential to make every effort to carry on . . . in order to maintain the orchestra's contribution to the musical activities of the nation'. On 7 October Charles Hambourg (the 'Stepney Slasher', as generations of orchestral players affectionately knew this workaday maestro) conducted the orchestra in the first Queen's Hall concert of the war. Played to a packed house, it was a statement of intent in more ways than one. The opening piece was the overture to Wagner's *Die Meistersinger*, followed by Beethoven's Piano Concerto No 4. Unlike in 1914, there was no perceptible objection to hearing 'the enemy's music'. It was as if the musical community had taken a tacit decision that the devil should not be allowed to claim the best tunes as his private property. The sound of Beethoven, in particular, was to become a remarkable anti-Nazi rallying cry as the war progressed.

The soloist in the concerto was a remarkable woman. London-born Myra Hess was forty-nine years old, and had been performing in public – without creating too much of a stir – almost as long as the LSO had. But the war was the making of her. Three days after playing with the LSO she began her series of lunchtime piano recitals in the National Gallery. They caught the public's imagination. The great paintings may have been removed for safe keeping, but this quiet, intense woman – playing her trademark Bach or Scarlatti in the very heart of London as the bombs fell – came to represent the flaming torch of civilisation: inextinguishable and inspirational. She was created a Dame of the British Empire in 1941, and rarely has that rather peculiar title been more aptly bestowed.

Something of her indomitable and stoic spirit infused London's other leading musicians as well. After the BBC had dithered and fretted over whether to continue the Proms during the war, Keith Douglas of the Royal Philharmonic Society decided to seize the initiative and announced that the

RPS would promote a 1940 Proms series instead. He hired the LSO, and invited the seventy-one-year-old Sir Henry Wood to conduct them once more. (All of the old tension between the LSO and Wood had long since disappeared; indeed, Wood had conducted the orchestra in some of the hastily arranged wartime concerts the previous winter.)

What a pity that the BBC, rather meanly, decided not to broadcast these 'unofficial' Proms. The microphones would have recorded history, as well as music, in the making. The first raid of the Blitz occurred on 26 August, and on several of the subsequent nights both orchestra and audience were effectively imprisoned in the Queen's Hall until dawn, when the Tubes started running again. The extraordinary circumstances produced both camaraderie and some bizarre entertainment. To while away the hours, the LSO gave impromptu concerts. Several of the principals took the opportunity to wheel out their party-piece concertos. There was chamber music galore, and even what we would now call 'stand-up comedy': one player, Ralph Nicholson, specialised in Beecham impressions.

'The audience took part,' recalled the LSO leader George Stratton, 'and there was much of interest, including Schubert's 'Trout' Quintet with Benno Moiseiwitsch turning the pages for Gerald Moore. Another time I played the Mendelssohn Concerto, but my chief contribution to these all-night musical orgies was to take round my big black hat which was fully filled with money for the Musicians' Benevolent Fund. The collections were heavy ones, and in consequence my poor hat was never the same after all was over.'

Then the players would snatch a few hours' sleep at the hall before assembling on the platform again for a 10 a.m. rehearsal. Those must have been remarkable days. But after a few weeks – with the solid mansions of Portland Place crashing down on all sides – the idea of spending the night playing Schubert quintets in an unprotected Victorian concert hall during a visit from the Luftwaffe seemed less like an act of defiance and more like mass suicide. For a while the starting time of the concerts was brought forward to 6.30 p.m. to avoid the raids and allow audiences to get the Tube home. But in the end the season was abandoned – fortunately, as it turned out.

The Prom on 7 September was to be the last ever in the Queen's Hall, which was reduced to ashes by an incendiary bomb on 10 May 1941. (It was a bad week for London's landmark buildings: the Houses of Parliament were badly damaged the following night.) Some historians claim, without a great deal of evidence, that the bombing of the Queen's Hall was a direct retaliation for the RAF's destruction of Berlin's Staatsoper a few days earlier. A more likely theory, however – if conspiracy theories carry any credence at all when applied to the haphazard business of air raids – is surely that the Luftwaffe was targeting the BBC's lavish new Broadcasting House, built nine years earlier right next door.

Whatever the bombers' intentions, that fateful night proved to be a doubly cruel blow for Adolf Lotter, the LSO's veteran principal double bass, who had studied with Dvořák in Prague as a youth. Lotter had left one of his instruments at the Queen's Hall overnight; it was of course destroyed. He then turned up the next day at Denham Studios (to the west of London) for a film-soundtrack session, and discovered that his other instrument had been destroyed in an air raid there. Some players said that he never recovered from the trauma; he died the following year.

The Proms were not killed off by the destruction of the Queen's Hall, but were immediately transferred to the much bigger Albert Hall, where the LSO again played under Henry Wood and Basil Cameron. Such was the remarkable thirst for music during the war that the Proms audience grew to fill even that capacious barn night after night. But the Proms alone were not going to be enough to keep the orchestra in business during the darkest days of the war. Nor were the weekly concerts in the Cambridge Theatre, organised by the impresario Jay Pomeroy. Something else was needed.

That something turned out to be the Carnegie Trust. The music committee of this big educational and philanthropic charity was chaired by the composer and Royal College of Music director, Sir George Dyson. He offered the LSO £50 per concert and a £50 guarantee against loss (plus a £200 reserve to cover what was terrifyingly known as 'catastrophic loss', meaning a bomb on the hall during a concert) if the orchestra would tour to the parts of Britain that rarely saw or heard professional musicians. The idea, which came from the Government, was to harness performers in a campaign to keep the morale of Britain's bombed and battered population high. Later in the war, ENSA (officially the 'Entertainments National Service Organisation'; unofficially 'Every Night Something Awful') would organise similar tours to barracks, naval ports and RAF stations across the country.

In this way the LSO began its peripatetic wartime existence. The orchestra visited venues and towns that no professional symphony orchestra had ever set foot in before, and possibly none has done since – the likes of Tiverton, Petersfield, Leamington Spa, High Wycombe. The tours were often incredibly demanding – sixteen concerts in eleven days in the autumn of 1942, for instance – and dangerous too. At one concert (according to LSO legend) a bomb went off so close to the hall that the solo pianist stopped playing and dived for cover under his grand piano, much to the amusement of the orchestra, which simply carried on as though nothing more untoward than a cough in the audience had disturbed the flow of the music.

Nor were food and accommodation easy to find for a whole orchestra, even one reduced by wartime conscription to forty-odd players. The endless journeys round small towns and army barracks became known as 'fish and chip tours', for obvious reasons – according to George Stratton, England's national dish was 'cooked in something strongly resembling train oil' during those war-rationed times. One trip to Dundee, however, became known as the 'salad cream tour'. In a grocery store there an LSO player discovered a whole storeroom of the stuff, which had become unobtainable in London. The orchestra promptly bought up the entire stock; whether this was for personal consumption or later resale on the black market is, perhaps wisely, not recorded in the annals.

One or two players may have found the long tours, coupled with the snatch-it-while-you-can attitude to sex in wartime, rather to their liking. Girls known as 'popsies' used to cluster round the stage door after performances, offering to 'knit sweaters' for the all-male orchestra. One trumpeter is said to have followed naval tradition and kept a girl in every port.

For most of the orchestra, however, those were difficult times. Stranded without a bed for the night after a concert in Plymouth, one player slept on the floor of the police station. In Hull, after another engagement, several string players found themselves accommodated in what was then known as a 'vagrants' house'. Things were so desperate after a Wolverhampton concert that Albert Coates, the conductor, appealed from the podium for people to take a player home for the night. And wherever the orchestra had been playing in southern England, the players invariably seemed to end up stranded at Didcot railway station in the early hours of the morning.

The biggest problem, however, was simply finding enough competent players to fill the orchestra's ranks at a time when more than sixty of its regular members were on active service. Bertram Lewis, the LSO's secretary, had a celebrated file with the name of every conceivable deputy for every orchestral section, and quite a few inconceivable ones as well. But even this comprehensive directory was exhausted one morning in 1944 when he was engaged in a desperate quest to find a third horn for that evening's concert. Finally, from the top of a bus, he spotted a guardsman going into Victoria Station clutching what could only be the case of a French horn (or a very oddly shaped bearskin). He raced after the man, who turned out to be a Welsh Guardsman on his way to an afternoon concert in Surrey. The soldier confirmed that he could be back in London by 5.30 p.m., and was engaged on the spot. No references, no audition, no rehearsal, no time! He proved to be a decent player.

In fact, the Welsh Guards band was a fertile recruiting ground for the LSO. Another of its alumni was the young trumpeter, Bram Wiggins. 'I was very lucky because there was a shortage of brass players during the war,' he recalls. 'And since the Welsh Guards band was stationed in London, we could creep away and do the odd date with the LSO. Lots of their players had been called up, yet they had loads of work to get through. In fact, I even played on a couple of wartime films with them while I was still a student.

'Well, one day, when I was in the Guards, I got a call from Bertram Lewis on a Friday night. 'Can you do the Albert Hall tomorrow?' he asked. It was fourth trumpet in *Roman Carnival*, I think. I said: 'I can't do the rehearsal, I've got military duties. But I could come for the concert.' He agreed to that. But when I got there I found that I was not way down the trumpet line as I had thought, but playing second trumpet. I also found that the concert began with a piece by Britten that I had never seen before, which started with a second trumpet solo! Fortunately it went all right. And as I came off the platform the LSO directors more or less offered me a permanent job on the strength of my playing that night.' Wiggins stayed in the orchestra for eleven years. 'I've always been rather glad I didn't do that rehearsal,' he says.

Seven LSO players lost their lives in the conflict. Among them was the violinist Simmon Latutin, a captain in the Somalia Gendarmerie, who was killed just after Christmas 1944. He had twice run into an ammunition store that was on fire to rescue a fellow officer and a Somalian boy who were trapped inside. He died of his injuries the next day. For this 'magnificent example of undaunted selflessness', he was posthumously awarded the George Cross.

*

War has the strangest and most unforeseen consequences. Before 1939, British orchestras, theatres, opera and ballet companies had to survive – if they did survive – on takings from the box office and the largesse of rich patrons. It was a ramshackle, patchy and hand-to-mouth system, but at least it meant that serious culture existed because there were people who wanted it badly enough to put their hands in their own pockets and pay for it.

By 1945, however, the country had somehow acquired a grand new institution whose donations to the arts would be more contentious. The new handouts were called state subsidy – money compulsorily extracted from taxpayers, whether they loved the arts, abhorred them, or were blissfully indifferent. A revolution had been accomplished, entirely by stealth. There had been virtually no public consultation or debate, except in the discreet Bloomsbury circle to which the ballet-mad economist John Maynard Keynes belonged. The Arts Council of Great Britain – a body that was to dominate the lives and thinking of the LSO players as no conductor or patron had ever done – was conceived, born, staffed and financed almost before anyone active in the arts had grasped what a leviathan of red tape had been created. As Keynes himself acknowledged in 1945: 'I do not believe it is yet realised what an important thing has happened. State patronage of the arts has crept in. It has happened in a very informal, unostentatious way – half-baked if you like.'

And half-baked is indeed what the Arts Council has often appeared to be in the subsequent sixty years. But in that glad dawn of 1945, nobody could doubt the idealism of Keynes's vision – nor, in practice, the necessity of State support. Another unexpected effect of war was that large numbers of the British public had been exposed to serious music, theatre and ballet for the first time in their lives, thanks to the wartime Government's decision to sponsor tours such as those described above as a means of keeping up morale. Astonishingly, the public had lapped up what was offered; almost by accident, the State had created a large market for serious culture. Now somebody had to carry on supplying and, of course, paying for it.

This new state of affairs chimed well with the inclination of the incoming 1945 Labour Government, which would extend the power and responsibility of the public sector into all sorts of different areas, from hospitals to coal mines. The notion that the arts, too, could be 'nationalised' was merely one more strand in the tapestry of the 'welfare state' – probably just as well, since there was certainly no chance that this huge new potential audience could be serviced by an arts world limping along as it had before 1939.

To understand what had changed in the economics of the arts, we need to turn the clock back a few decades. In retrospect it is obvious that the old patrons – the Church and the Court – were virtually exhausted as sources of serious money by the beginning of the twentieth century. New sources of support would have to be found – as they had been in the United States, which had no tradition of aristocratic patronage in any case. From the mid-nineteenth century onwards, the civic and social elite of American cities had begun to accept responsibility for funding their communities' orchestras, as they also accepted responsibility for public libraries, galleries, museums, universities and even hospitals. A magnificent tradition of enlightened and generous philanthropy sprang up, fostered by such visionaries as Andrew Carnegie. The tradition goes on to this day: witness the Los Angeles

Philharmonic's new home, the Walt Disney Hall, or the fabulous Getty Museum in the same city.

The need to find new sources of patronage for arts organisations was also recognised on the Continent, but here a very different solution was reached. Rather than turning to private wealth, orchestras and opera companies increasingly came to be subsidised, or even employed by, the State. Sometimes, as with Stalin's 'nationalisation' of music, literature, drama and ballet (a system of subsidy much admired by Keynes, incidentally), there were dubious, perhaps even odious, ideological factors driving the process. But elsewhere, as in nineteenth-century Germany, local councils and regional governments simply accepted that supporting a rich cultural life was an important communal obligation, like mending the roads or putting out fires.

Britain was different again. Rich and generous patrons did exist – though they generally had nothing like the wealth of America's new super-million-aires. However, there was no real tradition in Britain of the rich making art available to the poor, almost as a civic duty – indeed, there still isn't. Neither, however, had early twentieth-century Britain moved towards a continental-style system of state subsidy. True, Victorian England did see the birth of one publicly subsidised orchestra: the Municipal Orchestra of Bournemouth, direct forerunner of today's Bournemouth Symphony Orchestra – but this had only twenty-four players, so it was really more suited to teashop tinkling than the symphonic repertoire.

Why was Britain so late to embrace the idea of public subsidy? One reason, perhaps, is that the stark economic realities of running an arts organisation were masked for so long. The Victorian era's atmosphere of prosperity and stability lingered on, like an afterglow, when the country's wealth had in reality long vanished. Appearances were deceptive, in the music profession as everywhere else. But another, more insidious reason is surely that the Victorian ethos of self-reliance continued long after the Victorians themselves had disappeared. An Englishman was expected to stand on his own two feet, and so was an English orchestra or theatre.

The Great War and what came afterwards made that impossible. The raging inflation of the immediate post-war years, the Depression, the social anxiety and uncertainty of the late 1930s, and then another colossal and disruptive war followed by a prolonged period of austerity: all this had decimated traditional sources of revenue for the arts. Institutions such as the LSO, founded in palmy Edwardian days, were simply incapable, psychologically or practically, of 'scraping by somehow' for much longer.

The brilliant Keynes understood this, and also realised that if money could be prised from the State, the British arts scene could be revolutionised. He set about transforming an organisation set up in 1940 as a purely temporary wartime body, so stealthily and craftily that it seemed a natural metamorphosis. By 1945, he had succeeded in converting CEMA – the Council for the Encouragement of Music and the Arts – into a permanent Arts Council that would quickly come to dominate every facet of serious culture in Britain.

Just as Keynes had envisaged, public subsidy did change everything. In 2004, with national and local government pouring more than a billion pounds a year into culture of one sort or another, it is hard to imagine the arts world existing without it. The paradox is that it came into existence (like that other great edifice of the welfare state – the National Health Service) at the very moment when Britain, after two hundred years of burgeoning prosperity, had largely exhausted her resources and energies in a supreme effort to defeat Hitler. Subsidy of the arts in Britain was a shoestring operation from the outset, especially when compared with the lavish public funds available to French and German cultural institutions. That relative parsimony has been a source of endless agitation ever since.

Of course, that eternal, cynical maxim – 'There's no such thing as a free lunch' – is as true when the meal in question is supplied by the State as when the bill is settled with the swirl of a millionaire's pen. Keynes designed the Arts Council to be his own fiefdom – he would have been its first chairman, had he not died – and he was a natural meddler. 'I suffer from the congenital disability that, if I do join anything, I cannot manage to remain in a merely sleeping capacity,' he once told a friend. The quango he created in his own image has always exhibited a similar tendency. As London's orchestras have been finding to their discomfort over the past sixty years, the price of the 'free lunch' called state subsidy is eternal interference from the Arts Council.

The LSO discovered this truth sooner than most. In January 1943, the regional tours originally set up and financed by the Carnegie Trust were taken over by CEMA, Keynes's prototype Arts Council. At first the grant to the LSO continued as before. But in May 1944 an ominous letter arrived. Rather than continue to supply concert-by-concert support for the LSO's tours, as the Carnegie Trust had happily done, CEMA intended to supply a £1,000 grant for the whole year and a £4,000 guarantee against loss – provided that the LSO offered 'proper working conditions to your players by putting them on a salaried basis'. To Keynes's tidy mind, the LSO's 'musical republic' of self-employed shareholders was a nonsense, and so was the notion that humble orchestral players could be trusted to decide their own working conditions.

The LSO board played for time. With seventy per cent of its membership on military service, it argued, such a fundamental change to its constitution could not possibly be contemplated. The tactic was only temporarily successful. In February 1945 the orchestra received a sharp little letter from a sharp little woman who was almost as tidy-minded and meddlesome as Keynes himself – Mary Glasgow, CEMA's secretary. Later, she would run the Arts Council. 'It was our prime intention to give interim help to the LSO in the hope that its constitution could eventually be reconsidered,' she wrote. 'But the time has now come for me to warn you that, unless such a change is carried out, our Council will be unable to renew its association with the LSO.'

Thus was an orchestra that had survived all vicissitudes for more than forty years told to 'reform or die' by a bunch of bureaucrats who had been in office for less than four. The LSO promptly broke off the relationship, and stopped the tours. It was no great loss to the players: the wearisome journeys through English backwaters were by then making far bigger losses than CEMA could cover anyway. But the incident was a chill foretaste of things to come. Subsequent battles with CEMA's successor, the Arts Council itself, were to prove even more troublesome.

*

Meanwhile, Beecham was getting twitchy fingers again: it had been more than ten years since he had last founded an orchestra. The war was over, he could safely come back to Blighty, having passed the time very comfortably in America, and the only question to be settled was which distinguished set of musicians would have the honour of being conducted by him.

His first move was to try and re-establish his old relationship with the LPO, as if the bitter divorce of 1939 had never happened. That was never going to work. The LPO – which, like the LSO, had endured a tough and uncomfortable war – was now run by a bunch of proudly left-wing individuals who would rather have chewed their own music stands than turned the orchestra back into a baronet's fiefdom. And too many LSO players had vivid memories of 1932 for Beecham to find a congenial berth with that ensemble either.

The only path open to Beecham if he wanted to return to the centre of British musical life was to recruit yet another band of brilliant virtuosi to crew his showboat. It would be 1905, 1909, 1928 and 1932 all over again – what fun! His first attempt was a joint venture with Walter Legge, a bright and ambitious London tailor's son who had swiftly risen through the record-ing world to become EMI's top producer. Legge had realised, perhaps before anyone else, that advances in recording techniques would soon make pre-1939 discs sound very old-fashioned and inadequate. If he could hand-pick an orchestra specially for the recording studio and link it to the rising young conductors and soloists with whom he had assiduously cultivated contacts (he was soon to marry one of the greatest of them: the soprano Elisabeth Schwarzkopf), he would swiftly be running a very lucrative musical empire.

In the event, he didn't even have to hand-pick the orchestra. During the war many of the finest young instrumentalists in Britain had ended up in the RAF, which was consequently able to run what was probably the best sym-phony orchestra ever clad in military uniform. In 1946 most of them simply swapped their RAF barracks for Legge's EMI studio. Legge called them the Philharmonia – and thus another London orchestra was born.

Beecham, naturally, was implicated in all of this – in fact he conducted the Philharmonia's opening concert, in the dismal Kingsway Hall in 1946. Inevitably, however, he fell out with Legge. The producer was far too assertive a personality, too sure of his own tastes and too ambitious in his own right, to play second fiddle to Sir Thomas. In any case, Legge already had a whole raft of useful foreign conductors queuing up to conduct his new orchestra – the likes of Cantelli, Karajan, Klemperer, Toscanini. He really didn't need the ageing English maestro.

Beecham bounced right back. Having fallen out with three of the bands then playing in London, he promptly started another, resurrecting the cheeky title he had first dreamed up eighteen years earlier: the Royal Philharmonic Orchestra. (Naturally, he had asked neither the Royal Household nor the Royal Philharmonic Society if he could use the name.) True to London tra-dition, the star-spangled new orchestra swiftly plucked the most lucrative plums off the tree, usurping the LSO from Glyndebourne and winning a great deal of recording work. It was to be the last of Beecham's creations, and it took the number of symphony orchestras in London up to five. Nearly sixty years later, they all still exist – a matter of some astonishment to most observers of the scene.

*

All this must have been very irksome for the LSO directors, as they desper-ately tried to secure their own orchestra's future after the tumultuous celebra-tions of summer 1945 had faded from the memory and the dismal realities of 'austerity Britain' began to sink in. There were two priorities. One was to remind London concertgoers of the orchestra's quality. This required the players to make a considerable leap of faith. 'To get the orchestra back on its feet in the 1945–6 season,' Bram Wiggins recalls, 'we did some concerts called the LSO Celebrity Series for which we weren't paid – not for the extra rehearsals or anything. But if you couldn't do the concert, you still had to pay your deputy out of your own pocket! The next season we did get paid for the concerts, but we did the rehearsals free. And so it gradually got better.'

The other priority was to earn some real money. Luckily, there was no shortage of what would now be described as 'hack work' – engagements that weren't artistically satisfying, but at least paid the family's food bill. 'There was an even bigger boom in that sort of work than during the war,' George Stratton recalled. 'We went through a period of hard work that really became a test of endurance both physically and mentally.'

Many of these engagements must have been done on what later generations of musicians would call 'autopilot'. There were Tchaikovsky, Beethoven and 'Music from the Ballet' Nights galore. The same handful of piano concertos – Grieg, Rachmaninov Two and the 'Emperor' – would be endlessly repeated. Undemanding Sunday afternoon 'lollipops' concerts would be put on in the Albert Hall with virtually no rehearsal. In retrospect, the demand for these stupendously unadventurous programmes is easily explained. The nation had been traumatised, battered and bombed for the previous six years, and was now groping its way through a bleak period of acute shortages: food rationing didn't end completely until 1954. In addition, the winter of 1946–7 was one of the most bitter in living memory, with temperatures plunging to their lowest for eighty years and little fuel available to heat homes and halls (hot-water bottles became an essential accessory for concert audiences). At this stage in their history, the British people needed music to comfort the soul, not to stimulate the intellect.

In any case, over-familiar repertoire was not the worst problem encountered by an orchestra that couldn't turn down work. Much more galling was the rise of the dilettante conductor. According to Stratton, they were 'usually people who had some money to spare and thought that conducting was – oh so easy – just wagging a stick about'. Such performances were held together in the time-honoured tradition. 'I waved my violin about and the orchestra followed in the manner of a restaurant band, not looking at the conductor at all,' Stratton recalled. 'We endured this sort of thing for a time until the orchestra suddenly revolted and just refused to play with one conductor.'

It dawned on the LSO board in 1948 that such dispiriting engagements, no matter how profitable, could not go on indefinitely. The LSO's own winter concert series, abandoned in 1939, had to be permanently re-established. Apart from anything else, such a move would (as Gordon Walker, the LSO's chairman, colourfully put it) surprise 'other musicians who thought the LSO were just furniture removers to be hired to go from one engagement to another – with inevitable accidents on the way'.

More important still was the hope that the restoration of the London concert series would boost the orchestra's standards. By this time, of course, London's pool of orchestral talent was being split five ways, with the LSO all too often ending up with the fifth-choice players. Indeed, an internal Arts Council memo of that time described the LSO as 'dilapidated, artistically ruinous'. The ears of the bureaucrats hadn't detected anything that wasn't distressingly obvious to those running the band. George Stratton, the leader, put the matter with characteristic bluntness in a letter to the board:

Gentlemen, no doubt this will not come as a bombshell to you after the painful exhibitions we have all heard lately . . . The fact of the matter is that if we hope to survive as an orchestra in the face of present-day competition, the whole of the second violin section must be reconstructed, for there are very few of them that are worth their place in a first-class combination . . . This must be done very fast, for complaints from conductors are coming in thick and fast . . . There are quite a number of excellent players among students of the RCM, RAM, GSM, etc, who although short of experience would instil a new life and enthusiasm into our orchestra, and we might do worse than supplant our poor ones with some of these.

It would be another seven years before the LSO would take the radical step that Stratton was proposing, and bring in a new, young generation of players en masse. And even in 1955 the move was forced on the orchestra, rather than being instigated by its board. Perhaps ruthlessness on such a grand scale is constitutionally beyond the capability of a self-governing co-operative.

Instead, in 1948, the orchestra looked around for someone to galvanise its ranks and shake off its mediocrity. But who? The orchestra's pre-war stalwarts were either dead (Weingartner, Harty), ailing (Busch, Coates, Mengelberg) or tied to other orchestras (Beecham, Barbirolli, Boult). The players felt they needed a firm but humane figurehead: a conductor who would lift standards and enthuse audiences, but not act the tyrant. They found such a figure on 7 December 1948 when the forty-six year-old Josef Krips appeared in public with them for the first time.

The Albert Hall programme was quintessential Krips: Mozart and Brahms symphonies and Mahler's *Kindertotenlieder*, featuring a sensational English contralto called Kathleen Ferrier. It was love at first sight between conductor and orchestra. 'You know as well as I that the contact between the LSO and myself was the best company from the first minute when I met this wonderful orchestra,' Krips wrote, in his idiosyncratic English, to the LSO's chairman, Harry Dugarde. And his feelings were reciprocated. 'I have very happy memories of Joe,' said the bassoonist William Waterhouse. 'He used to stand in front with a blissful expression, head on one side, like a baby cooing. At first you might think: 'Why don't you wipe that stupid grin off your face?' But in fact he created an environment in which everyone could play nicely. He wasn't dictatorial; he just made it all happen very well.'

It took Krips two years to clear his Viennese commitments, but he became the LSO's principal conductor in November 1950. Sadly, he quit only four years later over a minor disagreement with the board at the start of the LSO's fiftieth-birthday celebrations – a contretemps that ended with Krips punching John Cruft, the LSO's secretary, on the nose, twice. In those four years, however, he restored the LSO's cohesion, its sense of artistic purpose and, to be blunt, its integrity.

By birth, temperament and training Krips was Viennese to his manicured fingertips. He was a choirboy in Vienna, a music student there (studying conducting with Weingartner), first violinist at the city's Volksoper, and then, after the usual teeth-cutting conducting jobs in minor German opera houses, permanent conductor at the Vienna State Opera and professor of music at the Vienna Academy of Music. All before he was thirty-six.

But although he was Catholic and quintessentially Austrian, he wasn't quite Catholic and Austrian enough for Nazi tastes. Because his grandparents were Jewish he was sacked from all his jobs in 1938. He fled to Belgrade, kept his head down, and passed the war as a packer in a food-processing factory. That counted in his favour in 1945, when the Russians gave him the task of reconstructing the Vienna State Opera – a task he carried out with conspicuous success. When he and Furtwängler brought the Staatsoper and the Vienna Philharmonic to Covent Garden in 1947 their performances of the big Mozart operas made, by all accounts, a remarkable impression. (Some London musicians, infuriated at how swiftly the Vienna Philharmonic had managed to put up the 'business as usual' notices after complying so shamelessly with the Nazis, picketed Covent Garden with placards reading: 'We can play as well as they.' Unfortunately, five minutes spent at the performance inside was enough to demonstrate the falsehood of this claim.)

With the LSO, Krips cannily played to his strengths. Each March he led the orchestra in a Beethoven cycle: all the symphonies and most or all of the concertos – Wilhelm Kempff and Claudio Arrau both completed concerto cycles. 'He got us to play in a more homogeneous way,' recalls Roger Lord, who had been recruited from the London Philharmonic to the LSO's principal oboe chair in 1952. 'He ironed out the differences in the styles of playing. Some said he ironed out too much, but we were certainly playing in a more suave, Austrian style, and this really showed in the Beethoven cycle.'

The cycle was important for another reason, too. 'You have to remember,' says Lord, 'that we were always in debt. The Beethoven cycle was the way that we could get back into the black on the balance sheet.' Besides Beethoven, Krips's programmes were full of Mozart, Brahms and Richard Strauss. But he also championed Mahler (the 'Resurrection' Symphony and *Das Lied von der Erde*, again with Ferrier) and Bruckner (the Eighth Symphony), at a time when the gigantically proportioned music of the two Austrians was generally considered to be too overwrought for English tastes.

Because his concerts were overwhelmingly Austro-Germanic occasions the LSO made sure that British music was well represented in the programmes of other conductors. What's surprising is how much of this native product was newly composed. In the six seasons from 1948 the LSO performed no fewer than thirty-eight works by living British composers. Admittedly, many of these were hardly *enfants terribles*. Vaughan Williams, Walton and Bax accounted for sixteen of the pieces. Even so, the younger generation was represented. Benjamin Britten, Lennox Berkeley, Malcom Arnold and the once highly rated Peter Racine Fricker were all given a platform. In many cases the new pieces were played twice in the same programme in order to give the audience a better chance to grasp the music – an admirable practice that should be more boldly followed today.

Such sterling service to living British composers was dangerous in box-office terms, of course. On 11 November 1949, the LSO played a fascinating Remembrance Day programme: *Banks of Green Willow* by George Butterworth (killed at the Somme); the cantata *Morning Heroes* by Arthur Bliss (himself a war hero); and Vaughan Williams's magnificent and tragic Sixth Symphony, conducted by the composer. 'The public', recalled John Cruft, the LSO's secretary, 'stayed away in thousands.'

Little wonder, then, that the LSO's championing of modern British music was the exception, not the norm, among London orchestras at that time. It would be another twenty years before the London Sinfonietta was founded specifically to specialise in the performance of new music. Indeed, the LSO's pioneering role was recognised in a letter the orchestra received in 1952 from Guy Warrack, the chairman of the Composers' Guild. 'We have so many disappointments from orchestras and programme-makers who invariably complain that contemporary British music empties the house,' Warrack wrote.

'We hope that the LSO's shining example will strike a blow that will be felt all over the country.'

In fact the LSO's commitment to living British composers helped to bring it a little commercial comfort. The innovative Decca Record Company was experimenting with 45 and 33 r.p.m. 'long-playing' records at a time when its more senior competitors were still stuck with 78s. It urgently needed a 'house' orchestra to supply a new catalogue of music for the new format, and the ubiquitous Victor Olof – a violinist turned conductor turned orchestral manager (for Beecham's RPO) turned record executive – recruited the LSO to supply the bulk of these. In the next few years the orchestra recorded most of the main symphonic repertoire under a host of illustrious (or soon to be illustrious) names, including Krips, Krauss, Sargent, Fistoulari and an up-and-coming Hungarian firebrand called Georg Solti. Not least of the LSO's achievements in the studio was a notable recording of Vaughan Williams's monumentally grim Sixth Symphony. 'It must have been hell to play it for three hours,' the ancient composer told the orchestra, after attending one session. 'I know it's been hell to listen to.'

What the LSO of the early 1950s was far less good at, however, was giving its audience a sense of the revolutionary musical trends sweeping the Continent. True, the orchestra gave one very important British première, of Messiaen's *Turangalîla-symphonie*, which took place at the Albert Hall under Walter Goehr's direction in 1952, only four years after the piece was completed. 'I remember the concert vividly,' recalls the trumpeter Bram Wiggins, 'because it's the only one I ever did at which half the audience was cheering like mad and the other half booing and hissing.'

Otherwise, if recent continental composers were included in LSO programmes at all, they tended to be neoclassicists or late-Romantics – names such as Bloch, Hindemith and Martinů. Schoenberg and Berg were closed books until Antal Doráti ventured into the Second Viennese School with the LSO in the late 1950s. As for Stockhausen, Boulez and Ligeti, one doubts whether the LSO players of the 1950s would even have known the names of these avant-garde pioneers, let alone played any of their music.

The LSO was hardly unique in its insularity: a cosy disdain for the strange noises being produced on the other side of the English Channel was a feature of all the British orchestral programmes of the 1950s, even the BBC's. That explains why William Glock, an avowed champion of the avant-garde, met with such hostility when he opened the hallowed doors of the Proms to Boulez and his serialist confrères in the early 1960s. Even Stravinsky was not often played by the LSO of that period – as the young Colin Davis discovered.

'I was a Stravinsky freak in those days, but they had played very little of his music,' he recalls. 'I particularly remember the tremendous tussle we had to go through in order to do the *Symphony in Three Movements*. We had to have extra rehearsals; in those days the strings simply couldn't cope with that sort of percussive music.' They must have learnt quickly: by the late 1960s no orchestra was playing Stravinsky with more panache than the LSO.

*

The LSO's rebellion against the meddling bureaucrats of the new Arts Council didn't last long. Survival comes a long way above principle in any orchestra's list of priorities, and in 1948 the LSO needed money and the Arts Council could supply it. So at an extraordinary general meeting on 24 September the players voted to alter their Articles of Association in order to bring them into line with the Arts Council view of what constituted a 'proper' way to run an orchestra. Henceforth the 'income and property' of the company would be 'applied solely towards the promotion of all or any of the objects of the company . . . and no part thereof should be paid or trans-ferred, directly or indirectly, by way of dividends, bonus or otherwise by way of profit to members of the company.' The alteration had the additional ben-efit of transforming the LSO into a 'non-profit-distributing' organisation (as its rivals were), and thus exempting it from entertainment tax. The players probably calculated that there was little point in being taxed as a profit-dis-tributing business when there were usually no profits to distribute.

A purely pragmatic rewording, then? Not entirely. Since its foundation, forty-four years earlier, the LSO players had been bound together by sharing equally in the profits and losses of their venture. There was a certain nobility of purpose about that self-reliance – and, naturally, a certain unease about giving it up. 'Any monetary benefit will result in loss of independence,' some players argued – and they were right. But in 1948 there was no alternative. Thus 'reformed', the orchestra finally qualified for an Arts Council grant. The reward for this fundamental change to its constitution? Just £2,000 a year. 'It could have been blown in one concert, once you paid a good soloist and conductor,' says Bram Wiggins. 'It was peanuts.' For that the orchestra was also obliged to allow an Arts Council assessor into its board meetings. The board was disconcerted, one imagines, to discover that the Arts Council representative was to be John Denison – a former horn player who had been a founder member of Beecham's LPO. At his first appearance, in December 1948, Denison took pains to reassure the LSO players that, as the Arts Council's representative, he couldn't vote and wasn't there to control the orchestra's policy in any way. As the subsequent decades have shown, that wasn't quite the whole truth.

*

The bomb that fell on the Queen's Hall in 1941 also blasted a crater in the musical life of London that has never been satisfactorily repaired. Everybody who heard concerts in that hall speaks, or spoke, warmly of its acoustics and atmosphere. It could seat more than 2,500, it was in the heart of the West End – by all accounts it was perfect. It should have been rebuilt after the war: there were plans, committees, even the start of a fundraising campaign. But it wasn't, and since then London has not had a symphonic concert hall that comes remotely close to perfection.

For a while after the war its musicians had no choice but to cope with the giant-bathroom reverberation of the Albert Hall. Then they had to adapt to the polar opposite – the disastrously dry acoustics of the Festival Hall, which, in Simon Rattle's immortal phrase, 'sap the will to live'. The Barbican Hall, when it arrived thirty years later, was also regarded as an acoustical calamity by most musicians who used it – though it has been greatly improved in recent years. But the sad fact remains that London, which can probably boast more professional music-making per square mile than any other city in the world, has not had a world-class concert hall since 1944 and will probably not have one again in the lifetime of any reader of this book.

The failure to rebuild the Queen's Hall after the war is a minor tragedy – why was it allowed to happen? The truth seems to be that the 1945 Labour Government, and particularly that all-powerful, behind-the-scenes fixer, Herbert Morrison, was determined that nothing should impede or eclipse its plans for the 1951 Festival of Britain, a £12 million jamboree to be mounted as 'a tonic to the nation' (as its director, Gerald Barry, put it) on twenty-seven acres of derelict or bombed land near Waterloo Station on the south bank of the Thames. And the cornerstone of those plans was the construction of a spanking new 'modernist' concert hall. The fact that the new Royal Festival Hall was in the wrong place, made of the wrong materials, and designed in the wrong shape, mattered not a whit.

The foundation stone of the new hall was laid in October 1949, and George VI opened it on 3 May 1951. The first concert was a combined effort, involving players from all the London orchestras. But the LSO was the first orchestra to transfer its regular concerts to the South Bank, and it made its début there on 9 May, playing Haydn, Handel, Elgar, Walton and Sibelius under Clarence Raybould.

That represented quite a moral victory for the beleaguered orchestra. Even before the Festival Hall had opened, the London Philharmonic had launched a propaganda war with the aim of getting itself appointed as 'resident orchestra' of the new venue, and thus having first claim on concert dates and rehearsal opportunities. Its idea – perfectly logical, seen through LPO eyes – was to establish the same sort of relationship with the Festival Hall as existed between the Amsterdam Orchestra and the Concertgebouw, or the Vienna Philharmonic and the Musikverein. In other words, a relationship so close that orchestra and hall were virtually inseparable in the public's mind.

The LPO, like the LSO, had survived the war by the skin of its teeth. Under a bizarre but apparently successful arrangement with the bandleader Jack Hylton, it, too, had toured the nether regions of the country, directed by Sargent and Basil Cameron. In 1943, however, it had chosen a different constitutional path from its senior competitor. Under the guidance of its inspirational managing director, a viola player and card-carrying Communist called Thomas Russell, the orchestra had become fully contracted and salaried. Provision was even made for its players to receive similar pensions to those offered by the BBC orchestras.

All these visionary ideas were subsequently abandoned in 1957 when the LPO players, faced with insolvency, reverted to the laissez-faire LSO model again. But in 1951 the LPO's case for residency of the Festival Hall rested on the very fact that its members were salaried and properly contracted, and the LSO's weren't.

The LSO couldn't really dispute this, but the LPO also implied that it was a proper, 'serious' orchestra and the LSO wasn't. 'When one orchestra organises at its own risk a series of symphony concerts over a wide area, and watches over the proper interests of its own members, while another sits around and waits to be engaged, leaving its members meanwhile to earn their living as best they can, it is no justice to treat both organisations alike,' argued the LPO's Russell, rather spitefully. His orchestra, he claimed, was putting on concerts 'for their cultural value, while film sessions and other remunerative sessions were not sought'. But as the LSO promptly pointed out, the LPO was at that time receiving a public subsidy of £25,000 a year from the London County Council – more than ten times the LSO's grant. With that sort of government backing, it could afford to put 'cultural value' first.

However, the LPO was about to hit the headlines for non-musical reasons. In 1949 Russell visited Moscow as a delegate on a 'peace conference'. His trip was seized upon by the press as evidence that the LPO was a rather unlikely hotbed of 'red subversion'. The London County Council withdrew its grant; and all notions of the LPO becoming resident orchestra at the LCC's new hall were squashed. This was the era of the McCarthy witch-hunts. British paranoia over Communist infiltration was not as pronounced as in the United States, but was present nonetheless. In those circumstances, Russell was foolish to accept a second dubious invitation – this time to the People's Republic of China in 1952. The Arts Council (rather shamefully) pressurised the LPO to get rid of its highly politicised secretary, and Russell was forced out in November of that year.

So instead of becoming home to one orchestra, the Festival Hall became what is now known in the arts world as a 'garage': a palace of varieties, available for hire by anybody and everybody. But the idea of a resident orchestra at the Festival Hall would not lie down and die. Indeed, in the late twentieth century it was touted more and more noisily as 'the solution' to 'the London orchestra problem'. In 1990 the LPO did finally win its coveted 'residency' at the Festival Hall – more than forty years after its players first asked for it. It proved to be not a gateway to orchestral excellence and stability but a poisoned chalice. Seven years later, it asked the Philharmonia (with which it had been locked in a vicious 'takeover' battle only a few years earlier) to share the residency, which rather seemed to destroy the point of having one. By then, however, the LSO was out of the equation altogether: safely anchored across the Thames with its own residency in a hall built on another prominent 1940s bombsite – the Barbican.

*

Every orchestra is a fairly rigid hierarchy. The best string players sit at the front; the rest are ranked behind them in order of ability. Those behind the front desks are even known officially as 'rank and file' – I often wonder why the Musicians' Union still allows the use of this mildly derogatory term in job advertisements. Between the string sections, too, is an unspoken but ever-present sense of hierarchy. The first violins feel perceptibly superior to the seconds (because their parts, generally, are higher and more exposed), and both groups lord it over the violas – the butt of the cruellest orchestral jokes.

It is the wind players, however, who regard themselves as the true aristocracy. They, after all, are all soloists; they cannot hide or seek security in the comparative anonymity of a string section. And even within that aristocracy there are degrees of pressure, and hence prestige. A principal trumpet or horn is the musical equivalent of an airline pilot: if he or she has a bad night, the whole performance comes crashing down. Arrogance goes with that territory;

without unshakeable self-confidence the job of playing, say, the stupendous trumpet call at the start of Mahler's Fifth Symphony couldn't be done.

Every hierarchy has inherent tensions, though. An orchestra's rank and file wouldn't be human if it didn't resent, or covet, the money and the adulation bestowed on the 'stars' of the band. Most of the time that resentment is mild and simmers under the surface. But the LSO of the mid-1950s was almost torn apart by it.

The ostensible cause of the dispute was film sessions. Increasingly an elite band within the LSO – basically, all the principals, and other leading string players – had been absenting themselves from concert work to undertake much better-paid session work for film companies. They virtually operated as a band-within-a-band, fixing work for each other. Indeed, there was even talk of turning the LSO into a full-time 'session band' for film and sound-recording purposes. To make matters worse, the LSO itself was going through a lean time with outside engagements. 'We had broken with Krips, and since he had the contract with Decca, we were not getting so much work from them,' Roger Lord recalled. 'It was a thin year after he left.'

In addition, many principals also accepted solo and chamber-music bookings. It would be another thirty years before the LSO management had the wisdom (and, of course, the income) to 'double-cast' its principal players, so that the finest instrumentalists could be retained by the orchestra without jettisoning all outside work. In the volatile atmosphere of autumn 1954 such a solution was inconceivable.

The LSO board was democratically elected, and therefore far more representative of the 'rank and file' majority than of the principals. In fact, the board had elected the first 'rank and file' chairman in the LSO's history, the cellist Harry Dugarde. Inevitably, the directors inclined to the view that if the orchestra's standards were to improve still further, these 'unofficial arrangements with conductors and others' had to end, and that all LSO members had to be available for all engagements bearing the orchestra's name.

As the principals quickly pointed out, this ruling was contrary to the original *raison d'être* of the orchestra. In any case, many of the principals were already unhappy with the board. 'The board of directors was very weak at that time,' says Bram Wiggins. 'It was unstable; you didn't know where you were. There was some feeling that the orchestra should get in a businessman as an orchestral manager.'

The usual arguments for and against deputies (by now rather whiskery) were wheeled out once more. Had the LSO not been founded expressly to uphold the deputy system? Were the board not trying to curtail individual members' 'liberty of action' – their right, in other words, to accept or decline whatever work they were offered?

The row turned nasty with the Fell affair, in spring 1955. Sidney Fell, the principal clarinettist, was dismissed for sending a deputy to an LSO concert 'without good reason'. Thirty LSO members demanded an extraordinary general meeting at which there was, by all accounts, 'vigorous' discussion of the orchestra's rules and traditions. The upshot was that on 11 May 1955, all the LSO's principal players – wind, brass and strings – resigned en masse. Their joint resignation letter was blunt and to the point. In the view of the departing players, it was not they who were jeopardising the orchestra's standards by their moonlighting, but the LSO board:

It is an indisputable fact that the orchestra is suffering from a serious decline – in number of engagements, standard of performance and esprit de corps, and it is our opinion that this is due to the faulty administration. Unless the principals could be give the opportunity of taking a full part in the administration, with a reconstituted organisation, we feel that the decline will continue. We deplore this situation, but it has been made quite clear at meetings that no such co-operation is encouraged by the existing board of directors, which is elected by an unfair representation of the string-playing majority. There was even an organised 'Rank and File' pre-election meeting. Later it was stated that the company is not interested in personalities but in the enforcement of rules and discipline. Making music to the best of our ability . . . is not possible under the existing frustrating conditions.

So the argument was out in the open. Great music-making was incompatible with democracy (or 'an unfair representation of the string-playing majority', as the principals put it). Or was it great money-making that was incompatible? Either way, the principals flounced out and set up the Sinfonia of London – exactly the sort of session band which they had wanted the LSO to become. Its name can be found on the end-credits of numerous 1950s films, and one or two rather good LPs – but then it just faded away, as the LSO would probably have done if it had gone down the same route. Nevertheless, the LSO board faced a sizeable problem in the summer of 1955. It had stuck to its principles, but lost its principals – all but one, at any rate. Roger Lord, the oboist whose extraordinarily supple playing arguably made him the true star of the 1950s LSO, was talked out of his resignation by the board.

'It was a difficult thing,' Lord recalls. 'I had just come back from holiday, and the other principals more or less presented me with this letter they were going to send into the management, and said 'of course you'll sign it,' and of course I did. But a week or so later I was talked by the management into staying with the orchestra. That was very unfortunate, because I made ene-mies of some of the principals. They left, and I stayed. But things like that happen in orchestras. Things go along smoothly for a time, then it goes wrong.' Roger Lord stayed on for thirty years.

As it turned out, the upheaval – and the urgent need to bring in new blood – was the best thing that could have happened to the band. 'The LSO's high standards of the 1960s came about basically because of the ideas of two men: John Cruft and Harry Dugarde,' recalled Stuart Knussen, the orches-tra's principal double bass and sometime chairman. 'Instead of signing up a series of established big musical names, they went around and searched for young men of talent.'

Forced to recruit quickly and boldly, the board skipped a generation or two, and snapped up a whole platoon of exceptional young players. The troublesome Fell was replaced on first clarinet by Gervase de Peyer. Hugh Maguire soon appeared as leader. An ambitious and mercurially clever thirty-year-old fiddler called Neville Marriner was recruited to lead the sec-onds. Denis Wick soon appeared as principal trombone, and William Waterhouse on bassoon.

Perhaps most significantly of all, the LSO poached from the Bournemouth Symphony Orchestra a young Australian horn player who seemed to have nerves of steel and an embouchure to match. He exhibited a pretty steely resolve, too – for within seven years Barry Tuckwell was running the LSO.

At nearly fifty years' distance, it is now almost impossible to disentangle the rights and wrongs of that turbulent year, 1955. 'Some years later,' Tuckwell recently recalled, 'I met my predecessor John Burden, who was the first horn and who had, of course, defected. "It's very ironic," he said. "Everything we wanted to achieve with the LSO has been achieved!" They were very good players who left, and they felt that the orchestra was seri-ously in the wrong hands – not morally, but in terms of their conception of what the LSO could be. They simply wanted the orchestra to be better.' And the strange thing is that it did get better, but without them.

'I certainly think that, when I joined, the LSO was way down the league table, perhaps at the bottom,' Tuckwell says.

The RPO and Philharmonia could pay better, and it's a regrettable thing, but money is the way to get the best players. I think the younger players amongst us thought that we had to do something. We got together, the rebels, the Young Turks – Gervase was there, Roger Lord was there, Neville was there – and it was decided: why don't we put up a candidate for the board? Well, everyone said, what a good idea, and then took two paces backwards. And then someone suggested that I should stand. I had never been on a board in my life. But I got elected because there was a block of votes for me, and that was the beginning of our influence to improve the orchestra.

These volcanic eruptions in the ranks of the LSO hardly made a paragraph in the national newspapers. Why should they have? In 1955 the nation was obsessed with the fate of Ruth Ellis, the last woman to be hanged in Britain, and with Churchill's exit from 10 Downing Street for the last time, and with the start of commercial television, and with the enforced termination of Princess Margaret's relationship with Group Captain Peter Townsend. But in that same torrid year, the LSO sowed the seeds of its future greatness – and changed the British music scene for ever.

6 Dealing with the maestro

Leonard Bernstein, 1980s

previous page In concert with the LSO – Claudio Abbado, 1980

Soon after the Duke of Wellington became Prime Minister, someone asked him how his first Cabinet Meeting with his new ministers had gone.

'Extraordinary,' the old general replied. 'I gave them their orders, and they wanted to stay and discuss them.'

Throughout the hundred years of the LSO, dozens of conductors must have felt much the same way about this orchestra. It had been formed in revolt against one conductor. It was the first British orchestra owned by the players themselves. Conductors were selected and, on numerous occasions, 'deselected' by the LSO members, not the other way round. So there was from the start a very different, democratic air about the LSO's relationship with its maestros. The conductor was *primus inter pares*, not the boss. In the orchestra's earliest days, especially, that came as a nasty surprise to conductors who expected the usual Edwardian squire-and-peasants sort of relationship with the players.

One early casualty was the amazingly pompous Sir Landon Ronald. In his 1931 memoirs he complains that he was 'not allowed [by the LSO] to appear more than six or eight times' in the orchestra's 1907 Albert Hall concerts, despite having (he thought) worked out a cosy deal with 'some good friends of mine on the Council of the Albert Hall'. His fury at the LSO's inability to know their place was still simmering, more than twenty years later. 'Looking back without any prejudice I consider that this was a very short-sighted policy. Had they had any foresight they would undoubtedly have realised that an ambitious young man like myself would not be content to sit down and take the crumbs thrown him by the Directors of the London Symphony Orchestra.'

Perhaps in any relationship between a conductor and a self-governing orchestra there is bound to be an inherent tension bordering on the paradoxical. It might be summed up as 'we, the orchestra, are hiring you, the conductor, to tell us what to do – but don't get too many airs and graces'. No wonder that so many podium autocrats, accustomed to unquestioning servility from German or American orchestras, found the LSO hard if not impossible to handle. And no wonder that LSO folklore contains so many tales of run-ins with conductors.

From the start, it seems, the LSO's principals gave conductors the impression that they deferred to nobody on musical matters. The young Ralph Vaughan Williams, nervous and unsure as a conductor – even though he was directing his own music – encountered the disdain of an LSO player more than once. 'I shyly approached Mr Solomon [the first trumpet] and said to him: "Did you play B flat or B natural at letter A?"' Vaughan Williams recalled many years later. Solomon replied: 'What was written in the part?' 'B flat,' said Vaughan Williams. 'If B flat was written, B flat was what I played,' Solomon retorted.

On another occasion Vaughan Williams was rebuffed again, this time by the saintly W. H. Reed. 'I know you will help me out if I miss that 9/8 bar,' said the composer to the LSO's leader after a rehearsal. 'My dear fellow,' Reed replied, 'we shan't be looking at you.'

But the LSO's offhand treatment of Vaughan Williams was tame compared with its merciless behaviour towards Ivor Atkins, the Worcester Cathedral organist and close friend of Elgar, during one Three Choirs Festival concert. Atkins was a pompous figure, more used to dealing with errant choirboys than hard-bitten London professionals, and at the rehearsal he made an extraordinary speech. 'Gentlemen,' he announced to the LSO, 'I have decided to introduce a new gesture when I conduct from now onwards. Whenever I raise my left hand to the level of my head, with my thumb pointing inwards, please understand that I am not satisfied.'

The words 'red rag' can rarely have been so aptly prefixed to 'bull'. At that night's concert Atkins started the last part of Tchaikovsky's *Capriccio Italien* too quickly and was unable to stop it from getting even faster. Up came his left hand with the thumb pointing inwards. 'The word flew around: he is NOT satisfied,' recalled Wynn Reeves, the violinist.

Gripped by a unanimous, telepathic urge to make mischief, the players forced the pace faster and faster. Reeves recounted what happened:

When an orchestra gets out of hand, it's the devil to pay. They are a thousand times worse than runaway horses. Our worthy conductor's hand was pumping up and down like a piston rod, turning over the score's pages and gesticulating wildly. Still the orchestra surged on: the bars flew by like the names of stations seen from an express train. Nobody knew where they were, I couldn't see the music for tears of concealed laughter, and I think most were in the same boat.

Eventually Henderson, the unperturbable timpanist, saved the day. He conjured from out of nowhere (certainly not from the part in front of him) a fortissimo fanfare on three drums at once – whereupon the orchestra blasted out the final chord as one man until, in Reeves's words, 'our worthy conductor decided to stop'. The audience apparently 'thought it was marvellous'.

In the cloisters the next day, Atkins happened to meet Alfred Hobday, the LSO's veteran principal viola. 'I fancy I took the *Capriccio* a little faster than usual last night, didn't I?' Atkins said. 'Oh, I didn't notice anything,' replied Hobday innocently. 'I'm a little worried about what Henderson played at the end,' Atkins continued. 'I have looked it up in the score and can't see anything like it.' Hobday pretended to ponder the matter deeply for a moment. 'Perhaps,' he finally replied, with a disarming smile, 'he was playing from a different edition.'

*

Such insouciance, concealed or overt, soon became a regular feature of the LSO's dealings with conductors who, for one reason or another, had irritated the orchestra. And it didn't take much to do that. 'I have seen the LSO give perfectly good conductors a hard time for no other reason than that it was raining outside,' says Howard Snell, the LSO's first trumpet and chairman in the 1970s.

André Previn agrees. 'A trait of the LSO which I find very sweet is that when they don't like a conductor, well, if the man blew up in front of them he still wouldn't get their sympathy. It's really quite extraordinary. And Colin Davis is exactly the same as his orchestra. He either admires colleagues boundlessly, or dismisses them with a short Anglo-Saxon word. I love it.'

Sometimes the LSO's fondness for talking back to conductors was nothing but good-spirited banter. The master of that was Jack Brymer, its immensely grand principal clarinettist in the 1970s. Asked by Previn, in a recording session for Messiaen's *Turangalîla-symphonie*, to play a passage very fast, he said: 'Well it is impossible of course, but I will try' – and proceeded to record the offending passage in a single take.

Another celebrated incident involved the avuncular conductor Norman Del Mar – the 'mass of life' as he was universally known to London orchestral players. Rehearsing Strauss's *Don Quixote*, Del Mar had the temerity to admonish Brymer for playing a phrase too loudly: 'Just a memory, Jack, just a memory,' Del Mar called out. 'Why are you playing it mezzo-forte?' 'Because Strauss told me to,' Brymer retorted. 'And I'm surprised that you don't remember, Norman, because you were playing second horn at the time.'

Other exchanges between LSO principals and conductors were not so equable. One of the most notorious involved Hugh Maguire, the orchestra's leader in the late 1950s, and Josef Krips. 'We were rehearsing the Beethoven "Emperor" Concerto with Rubinstein,' Maguire recalls, 'and Krips asked for some very exaggerated bowing effects. So I said: "You can't do that, Professor Krips" – he liked to be called Professor – "it's silly." Well, he stared at me and then exclaimed: "What do you say? Me silly? Me, the great conductor, silly?" And he burst into floods of tears in front of the whole orchestra. At ten in the morning!'

Krips stormed out of the hall. Rubinstein sat at the piano shaking with laughter. 'Rubinstein didn't want to rehearse anyway,' Maguire says. 'He'd played the "Emperor" hundreds of times.' Eventually the pianist said: 'Mr Maguire, why don't you conduct instead?' Maguire declined, and instead dashed off to persuade Krips to return. He found the conductor at his hotel, and eventually coaxed him back to the Festival Hall. But in the conductor's dressing room, Krips suddenly said to Maguire: 'Now before we go on, I want you to get down on your knees and pray. I will do the same.'

So, for perhaps the first and last time in LSO history, conductor and leader prayed together before a rehearsal. 'I looked at that great fat famous conductor,' Maguire recalls, 'and thought: what a silly child.'

The most frequent cause of disagreements was rehearsals. Since time immemorial London's top orchestral musicians had a tradition of 'flying by the seat of their pants' – getting by on the minimum of rehearsal, relying on superb sightreading skills and lightning reactions. Even today a school of thought exists in London (though not any more at the LSO) which says that British musicians are at their most galvanised when going into a performance virtually unrehearsed. Mendelssohn and Wagner both commented on the extraordinary sightreading skills they encountered when they came to England. But both also castigated the less desirable aspects of this tradition: the fact that, without a fair amount of rehearsal, it was virtually impossible for a conductor to obtain precise cohesion, refined phrasing and a large range of expression.

The LSO clearly inherited this disdain for 'over-rehearsing' when it came into existence – as the young Adrian Boult discovered when he was invited by the orchestra to conduct a Sunday-afternoon concert at the Palladium in 1919. 'The rehearsal consisted of three minutes' discussion on repeats, just before the curtain rose,' he recalled. Not that such skimpy preparation induced the performers to play safe. On the contrary, it seems.

'We were nothing if not adventurous,' Boult continued. 'We gave the first post-war performance of the three early Strauss tone-poems, which, owing to the reluctance to collect performing fees for enemies, had been totally neglected during the war. I think the nature of the performance, particularly of *Till Eulenspiegel*, without rehearsal after five years of neglect, will be better imagined than described.'

From those earliest days until comparatively recent times, the question of rehearsal time was always going to be an issue with the LSO's conductors. In the view of the orchestra through most of its history, too much rehearsal made things worse. It's an argument that André Previn can at least understand, if not endorse. 'London's orchestral musicians were, and are, the greatest sightreaders ever known,' he says. 'And the fascinating thing is that if you are doing a particularly complex piece, it usually tends to be better at the first reading than at the second. At the first reading, everyone is usually concentrating, while on the second time through they relax. They think they know it.'

On at least one occasion, however, Previn had reason to be grateful for the consummate ease with which the LSO performed even complicated music without prior rehearsal. It was during the so-called 'winter of discontent' (1978–9) when industrial action was intermittently disrupting Britain's power supplies. 'I had just joined the orchestra and never played Rachmaninov's Second Symphony before,' says John Lawley, the LSO's second oboist. 'Well, it was on a Shell tour, and at the rehearsal the lights went out. So André just said breezily: "Oh, don't worry – everybody knows this piece. Go back to the hotel and I'll see you at the concert tonight." So I found myself sightreading a Rachmaninov symphony in the concert! It went fine, but I was petrified.'

Not every LSO conductor reacted to the testing circumstances of London orchestral life with such equanimity. The tyrannical Klemperer, for instance, demanded four rehearsals for a single concert when he first came to the orchestra in the 1930s. 'Nobody could remember having more than two for anything,' recalls the veteran violinist Lionel Bentley. 'And at the end of the fourth rehearsal the orchestra was playing much worse than at the first. He had terrified them into such a state that it was very difficult to play at all.'

Bram Wiggins, the trumpeter, confirms how temperamental Klemperer could be. 'I can remember him coming and standing right in front of a bassoon player at rehearsal. The bassoonist said: "Don't stand there, you're making me nervous." Klemperer replied: "If you're nervous, go home."'

Klemperer also had an unpopular habit of extending a rehearsal beyond its allotted span. 'One day he went twenty minutes over, on a rehearsal that was supposed to finish at 1 p.m.,' Bentley says. 'So some players got up to leave because they had an afternoon engagement. Klemperer shouted at them: "What are you? Musicians or workmen?" One of them shouted back: "We're engaged as musicians, but you are treating us as workmen."'

That the LSO was not averse to rehearsing long and hard when properly motivated is clear from Pablo Casals's charming memoir of working with the orchestra in the 1920s. The great cellist who, like Rostropovich sixty years later, turned increasingly to conducting in his later life, came to the LSO four seasons in a row. For the first concert he declined a fee – provided he could have three rehearsals. 'After a fine rehearsal,' he recalled years later, 'the orchestra made me a present of a beautiful casket containing three Dunhill pipes – the Stradivarius of pipes! Deeply moved, I thanked them. Alas, that same morning I had consulted a doctor who advised me to stop smoking! For several days those pipes tormented me. The temptation was too great – and very soon I succumbed.'

It was the astonishing rehearsal demands of the Romanian conductor Sergiu Celibidache when he came to the LSO in the late 1970s that proved most divisive among the players. The initiative to approach him had come from Anthony Camden, then the LSO's chairman and principal oboe. 'I felt that we needed to spend some time looking at the orchestra's internal balance and phrasing,' Camden recalls. So Camden visited the notoriously pernickety Celibidache in Stuttgart. The Romanian proceeded to lay out the conditions under which he would work with the LSO. The principal one was that he should be given eight rehearsals for each concert – an astonishing demand, particularly since he was undertaking what, in other hands, would be termed standard repertoire. 'I mentioned to him that I had found out that he only asked for six rehearsals for a concert with the Stuttgart Radio Orchestra,' Camden says. 'His reply to me was: "Yes, that is true, but the better the orchestra is, the more rehearsals you need, as there is then far more that can be achieved."'

Much to Celibidache's surprise, the LSO board accepted his conditions – which also included the stipulation that for the entire month he was with the orchestra it should work with no other conductor and accept no other dates. But his intensive methods – sometimes working on half a dozen bars for an hour or more – sharply polarised the players.

'The first rehearsal was entirely spent on tuning,' recalls the cellist Francis Saunders. 'He was wonderful at making people listen to themselves and each other. And by doing that he was able to make people think differently about themselves, their lives, and what they were doing. I loved it, and I think about half the orchestra were mesmerised. The other half couldn't stand it, so they were allowed to be off for that period, and we got people in from other orchestras who really wanted to be there, to experience this legend for themselves. I think that's why the results were so terrific.'

Camden was also overwhelmed with the Celibidache experiment. 'Amazing! The phrasing and dynamics were beautiful, and the orchestra played with great precision, like a top-class Rolls Royce.'

But Mike Davis, who became the LSO's leader in 1979, was not quite so convinced.

'Chelly' was a species of person and conductor the like of which I had never come across in my life. This was clearly a man of extraordinary intellectual scope, with a view of music that was unique. During the week of rehearsals for the Fauré Requiem, I stopped putting rosin on my bow, because whatever you did, it was too loud. And some of the tempos! The girl singing 'Pie Jesu' must have been breathing through her ears, it was so slow. But I have to tell you it wasn't easy. His mood could change very fast. And I sometimes wondered whether he wasn't trying it on a bit – with those enormous silences between movements, for instance. As a down-to-earth Northern lad, I would look at all that and think: 'Oh, come on!'

At the other extreme, there were conductors who rehearsed too little, even for the LSO's taste. Stokowski, for instance, left Hugh Maguire perplexed. 'No preparation whatsoever! We would play through whatever piece it was, and at the end he would clap his hands and say: "Any questions? No questions? Next piece!" And so on, for days. There were never any questions, or suggestions. I suppose he got his marvellous sound by hypnosis, by using his hands and his eyes. But it was very strange.'

And one maestro – the great Stravinsky, conducting his own music – didn't rehearse at all. Not in person, anyway. He sent his assistant, Robert Craft, to convey his instructions instead – with predictable results, according to the LSO's harpist, Osian Ellis.

Craft would say: 'The maestro will conduct this movement in eight, and he'll start by beating 'five, six, seven, eight'. On the night, though, Stravinsky didn't do anything of the sort. He went straight into the movement, and everybody was baffled. A flute player started playing in four instead of eight, so Stravinsky called out 'Eight in a bar'. And this was all being broadcast! I remember the concert was in Oxford Town Hall, and very late starting. We all said, 'Oh, he must be late because he's waiting for his money,' because the rumour was that Stravinsky never went on a platform until he had been paid.

The amount of rehearsal was one bone of contention between the LSO and its conductors. Another was how conductors used or, in some cases, failed to use, the rehearsal time that had been allotted. One of the most out-spoken critics of conductors in this respect is Maurice Murphy, the LSO's principal trumpet. 'There are conductors who play things over and over again,' he says. 'So the pieces are over-played, yet not rehearsed. There are others who have their rehearsals mapped out exactly before they start, so if you get the same guy returning over ten years or so, you know exactly where he is going to stop, and exactly which bits he is going to rehearse. Still, at least you know it's coming.'

Though he admits that the LSO did 'some fantastic shows with him', Murphy reserves his most pungent observations for Claudio Abbado, the LSO's principal conductor in the 1980s. Softly spoken, and a believer in democracy, even socialism (if of the soft-cushioned Milanese variety), Abbado was reluctant to lay down the law to rebellious players, and in con-sequence his rehearsals – particularly early in his tenure – were astonishingly ill disciplined, even by the lax standards of that era. 'In the late 1970s and early 1980s,' recalls Clive Gillinson, who then played cello in the orchestra, 'something very close to anarchy prevailed at most rehearsals. People talking all the time, people playing on long after the conductor had stopped.'

In Maurice Murphy's view, Abbado's particular problems were largely his own doing.

We could hardly ever understand him. He was always going 'err-err' as if he had a mouthful of gobstoppers. We thought it might be because he wasn't confident with his English, but then people said he was like that in Italian as well. He was also very vain. He would never wear spectacles, and conducted without a score, which he com-mitted to vague recollection. And when he messed up two Prom concerts as a result – Petrushka and The Miraculous Mandarin – he blamed the orchestra. 'Some very bad playing last night,' he said the next morning. So of course we shouted back: 'What about you?' He was lost five or six times before the end of my first page. After both those shows he came off the platform with his face dead white. He knew he had blown it. And of course when a conductor doesn't have a score and it goes wrong, it's fatal. On loads of occasions the orchestra bailed Abbado out, but we would never get any thanks for it. He would just say that something had thrown him.

According to the bassoonist William Waterhouse, the LSO's sense of itself as being at least as important as the conductor in deciding how the music should go was evident even in the late 1950s – when most orchestras were still ruled (and that word is the right one) by ferocious autocrats of the old school. 'We were young, and belonged to a self-governing orchestra – which gave us even more *esprit de corps*,' he recalls. 'We felt: this is our performance, this is how we want to do it, and if you want to conduct us, this is what you will get. I think that many conductors found that attitude refreshing.'

And when they didn't, they were swiftly reminded that the LSO was not their personal fiefdom. Roger Lord, the principal oboist in those days, recalls:

I remember when George Szell turned up. I knew he was highly respected, but I could tell from the look in his face that he was going to be a difficult person, and sure enough he became very aggressive. I felt it was up to someone to speak up and not let him get too bossy, and sometimes that someone was me. I think it's important for players to retaliate a bit. And he was only a visiting conductor, after all. I don't suppose I would have stood up to him if I had been a member of the Cleveland Orchestra, his own band.

As the 1960s and 1970s progressed, that independence of spirit toppled into something rather more surly: an unwarranted rudeness or sarcasm which some conductors found disconcerting and others unbearable. 'LSO rehearsals were ferocious affairs in those days,' says Colin Davis. 'And if something went wrong, players would shout at the conductor: "Why don't you do your homework? We were only following your beat."'

A verbal barrage of that nature could be intensely distressing, even destructive, to younger conductors. 'We did a recording session with Simon Rattle in the mid-1970s,' Gillinson recalls. 'He was very young, just a kid really, and the orchestra treated him very badly, as they treated lots of people. Well, when I became manager it took me twelve or thirteen years to get Simon to be willing to work with us again. He did actually say: "I will never conduct the LSO again." I still tell people in the orchestra about that, to remind them of the reality that there are far more orchestras than great conductors.'

Rattle wasn't the only conductor to turn his back on the LSO in those unruly days, as Gillinson admits:

Giulini left the orchestra and would never come back because he was treated so badly. There was a huge blow-up with Jochum, and he wouldn't come back either. It was almost a question of the orchestra saying to the conductor: prove yourself to us! The culture is completely different now. We treat everyone as a guest, everyone as a partner. And if, in the end, people in the orchestra feel they don't want a conductor back again, we don't tell them while they are conducting! We just don't invite them back again. There's none of this 'battle for supremacy' thing in rehearsals any more.

Nobody appreciates that more than Colin Davis, the LSO's current principal conductor, who certainly had his difficulties with the 'bolshie' LSO of the

1960s and 1970s. 'It's so different now,' he says. 'We have had no angry words for eight years, and there seems to be no reason why we should start.'

But Davis is a very different sort of maestro from the old-style dictator. He detests displays of power, rather than revelling in them. And his relationship with the LSO now stretches back nearly half a century. The fact that the LSO of 2003 reveres him doesn't mean that the same players won't firmly reject a conductor whom they feel is overstepping his authority and expecting too much servile compliance. 'We did have one German conductor recently, a young chap – you probably know who I mean – who was a real tyrant,' a senior LSO violinist recalls. 'Well, we were very polite to him on the platform, which was certainly different from how the old LSO would have treated him. But afterwards everyone said: "No, we don't want to see him again." So the orchestra still has that power, and is prepared to use it. And rightly so. Music should be made in a pleasant environment.'

In the end, of course, it all comes down to chemistry. The LSO's chemistry has always been unique: combustible, dangerous but capable of powerful results when properly handled. Some conductors enjoy igniting that; some find it too hot to handle; some actively resent working with an orchestra that has a bigger personality than they do. Inevitably the most entertaining stories concern the relationships that failed. And sometimes that failure is through no fault of the orchestra's. Having assiduously cultivated the reclusive and demanding Carlos Kleiber to come and conduct the LSO in the early 1980s, for instance – and given what they thought was a once-in-a-lifetime sort of concert in the Festival Hall – the LSO players were mortified when what Anthony Camden describes as 'some crazy critic' wrote 'one negative remark' in a newspaper the following day. The critic had a perfect right to express his opinion, of course. The problem was that Kleiber learnt about the review, and decided never to conduct an orchestra in London again.

A rather different problem marred a promising relationship with the gifted Soviet conductor Yevgeny Svetlanov, who was one of the LSO's principal guest conductors for a time in the late 1970s. Like many Russians of his generation, he drank alcohol, heavily, even when he was working. 'There was a dangerous recording session of [Rimsky-Korsakov's] *Sheherazade* made at EMI's studios,' Camden recalls. 'Yevgeny brought a great many bottles of white wine with him. The piece was completed in one three-hour session, during which all the bottles became empty. The orchestra then suggested he ought to stop drinking, otherwise we should not renew his contract.'

Svetlanov did stop, and became a much pleasanter person. 'Unfortunately,' Camden continues, 'when he was sober his conducting was boring. So the orchestra asked me to persuade him to drink just a little. We were playing at the Edinburgh Festival, so that night I took him to the Festival Club, but he refused to drink any alcohol. So his contract was not renewed.'

It is worth pointing out that, from Nikisch to Bernstein, many famously volatile and demanding conductors have enjoyed long, happy and notably successful links with this orchestra. Perhaps the last word on this subject ought to go to André Previn, since he survived longer as principal conductor (eleven years) than anyone else in LSO history. In that time, he certainly experienced the LSO's capacity for internal politicking and feuding, but also its finer qualities of comradeship and generosity.

They gave me a lot of good advice, my friends in the LSO. You know – practical, cynical advice about how to get round technical problems. We were doing some Tippett that was extremely complex, and afterwards I went to have a drink with Barry Tuckwell [then the principal horn and LSO chairman]. He said: 'Let me tell you something. When you do a piece that is terribly complicated, if you ever get lost – and you will, everybody does from time to time – just look vague and elegant and we'll fix it. If you start flapping at us, we're all sunk. Everybody will go down the drain.

Well, a year or so later it happened in a concert. It was in a movement of Stravinsky's Symphony in C which is unreal in its complications. It's like *The Rite of Spring*, only multiplied by ten. Anyway, I got awfully lost. So I followed the LSO's advice: look vague and elegant. And as a result I still have a career.

7 Breaking the mould: the Fleischmann years 1956–67

Lord Harlech, Georg Solti, Barry Tuckwell, Ernest Fleischmann, 1964

previous page Ernest Fleischmann (General Secretary), 1963

All you really need to make a great orchestra are five things. Virtuoso players. Visionary management. Inspiring conductors. Money, plenty of it. And the willingness of all parties to work harmoniously together, on and off the platform. After the traumatic 'principals' revolt' of 1955, and the subsequent influx of young talent, the LSO certainly had a potential nucleus of virtuoso players. Visionary management and inspiring conductors were also to be acquired over the next few years, if sometimes more by luck than design.

All this carried the orchestra to heights of international prestige in the mid-1960s that must have been unimaginable ten years earlier. Even in those glory days, however, money was tight, the orchestra forever walking a tightrope. As for harmony behind the scenes: that was never a strong point of the buccaneering LSO of the 1960s and 70s. Quite the reverse: many of the dominant figures seem to have revelled in the hurly-burly of what could politely be called 'creative tension' but, more accurately, were flaming rows. Barry Tuckwell recalls:

It was like sitting on a volcano. There was trouble almost all the time. Yet I enjoyed that. On one tour an entire string section said, just before a concert: 'We are not going onto the platform if that person is playing.' So we went into a room and sorted it out, and I thought to myself: 'Hey, this is fun in a way, because there's a concert tonight!' It was exciting, because here was an orchestra on the verge of blowing up.

The trouble is that if you sit on a volcano for long enough, you get rather burnt. So it was with the LSO. The astonishing triumphs of the mid-1960s, the glamorous early years with Previn, the ebullient pride that enabled this impecunious, overworked British orchestra to swagger into Carnegie Hall or the Salzburg Festival and dazzle the world's sniffiest audiences – those are achievements that should never be derided or dismissed.

But that lack of harmony behind the scenes, coupled with an arrogant streak running through the orchestra that became more overweening and misplaced as the Swinging Sixties turned into the Cynical Seventies – that, in the end, led the LSO to the brink of catastrophe. It was an era of fireworks: brilliant displays in public; sudden, unpredictable flare-ups in private; a general feeling of uncontrollable combustibility; and an unwillingness to take responsibility for the inevitable moment when the revels end and the sky turns black again.

*

Little did the recently-recruited novice principals of the 'new LSO' realise it – either at the time or for three years afterwards – but a large part of their future destiny was decided in September 1956, when they boarded a plane and flew to Johannesburg to give five concerts in the city's first-ever festival. After the internal crisis of the previous year, the tour was seen as a crucial showcase for the orchestra. At that time the evils of South Africa's apartheid system did not weigh heavily on the conscience of most British people; indeed, there was still a multitude of trading, sporting and military links connecting Britain with her former colony. This would be the LSO's first major overseas visit since the war. It was a lucrative engagement, and a chance for the eager young players to show off their flexibility in repertoire that ranged from Haydn to Strauss, Mahler's Second Symphony and Walton's First.

It had begun badly. At the eleventh hour, Krips became ill and pulled out. The orchestra scrambled around for a replacement who could handle such wide-ranging repertoire with virtually no preparation. Finally, a suggestion came from the Johannesburg Festival's music director: 'What about Jascha Horenstein?'

It was an inspired idea. Russian-Jewish by ancestry, Viennese by upbringing, Horenstein had been a Furtwängler protégé who was guest-conducting the Berlin Philharmonic before he was thirty. He gave the world première of the string orchestra version of Berg's *Lyric Suite* with that orchestra in 1929, and became renowned as a champion of Schoenberg, Berg, Webern, Janáček, Stravinsky and all the other Young Turks whose astringent pieces shook the musical world in the 1930s.

But his abiding reputation was made in Mahler and Bruckner, and when he was forced to flee Nazi Germany and embark on a nomadic conducting life (which he maintained until his death in 1973) it was to these giants that he returned again and again. His performance of Mahler's colossal Eighth Symphony with the LSO in 1959 is widely credited with sparking the 'Mahler craze' in Britain.

Was he free to conduct the Johannesburg tour? He was. Did he wish to change any of the programmes? Not in the slightest. 'I know all the music except the Walton symphony,' he replied. 'I will learn that on the plane.'

'Horenstein was a terribly nervy figure, almost trembling with fear before he came on,' says Hugh Maguire, the Irish violinist whose first concerts as

LSO leader were on that tour. 'But he did such marvellous performances, very powerful, a bit like Klemperer.' The LSO was galvanised, and the Johannesburg concerts were triumphs. It was the first outward sign that the newly rejuvenated orchestra had the potential to be outstanding.

But the visit proved significant for quite a different reason. At the end of the final concert, Horenstein and the LSO's leader, Hugh Maguire, were publicly presented with laurel wreaths by the Festival's music director – the very person who had suggested Horenstein in the first place. He was a dynamic young man with a degree in music, an accountancy qualification and experience as an opera company répétiteur; he was also a conductor, a music critic and, of course, a festival administrator. Clearly he was going places. His name was Ernest Fleischmann. Three years later, he would hitch his rising star to the LSO's – and nothing would be quite the same again.

Many years later, Fleischmann would recall the series of events that transpired:

It hadn't been my intention to invite the LSO to Johannesburg at all. I had thought about the Philharmonia. This was in 1956, the Mozart bicentennial, and in those days the Philharmonia had the best reputation for the classical repertoire in London. But my protracted negotiations with that orchestra didn't seem to be going anywhere.

Then one day I had a visitor to my temporary London office in the South African Tourist Bureau. It was a gentleman by the name of John Cruft, who introduced himself as the Secretary of the LSO. 'Well,' I thought, 'why Secretary? Where is the manager?' Apparently this quaint term described someone with all the functions of the managing director but without the authority – which was jealously retained by the musicians on the board in those days, and in fact throughout my career with the orchestra.

Fleischmann told Cruft that he wanted to book the best London orchestra, and that from what he had heard on previous visits, this was not the LSO. ('Very opinionated I was then, and still am.') Cruft replied: 'Why don't you come and hear the orchestra again? There have been major personnel changes.'

Fleischmann took his advice:

I was bowled over. It was the orchestra in the very early stages of Barry Tuckwell, Neville Marriner, Gervase de Peyer and so on. I went back to the Philharmonia and gave them a deadline. They didn't meet it, so I called Mr Cruft and said: 'OK, let's talk business.' And the LSO came to South Africa and gave five wonderful concerts.

Three years passed. Fleischmann, still toying with the idea of being a conductor, had applied to be music director of Cape Town's leading orchestra:

Since I was to be employed by the city council, I had to get five testimonials from independent sources. So I asked the LSO for one, and they sent a really nice letter. Then they suddenly contacted me again and asked how the application was going. I said: 'I'm glad you asked because tomorrow or the day after I am meant to sign my contract. I've got the job, to my great surprise.'

Orchestras can move fast when they have to. John Cruft, who had stoically seen the LSO through all the crises of the 1950s, had resigned as Secretary to join the British Council. The LSO's new, young members were pressing for a different management style, complaining that what had sufficed since 1904 was 'creaky, old-fashioned and periodically ineffectual' (to cite one letter of complaint to the directors). The board was considering seven replacements, none of whom inspired great enthusiasm. Then Fleischmann's request for a testimonial arrived, and jogged memories of the sparky young South African. The LSO board sent a cable the next day offering him Cruft's old job.

Fleischmann recalls:

I had twenty-four hours to decide whether my future was to be a conductor or administrator. I felt that as a conductor I had a certain amount of talent, and had a magnificent musician, Albert Coates, as my mentor. But I also knew how difficult it was to study a score and absorb it so that you knew it better than every musician in front of you. I got cold feet. I felt I couldn't tell the principal oboe of a great orchestra how to phrase the solo in *Don Juan*. So I decided, more or less overnight, that I would go to London. The LSO's offer also gave me the chance to leave South Africa fast and say goodbye to apartheid.

So about five weeks later I came to the LSO. And from my point of view it was a good decision. I was associated with an orchestra that was clearly on the rise. All I had to do was sit back and watch them get better.

This, of course, is nonsense. The idea of the young, impatient and volatile Ernest Fleischmann passively 'sitting back' in any organisation is inconceivable. Knowingly or unknowingly, the LSO had hired an administrative whizzkid – perhaps the very first to hit the London music scene. Within days of his arrival in November 1959, everybody could feel the difference.

He was employed specifically to 'sell' the orchestra. 'We all felt very excited,' the bassoonist William Waterhouse recalls, 'that here was someone who had done great things in South Africa, who had tremendous energy and insight and high standards – in a way, the same qualities that Walter Legge had, of being able to pick winners and create a set-up whereby the best conductors and soloists wanted to come to the LSO.'

That last point is crucial. Cannily, Fleischmann realised that what sold orchestras to the general public was the company they kept: the quality of the conductors and soloists with whom they regularly appeared. 'It wasn't difficult to change the list of conductors that the orchestra worked with, because one couldn't do much worse, really,' he recalls. 'Virtually anybody who had the requisite amount of money was able to hire the LSO.'

That sweeping denunciation isn't entirely fair. But certainly the LSO was still filling up its order-books with far too many dates that did its image no favours – especially at a time when the Philharmonia was conducted by Klemperer and the RPO had Beecham. Fleischmann somehow needed to shift the public's perception of the LSO, and one obvious way to do that was to increase its outings with charismatic conductors and soloists who excited audiences.

In the four years before he had arrived the new-look LSO had already made some significant liaisons. One was with the mesmeric Leopold Stokowski, who had last conducted the orchestra in 1912. Since then he had gone on to turn a provincial American band into the 'fabulous Philadelphians', make himself a millionaire several times over, enjoy well-publicised affairs and/or marriages with a string of beautiful and/or rich women, and win himself worldwide fame as the conductor who, in the Disney cartoon film *Fantasia*, shook hands with Mickey Mouse (a remarkable technological achievement for 1939).

He also had a capacity for affectation that was not only limitless but legendary. He might have been Polish by descent, but he had been born and bred in London. Indeed, as plain Leonard Stokes he had trained at the Royal College of Music and been organist for a while at fashionable St James's Church in Piccadilly. Yet one would never have guessed his Cockney roots from the bizarre succession of fake European accents that he affected in later life. Nor from his behaviour. He once astonished two LSO members who were travelling with him in a taxi across Westminster Bridge by pointing to Big Ben and saying: 'Vot ees zat?'

'He put on this phoney Polish accent,' says the LSO bassoonist William Waterhouse. 'In the recording studio he would ask for extra "meekroferns", then say: "Send for Herr Yonas." After a while we discovered that Herr Yonas was really Mr Jones, the sound engineer.'

There was an element of trickery about his musicianship, too. A brilliant conjuror of orchestral sound, he controversially massaged and doctored the classics until, in the immortal verdict of the critic Neville Cardus, he had near enough 'embalmed the music'.

Nevertheless, attracting the seventy-three-year-old maestro back to London was a terrific coup for the LSO, particularly in 1955 – the year of such disquieting upheaval inside the band. Significantly, the initiative came from Barry Tuckwell, who had just joined the orchestra. 'We were doing a film with Bernard Herrmann,' the horn player recalls. 'He and I got chatting about the LSO, and he said: "You ought to get Stokowski to conduct." I said: "How?" He replied: "I'll phone him up."'

Tuckwell maintains that Stokowski's first concert was a turning point for the young orchestra:

You have to bear in mind, Stokey was not what is now known as a dynamic conductor. He stood there and beat semaphore – one, two, three, four. But he got near the end of the *Roman Carnival* overture, and he suddenly held a chord – and the orchestra followed him. Then another. We followed again. And then at the end he suddenly made a big gesture and we played four times louder! I can still feel it today. He made us feel like we were a good orchestra. And I think he liked the LSO because we were young and eager and flexible and wanted to get better.

The oboist Roger Lord supports this view:

Don't forget that by then nearly everybody had seen *Fantasia*. Stokowski was a great hero, the most famous conductor around. Everybody was really frightened of him; we knew we had to do something special. And he wasn't slow to jump on somebody. Quite often it was somebody who was doing their job perfectly well.

The LSO quickly learnt Stokowski's little tricks. One was to seat the orchestra oddly, with double basses in a long row at the back, the remaining strings to one side, and woodwind to the other. Some of his ploys were less visible, as William Waterhouse relates:

I recall a extraordinary incident when we were rehearsing Schoenberg's *Gurrelieder*. There is a passage in which the piccolo has to sustain a very high B, *pianissimo*, for many bars. Stokowski walked right up to the player, put his hand in his breast pocket and pulled out a flageolet, a little recorder which had been made to his specific instructions in Philadelphia. It was magical, because when you blew it you could produce this top B, pianissimo, without any problem at all!

The other grand old man to strike up an alliance with the LSO in the late 1950s was the polar opposite of the showman Stokowski. Pierre Monteux had achieved virtually everything in music except the universal acclaim in which far less deserving conductors basked. That comparative obscurity can perhaps be attributed to his self-effacing personality and abhorrence of platform histrionics. Perhaps he had seen too much real tragedy in his life to be comfortable with too much showmanship on the podium. Several of his family, who were in the French Resistance, were executed by the Nazis.

His reputation within the orchestral world, however, was *sans pareil*, as was the breadth of his experience. He was playing in the pit-band of the Folies Bergère ten years before the LSO was founded. Then, as music director for Diaghilev's Ballets Russes, he had gone on to direct the premières of a whole array of early twentieth-century masterpieces, including Stravinsky's *Petrushka* and *The Rite of Spring* (perhaps the most riotous first performance in the history of ballet), Debussy's *Jeux* and Ravel's *Daphnis et Chloé*. To steer not particularly skilled pit bands through those complex scores must have required nerves of steel and the concentration of a Buddhist monk. As for his conducting style, Toscanini declared that Monteux had the best baton technique he had ever seen.

When he came to the LSO, however, he was eighty-three. 'More than once he collapsed on the box in front of us,' William Waterhouse said. 'We were terrified, because he was so old. I remember when we were doing Brahms Four, he kept on asking the triangle player to play louder and louder, because of course when you are that old you lose your hearing of the high frequencies. By the end the triangle was almost deafening, and we just sat there embarrassed.'

Yet the three LSO concerts that Monteux conducted in the summer of 1958 created a sensation with players, press and public alike. 'My second horn once worked out how Monteux got the musical climaxes that he did,' Barry Tuckwell recalled. 'He said: "He just moves!" And it was true. Most of the time he was incredibly still, like a character in a Noh play. If he moved, that was volcanic.'

In the French repertoire, he was utterly unchallenged. Waterhouse says:

I have done those pieces with other conductors, also of French birth, and they are not in the same class. Monteux was a wonderful psychologist, too. He was a father figure to the orchestra. Everything he did was magisterial. He could present a performance so the whole thing was like an architectural structure. And he had a wonderful ear for balance. Those are the two things most important in a conductor.

Of course, part of Monteux's appeal to the LSO was also that they knew 'he wouldn't disturb them, he was safe' – as Hugh Maguire perceptively notes. 'He wouldn't want to have a new horn section next week. He wasn't trying to make a career for himself. He never did. He always put the music first.'

He had an impish sense of humour, too. 'Once we finished a Berlioz recording early,' Maguire says. 'As I was putting my fiddle away, I said: "*Maître*, it's great to finish early. My wife will be surprised." He answered: "Be careful. It's you who might be surprised." Not bad for a man of eighty-eight, I thought.'

With Stokowski and Monteux, and with the rising Hungarian firebrand Georg Solti also available, Fleischmann was able to pull off his first big coup. For all orchestras, Vienna was – and to a certain extent, still is – the 'fantasy place' (Fleischmann's phrase) in which to perform: the city with the greatest musical tradition and the highest audience expectations.

The South African was nothing if not brash about storming such citadels. He contacted the organisers of the Vienna Festwochen and said: 'If I produce for 1961 Monteux, Solti and Stokowski, will you take us?' It was an offer that even Vienna could not disdain, and the LSO was booked.

'Suddenly we found ourselves playing at the Vienna Festival and staying not in some cheap out-of-town B and B, but the Hôtel de France,' says Denis Wick, who had recently come from the City of Birmingham Orchestra to be the LSO's first trombone. 'We were living the sort of life that American orchestras lived. That typified Fleischmann's style. He valued us much more highly than we did ourselves.'

That visit had an even more memorable denouement, as Fleischmann notes:

It all happened on 4 June 1961. That date is quite important for other reasons, because Khrushchev and Kennedy were also in Vienna, holding the fateful summit at which they tried to save the world from the brink of disaster, and actually failed. Well, a few of us went to dinner at the Imperial Hotel, where Khrushchev and Kennedy were meeting. Everyone was in high spirits because we had just given a wonderful performance in the festival, and at one point in the conversation Monteux turned to me and said: 'I really love this orchestra and I wish there was something I could do for them.' 'I replied: 'You can. Become our principal conductor.' Monteux then said: 'Done! But I want a twenty-five-year contract, with a twenty-five-year option!'

This was exactly what he got, at the age of eighty-six. 'It was sort of ironic,' Fleischmann says. 'Khrushchev and Kennedy were trying to reach an agreement, and failed. We didn't set out to reach any agreement, and we came out with a wonderful one!'

Sadly, Monteux died after fulfilling only three years of his twenty-five-year contract. But his concerts with the LSO during the last six years of his life were, by all accounts, stirring occasions, imbued with an urgency and an intensity that perhaps only comes from a performer who knows that, for him, the clock stands at two minutes to midnight.

The performance that is best remembered, if only for the wrong reasons, is *The Rite of Spring* in the Albert Hall on 29 May 1963, fifty years to the day after he conducted the première. Ironically Monteux, so associated with the work, hadn't conducted it in years. 'He didn't like the piece,' says Tuckwell. 'He was actually sick of it.'

There were other complications. 'He brought along his own orchestral parts, written out in manuscript,' recalls William Waterhouse. 'The metrical divisions at the end were quite different in his version – and, I may say, a good deal less complicated.'

Others disagree, including the trombonist Denis Wick:

These were the original parts which Monteux had prepared for the première. Apart from all the different barring, which meant his beats were coming in places we didn't recognise, they were covered in cigarette burns and stains. After the rehearsal I was so worried that I went to our librarian and asked if he had the usual trombone parts for the *Rite*. 'You as well?' he replied. It turned out that Barry Tuckwell and some of the other principals had all had the same idea.

According to Tuckwell, the ensuing performance was 'nearly a train wreck'. Fleischmann agrees. 'If you listen to the tape, the performance is really sort of worrisome, shall we say. Nonetheless, it was a great occasion, and the audience went crazy.'

The truly extraordinary part came afterwards. Stravinsky, who was in London at the time, had initially decided not to attend, but then arrived late and sat in a box with Fleischmann. As the performance ended, Monteux gestured up to the composer, inviting him to take the applause. And then, while the composer bowed to the audience, the eighty-nine-year-old conductor set off to climb the Albert Hall's daunting stairs to Stravinsky's box.

'I was only involved in the *Meistersinger* overture in the first half of the concert,' says Osian Ellis, then the LSO's harpist. 'So Madame Monteux had said: "Come and sit with me in the second half." Well, at the end of the *Rite*, when Monteux started galloping past us up the stairs, Madame Monteux said to me: "Oh please go after him, he might fall!" But he was leaping up the steps almost two at a time, and I had great difficulty keeping up with him.'

Fleischmann continues the story:

It was an incredible gesture, at his age. But the sad thing was that, as he was making that climb, Stravinsky was saying things like 'terrible, shit, awful' under his breath, while grinning at the crowd. Of course I felt: 'How dare you?' However great a composer Stravinsky was, it wasn't fair to use those words to describe what Monteux had done with love. Monteux had relearnt the piece. He hadn't conducted it over twenty years. That night I discovered that one of my idols seemed to have, if not feet of clay, then a heart of stone.

One other conductor, of a younger generation, made a big impact on the LSO in the late 1950s. He was Antal Doráti, a tempestuous Hungarian émigré who stormed into the lives of dozens of American and English orchestras – and in most cases, out again pretty quickly. Doráti's personality was much like the orchestral sound he produced: hard, shorn of frills and frippery, ruthlessly precise. He was not lovable, nor did he try to be. But he was a tough and methodical organiser of orchestral sound: painstaking, nit-picking and shin-kicking in pretty well equal proportions.

'He was a bully, not an orchestral trainer,' says Barry Tuckwell contemptuously. 'That was the mistake Glock made when he got him for the BBC.' But it is obvious when you listen to the dozens of fine recordings they made together that Doráti had a very beneficial effect on the young LSO players.

The trumpeter Howard Snell, who joined the LSO in 1960, recalls

His conducting was actually fairly shambling. You would not look up and get a 'one, two, three, four'. You would just have some pushing and pulling gestures, which made you very quickly look down at your part again. But he had a great fund of orchestral knowledge. He knew how things fitted together, and if you didn't do what he wanted he got short-tempered in a very quick time. His shriekings in a high-pitched little voice became a regular feature. After a while one shut it out. But on the other hand, he was almost always right about the things he said.

Doráti was contracted by the ambitious Mercury label to make 150 LPs, of both standard and more adventurous repertoire. In our present crossover-obsessed age, when the recording of a single Mahler symphony by, say, the Berlin Philharmonic and Rattle is regarded as a newsworthy event, such a gargantuan project seems astonishing. But the competition among record companies at the dawn of the stereo age was so cut-throat that Doráti's contract was by no means exceptional. About a hundred of those recordings were undertaken with his own orchestra in Minneapolis. But Harold Lawrence, Mercury's classical manager, allotted the remaining fifty to the LSO, a respite for which the Minneapolis players must have been truly grateful.

For the Londoners, the sessions – sometimes three a day, out in Watford, for six or seven days a week – must have seemed akin to being flung into a whirlpool when you have only just learnt how to swim. 'There was no question of preparation,' says Denis Wick. 'You got it right first time. You had to. If it wasn't, Harold Lawrence's voice would come over the loudspeakers: "Gentlemen, first violins not together, first measure letter B." No one would want to be criticised, so within the first hour of a session the LSO's standard would go from also-rans to something quite special.'

'It was boot camp,' says Tuckwell. 'But the hard work was good for us.' And because it made sense, economically, for the music recorded in the studio then to be performed in the concert hall, the LSO saw an awful lot of Doráti.

'He should really have been given a title of some sort,' Roger Lord says, 'because he brought very good business, and we did cover a big range of music.' That is a view with which the conductor himself would have concurred. 'Though I never had an official position,' Doráti later recalled, 'I was more or less the LSO's permanent conductor for some five or six years, touring with it in Europe, Israel, Japan and in England itself.'

Doráti's repertoire included a whole raft of mid-twentieth century pieces – by Schoenberg, Berg, Stravinsky, Bartók and Copland – which are virtually standard repertoire today, but were rarely played in England before 1960. For the players it was a baptism of fire, and the LSO certainly emerged from those exhausting sessions a much more technically accomplished and confident orchestra. Doráti himself, never a man to underestimate his own influence, happily acknowledged the fact in his memoirs: 'It can be said,' he wrote modestly, 'that the period of our close collaboration coincided with that of the orchestra's rise to the top international rank.'

But he argued with Fleischmann. 'He was not always easy to get on with,' Doráti wrote. 'But neither was I. And regrettably neither of us restrained our clashing temperaments. No single incident proved fatal to our relationship, but the gradual erosion which it suffered was undeniable.'

The significant point about that remark, surely, is not so much that Doráti and Fleischmann had arguments. It is the remarkable fact that, after just a year or two in the job, Fleischmann – who was, after all, a mere non-playing administrator employed by the LSO members – had acquired enough clout to stand up to the toughest conductor on the circuit. 'The "secretaries" of orchestras really were secretaries in those days,' notes Hugh Maguire. 'Someone told them that the orchestra wanted Karajan or whoever, and they would go out and try to fix it. Ernest was not that. He was music director, artistic director, total director. And he did it in a very subtle way, at least at the beginning.'

In short, Fleischmann had wrought a backstairs revolution at the LSO. How had this been achieved? The answer is that, in his early years at least, he and Tuckwell – unquestionably the dominant personality in the orchestra, even before he officially became chairman in 1962 – formed an unstoppable and, at times, pretty ruthless alliance for change and improvement. The methods were far too forceful for some tastes. 'Ernest,' one player remarked wearily, 'would win an Oscar for battering at doors which would otherwise open to a gentle push.' And when Neville Marriner nicknamed him 'flick-knife Fleischmann', the soubriquet stuck. Its recipient probably took it as a compliment.

'There was a very receptive board in those days,' Fleischmann says. 'They were raring to go, and so was I. And at that time the music business didn't plan far ahead. So we were quickly able – sometimes through sheer luck, or sheer cussedness – to attract interesting people and make radical changes.'

Some of those changes were behind the scenes; they had no impact on the public, but they fundamentally altered the LSO members' lives. For the first time, players were paid through their banks. A full-time orchestral manager and a librarian were employed; previously, those roles had been taken by players in their spare time. Most important of all, Fleischmann and Tuckwell established an LSO Trust – a fund that would help to finance tours, as well as sickness benefits and holiday payments for the players. After nearly sixty years of 'no play, no pay', this was a revolution.

What's more, the LSO Trust for the first time formalised, and gave public recognition to, the circle of rich patrons who had traditionally kept the orchestra afloat since its first days. The first trustees and management committee included such figures as Edward Heath (who resigned only when he became Prime Minister in 1970, but maintained his links with the orchestra and conducted it on several occasions), Benjamin Britten, Robert Mayer and the tobacco heir John Spencer Wills.

But perhaps the most influential figure was a Yorkshire businessman called Jack Lyons. As a child he was the only one of six siblings who had not been allowed music lessons. Perhaps the sense of 'what might have been' shaped his whole life, because few twentieth-century Englishmen have poured more passion and cash into supporting music-making by others. A former Leeds Festival chairman, Lyons had been 'bagged' by the alert Fleischmann when he moved from the north to London. Although he poured hundreds of thousands of pounds of his fortune into musical ventures in London and Yorkshire over several decades – both the Royal Academy of Music and the University of York have concert halls named after him – it was the LSO that became the prime beneficiary of his money and energy. Bustling and glad-handing behind the scenes, he fuelled the jet that allowed the LSO to soar in the 1960s.

Indeed, you can argue that the LSO's transformation into a globe-trotting orchestra was as much due to Lyons's indefatigable financial resourcefulness as to the vision of Fleischmann and Tuckwell.

Some of Fleischmann's other changes would certainly have been noticed by the audiences. The design and content of the printed concert programmes was hugely improved. Vouchers were introduced to encourage booking for concerts well in advance at reduced rates – the forerunner of today's sophisticated subscriber schemes.

And there was another innovation: industrial sponsorship. Of course, the arts had long been the recipient of philanthropy from wealthy industrialists. One need only look at the names of great institutions such as the Tate Gallery, Carnegie Hall or the Courtauld Institute. But the LSO's association with the Peter Stuyvesant Foundation, which began in 1963, was something very different: a business deal, conferring benefits to both parties, which established many of the ground rules that have governed business sponsorship of the arts in Britain ever since.

On one side was an immensely rich tobacco company keen to generate a more caring, community-conscious image for itself. On the other was a hard-up orchestra that was now led by a brash young Australian and an even brasher South African who were perfectly prepared to entertain American notions of 'product endorsement' in the sacred temples of art. In 1963, this was something new and perhaps rather shocking. So was the clarity of the sponsorship deal thrashed out by Fleischmann and, for Stuyvesant, an executive called Michael Kaye. The orchestra insisted on there being no artistic interference. Stuyvesant (which also, rather bravely, put money into the avant-garde Whitechapel Art Gallery) insisted that its money not only had to make a difference, but had to be seen making a difference. In other words, it wanted to support new initiatives: particularly the commissioning of works (often surreptitiously slipped into concerts as 'item to be announced', so as not to frighten the more traditional members of the audience) and the touring of new and neglected venues.

The first of these helped to spur the LSO into one of its most fruitful periods of collaboration with living composers. Names such as Alun Hoddinott, Richard Rodney Bennett, Aaron Copland and the Australian composer Don Banks started to appear on the programmes. But the most significant liaison was with Britten who, by the early 1960s, had consolidated his reputation as one of the four or five most significant composers in the world.

The orchestra's relationship with him went back for years. Indeed, it was the LSO, conducted by Sargent, that was featured on *The Instruments of the Orchestra*, the famous 1946 Ministry of Education film of Britten's *Young Person's Guide to the Orchestra* – perhaps the most influential music-teaching film of the twentieth century. In the late 1950s and early 1960s the relationship became much stronger. 'We were the orchestra he chose, for a period of his life, to do all his orchestral recordings,' William Waterhouse says. 'And he conducted us a lot in other people's music as well. I remember doing a Mahler Four with Ben in Orford Church.' That must have been an overwhelming occasion; Orford Church, not far from Britten's Suffolk home in Aldeburgh, is about the size of the Wigmore Hall.

Another remarkable experience was the recording of Britten's *War Requiem* in January 1963. The LSO had not been involved in the première of this extraordinary work. That took place on 30 May 1962 in Basil Spence's Coventry Cathedral, a spectacular modern building that had risen alongside the bombed ruins of the medieval cathedral, and was already filled with startlingly modern pieces of art and sculpture by the likes of Graham Sutherland, Jacob Epstein and John Piper.

The preparations had been fraught. Britten had wanted the soloists to be the Russian soprano Galina Vishnevskaya, the German baritone Dietrich Fischer-Dieskau and the British tenor Peter Pears, since he considered the Soviet Union, Germany and Britain to be 'the three countries that had suffered most during the war' (a comment that might not have impressed the Poles, among others). This was the height of the Cold War, however, and Vishnevskaya was expressly forbidden by her own Culture Minister to stand as a 'Soviet woman' next to a German and an Englishman and perform 'a political work'. The English soprano Heather Harper valiantly replaced her, with only days to learn the testing coloratura part. Then Britten discovered that the new cathedral's acoustics were (in his words) 'appalling', and the cathedral staff engaged in 'really Trollopian clerical battles, but with modern weapons'. The final straw was when the clergy refused to open up more than one small door for the audience at the première itself, resulting in a long queue and a very late start.

Yet the work made a huge impact. In the era of CND, the arms race, and such pacifist theatre pieces as Joan Littlewood's *Oh What a Lovely War*, the *War Requiem* chimed with a very strong public mood. When the LSO and Britten recorded it for Decca in Kingsway Hall the following January (with

Vishnevskaya, finally, allowed to sing her part, thus allowing Britten's multi-national concept to be appreciated for the first time), the resulting boxed set sold an astonishing two hundred thousand copies in five months – unprecedented for a new piece of 'serious' classical music.

Britten was a superb conductor: clear, incisive and supremely intelligent. Some of his recordings with the LSO remain stunning to this day. They range from *Billy Budd*, *A Midsummer Night's Dream*, the *Nocturne* and the *Serenade for Tenor, Horn and Strings* (with Tuckwell as the horn soloist) in the early 1960s to a classic interpretation of Elgar's *The Dream of Gerontius*, taped at the Snape Maltings in 1971. But Britten had a prickly and rather aloof aspect that was never going to endear him to all LSO players. 'He was severe in some ways,' says Waterhouse. 'Someone likened him to a candle with moths round it. You were attracted to him, but in time you often got your wings burnt.'

*

The relationship with Britten was just one of many dazzling partnerships that the LSO struck up in the heyday of the Fleischmann/Tuckwell era. During the early 1960s, perhaps for the first time since the orchestra's early years, there was a real 'can do' spirit in the LSO, as Waterhouse remembers:

I know it's fairly common today for orchestral noticeboards to have newspaper reviews pinned on them. But I had never encountered it until I came to the LSO. And I think it did reflect how much the orchestra wanted to know how well they were doing, whether they were going to get this or that recording or tour, whether they had impressed people. We were all from a younger generation – the principals, anyway – and we probably rather big-headedly thought we were doing much better than the older generation we had replaced.

Fleischmann nurtured that optimism by booking not only the established big-name soloists or conductors of the day, but also those who would become superstars in the coming decades. His knowledge of the international scene seemed encyclopaedic. 'He was very much in touch with that great German-Jewish cultural tradition,' Hugh Maguire says. 'He was born into it; it was in his bloodstream.'

But Fleischmann himself put it down to insatiable wanderlust and curiosity:

I had made it my business to find out what was going on. Even when I lived in South Africa I came to Europe virtually every year – travelling steerage at the back of the boat – and paid my way across Europe by writing articles for South African publications and recording pieces for radio. Every night, wherever I was, I went to concerts. So it wasn't difficult to find out who was worth inviting and what music was worth performing.

Whether or not it was quite as easy as that, the results of Fleischmann's research were remarkable. Virtually his first decision, in early 1960, was to recommend a twenty-three-year-old Indian called Zubin Mehta to take over a series of concerts when Krips pulled out. The LSO board decided Mehta was too unknown and too untested for such a big set of Festival Hall dates – which was a pity, because the following year Mehta became the youngest-ever conductor to direct the Vienna and Berlin Philharmonics, and shortly afterwards he was appointed principal conductor in Los Angeles.

After that, the LSO must have been more inclined to back Fleischmann's hunches. Certainly, the orchestra's 1963 and 1964 seasons were crammed with names that would go on to dominate the international music scene for the rest of the twentieth century: they included Abbado, Solti, Mehta, Maazel, Boulez, Kertész and a young English clarinettist-turned-conductor who had made a sensational Festival Hall début standing in for Klemperer a few seasons earlier – Colin Davis. The soloists were of a similar calibre: musicians soon to become renowned, but whom the average London concert-goer might be hearing for the first time.

One in particular created a sensation. Mstislav Rostropovich, then in his late thirties, was at the height of his powers as a cellist. But the repressive policies of the Soviet Union, brought down with particular force on a man inclined to side with dissidents, meant that his opportunities to exhibit his incredible musicianship to Western audiences had been restricted.

The fog of official hindrance briefly lifted in 1965 when, after months of negotiation with the implacable monolith of Soviet bureaucracy, Rostropovich was allowed to give a series of London concerts with the LSO, conducted by another Russian, Gennadi Rozhdestvensky. As if to make up for lost time, he delivered one of the most awesome displays of instrumental virtuosity in concert history, playing no fewer than thirty-one concertos over the course of nine concerts in just three weeks. (The whole series was then repeated in New York.) Besides the familiar Dvořák, Schumann, Elgar and Haydn, they ranged from Vivaldi and J. C. Bach to the masterpieces written for him by the three great composers he personally knew and revered: Prokofiev, Shostakovich and Britten.

At the conclusion of this epic journey through what seemed like the entire concerto repertoire of his instrument, the LSO presented the great cellist with a medal struck in his honour. It would be another ten years, many of them spent in abject misery and what was virtually internal exile, before Rostropovich and his wife, Galina Vishnevskaya, left the Soviet Union. But the link forged with the LSO and with Britain would endure.

Over the next four decades Rostropovich would inspire some of the LSO's most enthralling evenings. both as cellist and conductor. His series gave Fleischmann an unexpected bonus, too:

I had always wanted somehow to get hold of Leonard Bernstein. But he was very elusive. I got news that he was in town and through mutual friends I found out he was at the Savoy. So I just picked up the phone and asked for him. He answered, and I said, 'Mr Bernstein, there's something very special happening tomorrow night, namely Rostropovich ending this remarkable cycle, and the orchestra and I would really appreciate you being at this concert, and maybe you will join us for dinner?'

Well, he enjoyed the concert, but afterwards he told me he wasn't coming back to London to conduct because he didn't like doing rehearsals in draughty halls. I said: 'It's all changed. Tell me how many rehearsals you need and, although I may argue with you, you will get virtually everything you want and I promise you there won't be any draughts.' Bernstein said: 'Well, come and see me in New York and we'll make some programmes.' I did, and the first thing that happened was the Shostakovich Five, which Humphrey Burton took into the studio to film. Which must have been live, because the rehearsal was so engrossing that BBC2 postponed the late-night news to allow it to finish. You could do things like that on TV in those days, and get an audience for it.

Once wooed back to London's 'draughty halls', Bernstein's relationship with the LSO lasted until his death, nearly thirty years later. Other relationships that the orchestra attempted to establish didn't work out so well. One was with George Szell, the chillingly severe perfectionist who had ruled the Cleveland Orchestra with a baton of iron for twenty years, and would continue to do so until his death in 1970. Szell was an out-and-out tyrant, but his insistence on pure intonation and rhythmic precision was respected throughout the orchestral world. 'He was quite the most unpleasant conductor I ever played under,' Barry Tuckwell says, 'but we invited him to the LSO because we wanted to become a better orchestra, and we knew he would make us better.'

The relationship was fraught. The orchestra made a number of recordings with him, including Harty's arrangements of Handel's *Water Music* and *Fireworks Music*, and Brahms's First Piano Concerto with Clifford Curzon as the soloist ('to my mind, still one of the most superb concerto recordings ever,' says Fleischmann). Then came catastrophe. When Szell returned to conduct Beethoven's 'Eroica' Symphony in concert, the LSO had a new leader. As Fleischmann recalls:

In his zeal to show how industrious he was, the new leader had changed all the bowings he found in the parts. He didn't realise that Szell's orchestral parts are sacred, like the Bible, to musicians in America and elsewhere. At the rehearsal break Szell called me in and said: 'I'm going home, you had better find another conductor.'

I talked him into staying and doing his programmes, but after that he said: 'While you are self-destructing, I want no part of it. The moment you call me and tell me you have a new leader, I'll come and conduct my first concert with you without a fee.'

Three years later, when the LSO was touring Israel under another conductor, the same leader was the focus of a rebellion among the violins. They refused to take the stage unless he was replaced. 'Well, at that point the board finally decided that we needed a change of leader,' Fleischmann says. 'From Tel Aviv I somehow got through to Szell in Cleveland, and said: "George, you remember three years ago you promised me something?" "Don't tell me you've got rid of him," Szell replied. "He's resigning," I said. "Have you got your diary handy?" And Szell came and conducted without a fee, just as he promised.'

*

When Pierre Monteux died in July 1964, the debate within the orchestra on the merits or otherwise of the conductors introduced by Fleischmann and Tuckwell suddenly took on a new urgency. There was, of course, no constitutional rule compelling the LSO to have a principal conductor; indeed, there had been a six-year gap between Krips's resignation and Monteux's appointment, and a sixteen-year gap between Harty and Krips.

Things were different now, though. Much of the financial well-being of an orchestra depended on recording work, but the record companies contracted conductors, not orchestras, and a conductor would usually choose to record with the orchestra of which he was principal conductor. This was the commercial reality lying behind every principal-conductor appointment in every orchestra from the heyday of the classical recording industry in the late 1950s and 1960s until its sudden startling implosion in the early 1990s.

What were the LSO's options in 1964? 'We had a shortlist of István Kertész, Lorin Maazel, Georg Solti, Colin Davis and Gennadi Rozhdestvensky,' Tuckwell says. The fact that Rozhdestvensky was a Soviet artist was always going to cause complications at the height of the Cold War. 'Solti, we could see, was going to be trouble, though we liked working with him,' Tuckwell continues. 'The same with Maazel: a little bit too much friction. Colin wasn't rejected as such. But at that time, for what we wanted to achieve musically, Kertész was better for us than any of the others. We needed help where we were weak. We could play Stravinsky and Berlioz brilliantly already.'

That is not how others saw it. Colin Davis had conducted a performance of Berlioz's *Grande messe des morts* in memory of Monteux, and the thirty-seven-year-old Englishman was clearly being lined up in some quarters as the great Frenchman's successor. 'I quite frankly wanted him to get the job,' Fleischmann admits, 'but the majority of the players voted against it. Kertész was a wonderful conductor and a very sweet man. But Colin would have been a better choice. In those days the LSO was a young orchestra and he was a young conductor, and they were both British. Well, I'm glad he got the job in the end.' He did, but it was thirty-one years later.

Some detected a campaign in high places against Davis. 'I think Barry Tuckwell would sometimes make difficulties for him,' says the harpist, Osian Ellis. 'But I expect that Barry Tuckwell has grown up by now.' More significantly, Davis himself – a much more prickly and impetuous character as a young man than later in his career – was struggling to deal with the break-up of his marriage and a certain amount of inner turmoil during his leg of the LSO's 1964 world tour, at the very moment when he needed to be at his most persuasive on the podium.

Nearly forty years later, Davis recalled:

I didn't expect to get it anyway. I thought it might have happened at one stage. But I'm glad it didn't, because I was too young. In the next few years they offered me the job several times, but I declined. Though whether that was out of pique or good common sense is not for me to say. Now, of course, the orchestra is completely different.

Kertész was finally given the job. It was an ominous warning to Fleischmann, if he but knew it, that the LSO players (or at least the ones with most influence) were beginning to resent his influence on artistic matters. Still, the appointment was widely welcomed as being an enlightened choice. Just turned thirty-five, Kertész was one of a generation of gifted Hungarians who had emerged in the West after the 1956 uprising. Though he had done most of his subsequent work in Germany, he had conducted the LSO as early as 1960, and made a big impact on the players, especially with Romantic repertoire such as the Dvořák symphonies.

'He brought a lovely singing quality to the orchestra,' Roger Lord recalls. 'He had that poetic touch that, say, Doráti lacked. It's something to do with a feeling of mystery in music or painting: if it isn't there, the art is too prosaic. And he had a pleasant personality, as well. I think he was pleased to get out of Hungary and have an orchestra to conduct.'

Pleasant personality or not, Kertész's brief era with the LSO was destined to be one of the stormiest in the orchestra's history. He gave his first concert in October 1965. Within three years his relationship with his new band was in tatters.

*

As if dealing with the death of Monteux and the succession problem was not stressful enough, the LSO management was faced, in the autumn of 1964, with the pressing task of preparing evidence for the Goodman Committee on the London orchestras. It mattered. London's four independent symphony orchestras were all in financial disarray. The Royal Philharmonic – left stranded after Beecham's death in 1961 and now run, LSO-style, by its players – had needed an emergency Arts Council bail-out in December 1963 to keep it from bankruptcy. The Philharmonia was reeling in 1964 from the cold-hearted withdrawal of Walter Legge from its affairs, and the LSO and LPO were also hit by dismal attendance figures for many Festival Hall concerts. In 1963 the LSO sold only 745 seats (out of 2982) for a programme of Britten, Mahler and Brahms conducted by Solti. Kertész had fared even worse for a Mozart, Bartók and Dvořák concert: just 593 tickets sold.

Since 1945 the Arts Council had become an increasingly important source of funds to orchestras. But with each increase in subsidy, the bureaucrats' desire to 'sort out the orchestras' became ever harder to resist. The post-war era was, in any case, one in which the Government or quasi-Government agencies were expected to intervene in, and solve the problems of, a great many areas, from the ailing British car industry to the expansion of higher education. The Arts Council was only following the prevailing trend.

The London orchestras clearly needed some sorting out in 1964, at least financially. With the BBC Symphony Orchestra also presenting concerts in the Festival Hall, and the vibrant new Academy of St Martin-in-the-Fields and English Chamber Orchestra also competing in the same market place, the audience for orchestral music was being stretched far too thinly to support so many bands.

That obvious fact raised a bigger question that would recur like some ominous Wagnerian leitmotif for at least the next thirty years. Did London have too many orchestras, even for the good times? Wouldn't taxpayers' money be better invested in supporting two symphony orchestras well, rather than four inadequately?

That the public was confused by the alphabet stew of orchestral titles in London concert programmes was not seriously in doubt. In the early 1980s a survey was carried out of audiences emerging from Festival Hall concerts. Most concertgoers had no trouble remembering the names of the conductor and soloists they had just seen. But many couldn't remember which orchestra had been playing. Or perhaps the name had never registered in the first place.

That didn't matter so much (except to the various orchestras' self-esteem) when the halls were full and the music-making riveting. But in bad times, such interchangeability of product in the same venue made Arts Council bureaucrats nervous. They felt they had to 'rationalise' – use their power of subsidy to force orchestras to move, or merge, or disband altogether.

The problem, however, was that the subsidy they offered wasn't enormous, so withdrawing it would not necessarily kill off an orchestra. Indeed, the reverse would often happen. Decades of struggle and insecurity had made the London orchestral profession world-class exponents in the art of survival. A threatened orchestra would (and still does) harness every propaganda weapon at its disposal: sympathetic press; high-placed patrons; statistics on Arts Council waste in other areas. The players would tighten their belts, play without fees for a while if necessary. In the end, their will to survive would be stronger than the bureaucrats' will to reform.

Antal Doráti once observed:

It is said periodically that there are too many London orchestras and that one – or more – should be eliminated. Actually, none can be 'eliminated', that is, forced not to exist, except through an act of murder. These orchestras live by their own strengths. At one time I told an official enquiry that to cut off one symphony orchestra from London because there seemed to be 'too many' would be as stupid as finding an animal whose natural endowment was five legs and cutting off one of them because most animals only have four. London, with all its orchestras, is such an animal. We should accept the fact, and glory in it.

But for fifty years the Arts Council rarely accepted the fact, and never gloried in it. For generation after generation of bureaucrats, the imbalance in 'orchestral provision' around Britain was like some ugly stain on their immaculate desktops: it had to be cleansed, erased, made neat and logical. The competitive traditions of London's orchestral life counted for nothing. Nor did the views of London audiences and the millions of cultural tourists attracted to the capital who, on the whole, rather liked finding a choice of eight or ten different orchestral programmes each week. After all, if they had wanted to enjoy a single orchestra repeating the same programme four times a week they would have visited Cincinnati or Denver.

Such arguments cut no ice with the Arts Council mandarins. What infuriated them was that London had no fewer than eight large-scale orchestras (the four independents, the two opera-house bands, plus the BBC Symphony and Concert Orchestras), that north-west Lancashire and Glasgow boasted three each, but that due to a historical quirk, the poor, benighted 'East' – from East Anglia up through the East Midlands, Yorkshire, Northumbria and Scotland to Aberdeen – couldn't boast a single resident symphony orchestra at all.

This was clearly a scandal. Something had to be done, even if it meant forcibly 'relocating' a London orchestra to, say, Nottingham. Bureaucratic propriety demanded nothing less. On no fewer than twenty occasions over fifty years the Arts Council produced a new report which sought to 'solve the orchestral problem', usually on some such terms. One hesitates to calculate the cost in bureaucrat hours and paperclips, but the total would surely have been enough to pay for the entire population of Nottingham to travel to London twice a week in perpetuity and enjoy LSO concerts at the taxpayers' expense.

Eleven of those reports were solely on the London orchestras, whose players were generally perceived by the bureaucrats to be either 'fat cats' flitting from one lucrative film session to another, progress-resisting Luddites, or simple villains. But nearly all of the reports regarded London as being at the crux of the problem. And the first really important one was the 1964–5 inquiry presided over by Arnold Goodman, solicitor to the very rich and powerful.

It was possibly unique in British bureaucratic history in being chaired and written by a man who knew that, since he had been promised the job of Arts Council chairman by the incoming Wilson Government, he would be presenting his own report to himself for implementation. W. S. Gilbert's Pooh-Bah would have doffed his many hats in admiration. But Goodman's bizarre ubiquity didn't really matter, because in page after page of elegant blather – compiled after each orchestra had been required to spend hundreds of hours of management time submitting evidence over the winter of 1964–5 – his report basically said: do nothing. The report's most famous conclusion was that the demand for orchestral music in London justified 'the existence of rather more than three but less than four orchestras'.

Goodman's main intention was plainly to quash a move inside his own music department to withdraw their subsidy from the Royal Philharmonic. In that he succeeded. Wearing his Arts Council chairman hat, he then created a creature called the London Orchestral Concerts Board, a kind of sub-quango to his quango, which (as the LSO management tartly pointed out to the Arts Council), subsequently managed to run up £10,000 of administration costs each year while distributing basic subsidies of just £40,000 to each of the four London orchestras.

Still, the necessity of preparing evidence for Goodman did at least focus the minds of LSO board members on what would be vital and/or desirable in order to increase the quality of their own orchestra. They argued for a string section of sixty rather than fifty, for co-principals throughout the wind sections, and for quadruple woodwind – taking the orchestral size from seventy-eight to ninety-eight, and ideally to a hundred and fifteen. 'A situation is rapidly approaching when, as a result of acute overwork and borderline finance, it will be impossible to maintain standards, let alone raise them,' the LSO's submission to Goodman argued. It would be another twenty-five years before the orchestra achieved such luxurious numbers. But that, one suspects, is still rather sooner than the LSO board might have expected when asked to compile this wish list back in 1964.

Life, and this book, are too short to catalogue all the Arts Council's later reports into London orchestral life, but here are the more famous of them. In 1970, five years after Goodman, the economist Alan Peacock had his chance to set the London orchestras straight. His effort was rather more astringent. He wanted the Arts Council to end altogether its funding to two London orchestras (which he did not select), and bolster the regional orchestras instead. Unfortunately for him, his meticulously prepared screed of tables and dry financial reasoning was utterly undermined by an introduction from Lord Goodman which more or less said that the Arts Council would do nothing of the kind.

Then came Sir Frank Figgures' 1978 report. This advocated 'no further assistance to [London orchestral] managements in difficulty', which suited the Arts Council fine, because it was then flirting with the idea of creating a Berlin Philharmonic-style 'super-orchestra' – dubbed 'The Million Pound Band' by the press – by giving all the available subsidy to just one of the four London orchestras. This Beechamesque notion was not exactly new. Seven years earlier, EMI had been pushing the Arts Council to bring about the merger of the LPO and the (then floundering) New Philharmonia, in order to create a 'dream-team' plaything for its star conductor/pianist, Daniel Barenboim. That fell apart because, in all the excitement of plotting in smoke-filled rooms, nobody had bothered to consult the musicians of the two orchestras. It emerged that the Philharmonia's, in particular, were not exactly ecstatic at the prospect of spending the rest of their lives playing bit parts in the career of Daniel Barenboim.

The 1978 'million-pound orchestra' scheme was mooted for well over a year – creating the usual upheaval in orchestral circles, and a small mountain of paperwork – before being abandoned. The reason? Someone pointed out that, to match the funding of the Berlin Philharmonic, London's new super-orchestra would need not £1 million of subsidy, but two or three times that amount. At which point the Arts Council – doubtless contemplating the implications of Margaret Thatcher's arrival in 10 Downing Street – went strangely quiet.

Moving on to 1984, we arrive at *The Glory of the Garden* – an enormously influential strategy document by William Rees-Mogg, the former *Times* editor who chaired the Arts Council in the early 1980s. This advocated much more attention being paid (and subsidy diverted) to the regions, as opposed to London. Along the way, almost as an afterthought, it proposed creating a 'great eastern symphony orchestra' based in Nottingham. The RPO was supposed to embrace this relocation.

At more or less the same time, a veteran Arts Council pen-pusher called Neil Duncan produced his report on the London orchestras, which came up with the blindingly original suggestions that the Arts Council should withdraw support from any orchestra in trouble, that all the capital's orchestras should tour outside London more often, and that the RPO (when it wasn't in Nottingham, presumably) should replace the LSO as resident orchestra at the Barbican. (The LSO's torrid first years in the Barbican are discussed in chapter 9.) Another waste of good trees. Duncan quickly disappeared to run something in Hong Kong after his report was published, but not so quickly that he wasn't around to see his report sink without trace.

By contrast, Robert Ponsonby's report, written a mere three years later, was a careful examination of the case for one orchestra to become resident at the Festival Hall – an idea mooted by the LPO nearly forty years earlier and realised by the same band three years later. Unfortunately for Ponsonby, his earnest musings were overtaken by events: the LPO launched a bid to merge with, or take over (the terminology differed, depending on your affiliation), the Philharmonia. For several months the London orchestral world was in a state of civil war. In 1990, when the dust finally settled and the Festival Hall residency was duly awarded to the LPO, the strings attached to the appointment were so tangled and restrictive that the orchestra was staring at insolvency only four years later.

Passing over the half-baked scheme floated in 1991 by another ennobled Arts Council chairman, the whimsical Lord Palumbo, to create a 'super-orchestra to rival the Berlin Philharmonic', this time to be conducted by

Georg Solti, we arrive finally at the infamous Hoffman report of 1993. This was a beauty contest, pure and simple, between the three London orchestras based at the Festival Hall (the Arts Council said that the LSO was 'self-selecting'), in which the prize would be to collect all the subsidy. The two losers would be left out in the cold.

But there turned out to be nothing simple, and certainly nothing pure, about this débâcle, which had been secretly concocted as a way of cutting subsidy to the orchestras (though the secret was soon out). It roused the ire of practically every eminent musician in Britain, provoked hostile commentary even in the tabloid press, and turned the Arts Council from a minor laughing-stock into a object of national scorn. Even the composer Sir Peter Maxwell Davies was roused from his Orkney cottage to thunder in the *Daily Mail*:

The Arts Council appears not only determined to cut music as much as possible out of our lives; but worse, it is wantonly sowing despair, disillusion and enmity in a profession where hitherto there were only friendly rivalries. Its dogmas are as demeaning and disrespectful of human values as anything dreamt up by the Communists.

Worst of all, though, the upheaval achieved absolutely nothing. For after months of turmoil, consultation and pondering, Lord Justice Sir Leonard Hoffman hilariously announced that he was 'unable to offer the Arts Council the clear advice for which it asked', and we were all back where we started. It was a solution worthy of Lord Goodman, thirty years earlier. Which isn't surprising, because back in 1965 Goodman's chief aide when writing his orchestral report had been a bright young South African barrister called Leonard Hoffman. As the nursery song tells us, 'The wheels on the bus go round and round, round and round, round and round.'

Fifty years of Arts Council meddling, and London still has exactly the same number of London orchestras, doing precisely the same sort of things on more or less the same amount of inadequate central Government subsidy, as it had in 1950. In a way, that's reassuring. London's teeming musical and theatrical life may be chaotic, ungovernable and sometimes unfathomable. But it has a thousand times more zest, energy and imagination than those tidy continental cities which organise their cultural affairs like train timetables. At least, that's how Londoners see it.

*

Notwithstanding the uncertainty caused by Monteux's death, the Goodman Committee's inquiries and erratic concert attendances in London, the years from 1963 to 1965 must be viewed as the high noon of the Tuckwell/ Fleischmann era. The trumpeter Howard Snell confirms this view:

By then the orchestra had developed a new style, very much as it is now. It was a very forward, very attacking orchestra. The brilliance of the attack and the sheer panache of the leading players carried it along, really. And of course that was in marked contrast to the Philharmonia, which had an 'olde worlde' sonority – a rather fat and happy-sounding orchestra. The LSO came on the scene, young and hungry and with a manager, Ernest Fleischmann, who was similarly a ball of fire, and proceeded to cut a swathe through the London orchestral scene. There were many noses put out of joint among the elder statesmen, the Walter Legges and so on, at the appearance of this rather garish new ensemble.

To ambitious young men such as Fleischmann and Tuckwell, the logical next step was to display this 'garish new ensemble' to a wider public than the one that flocked (or sometimes didn't) to the Festival Hall. And so, in the autumn of 1964, at a time when it had virtually no money in the bank, the LSO embarked on nothing less than a world tour.

In its way, this 'diamond jubilee' tour was as epic an undertaking, and as breathtakingly brash a concept, as the LSO's groundbreaking American trip had been in 1912. Partly financed by the Stuyvesant Foundation and partly by the prodigious fundraising powers of Jack Lyons and his LSO Trust colleagues, the 1964 tour took in the United States, Japan, South Korea, Hong Kong, India, Israel, Turkey and what was then Persia (now Iran). In all, thirty-two thousand miles, fifty-one concerts, thirty-one cities, seventy-eight days – and a 'baton relay' of conductors that included Davis, Solti, Stokowski, Sargent and the composer Arthur Bliss.

'It was because the Festival Hall was closed for three months,' says Tuckwell. 'There was nowhere to give concerts in London except the Albert Hall. So it seemed like a good idea to play a few weeks in the United States, then move to Japan, and so on.'

If that was indeed the origin of the tour, then pragmatism can rarely have been so inspired. The billing – 'the world-renowned London Symphony Orchestra' – might have seemed a touch disingenuous on 27 September, the day the players embarked, but by the time they returned on 11 December they were indeed world-renowned. They had performed to an estimated hundred million people, either live or via TV and radio. They had won positive reviews nearly everywhere, and made a particularly big impact in New York, with both a tremendous concert under Stokowski in Carnegie Hall ('We played as if our lives depended on it,' Tuckwell told a *Newsweek* journalist, who went on to hymn the LSO's 'new young look and profound artistry'), and a performance at the United Nations building on United Nations Day that was televised coast to coast.

As a result the Mayor of New York declared a 'London Symphony Orchestra Day', and the orchestra was invited to return to New York every spring. That proved financially impossible, much as the invitation must have appealed to the ambitious Fleischmann and Tuckwell. The 1964 tour had exhausted even Jack Lyons' cash-conjuring abilities for a while. But in 1966, the LSO embarked on a tour that was scarcely less ambitious than that of 1964, this time to Hong Kong, Singapore, Australia, the United States and Switzerland. After that, a schedule that included at least one glamorous foreign tour a year was regarded as essential to the preservation of the LSO's new, swaggering image.

That was particularly true when the players discovered a place that transformed their notion of foreign touring from a high-pressure chore into what *Time* magazine described as 'a continuous round of sun and surf'. As part of their 1966 American visit, they were invited to take up residency at the inaugural Florida Music Festival, based at Daytona Beach. The orchestra's duties were not arduous: a few concerts and chamber recitals, some public rehearsals and educational work. This left a great deal of time for rest and recreation. *Time* magazine's reporter caught the spirit of that first residency rather well:

'It is so mad, so utterly wild a scheme that we can't resist!' So saying, the management of the London Symphony cancelled twenty recording sessions, five concerts, refused an invitation to the Athens Festival and, with the abandon of undergrads leaving for spring vacation, bundled the orchestra off to that big sandbox in the sun, Daytona Beach, Florida. Scheduled for a month-long stay, the London Symphony is the first European orchestra to settle in a US city for such an extended engagement. When they arrived two weeks ago – ninety-six musicians, forty-three wives and thirty-six children – they were met by a caravan of forty cars and treated to a wee-hour spin across Daytona's famed beach.

Whether or not the LSO did cancel twenty recording sessions (it seems rather uncharacteristic behaviour for this particular generation of players), the lure of Daytona did prove irresistible, and the orchestra returned for each of the next three years. After that there was a prolonged break, but the link with the Florida resort was renewed in the early 1980s, and since then the LSO has visited Daytona every two years. That the nature of the visit, or the lavish hospitality, hasn't much altered since 1966 (though it now costs the Florida town well over a million dollars to host one LSO visit), is evident from this breathless account of the 1993 visit in the *Daily Mirror*:

It's a place even locals call 'The Redneck Riviera'. A mecca for Hell's Angels. Where culture means eating your hamburger with a napkin. That's Florida's Daytona Beach, where ears were made for earrings – not hearings.

But listen up. This tiny town of sixty-five thousand sweating citizens also plays host to the world-renowned London Symphony Orchestra . . . The scale of the operation is reflected in the thirty spotless limos assembled before the orchestra arrives in three Delta airliners at the town's brand-new airport. The red carpet extends to the orchestra's beachside dwelling where the players are showered with a fountain spouting champagne cocktails.

'We have sixty-five invitations to parties, and that's just for the next five days,' says violinist Lennie Mackenzie in his Stars-and-Stripes swimming trunks. 'I suppose it's all a matter of pacing yourself.'

*

The LSO's fun and games at Daytona Beach in the late 1960s were as nothing, however, compared with the fun and games back home. Within the space of a few tempestuous months in 1967, every faultline in the orchestra's constitution was relentlessly exposed, every tension between individuals brought to the surface, every concealed resentment aired, every grudge revenged in a triple-whammy of carelessness that would not have impressed Lady Bracknell.

There is the feeling almost of Greek tragedy about the way in which the LSO's wonderful outward exuberance was suddenly soured by this brutal season of back-stabbing. To heap all the blame for the latter on the three principal characters – Fleischmann, Tuckwell and Kertész – is an unfair over-simplification. The LSO of the early 1960s was full of outspoken individualists, quick to criticise, hard to please. Instrumental sections were constantly being reshuffled in those years to accommodate 'personal incompatibilities', and on one famous occasion in 1965 the entire violin section refused to take the platform unless the unfortunate leader was replaced. The impatience of the most influential players with anything less than perfection is probably the main reason why the LSO's playing standards rose so dramatically in those years. But it also made for a continuous stream of low-level invective behind the scenes.

'That's why we appointed John Georgiadis as leader,' Tuckwell remarks. Georgiadis appeared in 1965 after the episode referred to above, served an eight-year stint with the orchestra, then returned for a period in the late 1970s before developing his own solo and conducting career. 'He had that kind of arrogance and strength. When someone in the section tried to tell him what to do, he didn't exactly take his jacket off and prepare to fight, but that was the attitude. That was what we needed. We were a rough lot.'

One of Tuckwell's great strengths, too, was his ability to deal effectively with all that. He could, in short, tough it out with the toughest of them. He recalls:

When I became the chairman, I remember speaking to a very distinguished colleague, a very intelligent and mercurial man, a good friend, but a person who was forever sniping. I won't reveal who it was. I said: 'Neville, I've got a job to do. If you don't stop sniping, I'm going to start attacking you.' I felt my responsibility was to the orchestra; I couldn't look after friends who I thought were misbehaving. After all, we had to pull ourselves up by our own boot strings.

Other players must sometimes have been made to feel vulnerable by the arrogance, or perceived arrogance of those in the 'inner circle' of principals and board members. The trumpeter Bram Wiggins tells a revealing story. In 1956, after twelve years in the LSO, he emigrated to Canada. After a few years, he decided to return. 'I missed the big occasions,' he says. He was phoned by an LSO board member. 'Would you come back as co-principal and do the high trumpet parts?' the man asked. Wiggins said he would consider it. A few days later, Fleischmann phoned him. 'Will you do an audition?' he asked. 'Not for a job I did for twelve years, and never auditioned for in the first place,' Wiggins replied. 'You approached me, I didn't approach you.'

So Wiggins came back to London, but not to the LSO. 'Within four days of returning, I was working again – for the Philharmonia, the Royal Philharmonic and the English Chamber Orchestra,' he recalls. 'But after a couple of months I got another call from the LSO: "We'd like to get you back in the business," they said. "Do you want to do a concert with us?" I replied: "You're not getting me back in the business; I've been very busy with other orchestras. What will you pay me?" The man replied: "Union rates." I said: "I'm getting more than that from other people. Get someone else." I found the LSO's attitude very peculiar, and rather sad.'

This insider/outsider tension at the LSO – if that is what it was – came to a head in the season of 1965. Spurred, perhaps, by the process of compiling evidence for the Goodman committee on the future of the London orchestras, Tuckwell began a series of semi-private inquests on playing standards and conditions, conducted by his board members who interviewed each principal in turn. Rumours flew around the orchestra – that 'star' players were to be given red-carpet treatment to stop them defecting to other bands; that Tuckwell was planning a purge of the rank-and-file.

Stuart Knussen, the principal double bass (and later the LSO's chairman), stoked up the discontent when he threatened to leave the LSO for the New

Philharmonia, claiming that the latter's second violins were better than the LSO's firsts, and that its cellos were in a different class. 'Stuart was a really powerful influence on the LSO then,' says Denis Wick, the trombonist. 'A number of back-desk cellos left the orchestra because Stuart would be standing right behind them and clear his throat in this very loud and distinctive way in rehearsal if they played something less than perfectly.'

Neville Marriner, who favoured 'differentials' in pay even between the various rank-and-file fiddle desks, put his finger on another problem: 'The amount of work the orchestra is obliged to undertake [about 750 three-hour sessions a year at that time] not only inhibits personal attention to one's technical ability, but is physically and mentally enervating,' he told the board. There was also heated discussion of an old problem: principals who were in demand as soloists, such as the clarinettist Gervase de Peyer. They often absented themselves from LSO concerts, a trait that inevitably exposed any deficiencies lower down the section.

It is against this volatile background that the dramas of 1966 and 1967 must be viewed. In a curious way, the atmosphere inside the LSO mirrored the general mood in Britain at that time. The 1960s were in some respects an era of great optimism and social liberation, in which old imperial attitudes and pompous authoritarianism were mocked on satirical shows such as *Beyond the Fringe* and *That Was the Week That Was*, when popular broadcasting was hijacked by 'pirate' radio stations, and when London briefly became a hothouse of youth culture and fashion. But it was also an era of dire economic crises, of industrial decline, of continual currency devaluations and galloping inflation, of Government impotence and financially catastrophic strikes. In short, it was a time when Britain was, in that splendid northern phrase, 'all fur coat and no knickers'. With the devastating blackouts of 1972 and the three-day weeks of 1973, even the fur coat was rudely ripped away. It isn't too fanciful, perhaps, to regard the LSO's propensity for swanning grandly around the world and consorting with the finest conductors, while failing to solve basic and highly divisive problems, as being rather similar.

What's more, the anomalies of Fleischmann's position were becoming increasingly evident as his personal ambitions became more apparent. When he was recruited from South Africa in 1959, the LSO board had been comparatively tame. Moreover, the orchestra's workload – particularly from recording sessions – had increased to such an extent that the LSO's directors (all working players, of course) were, by necessity, increasingly distanced from the day-to-day management of the orchestra. That left a large and inviting gap, which Fleischmann swiftly filled – and filled so well that, to the musical world outside, he swiftly became the voice and the face of the LSO.

Nor did the players complain, at first. After all, Fleischmann filled the LSO's diary not just with lucrative work but with quality engagements and glamorous tours as well. But as the board, led by Tuckwell, became more assertive – and as the LSO players themselves started to question who was really running the orchestra – Fleischmann's high-profile image began to be resented. So did his very un-British brashness. 'People started saying: who does this South African guy think he is?' Hugh Maguire recalls. 'Ernest really loved music very much,' says Colin Davis. 'But he was also dictatorial, and this mattered at the time when the LSO board gave themselves airs, which they don't do any more.'

'We had our fights,' Tuckwell admits. 'Ernest was a first-class salesman and entrepreneur. But he wanted to have his own musical thoughts as well. That is where we got jealous and said: "No, this is our business." I got a lot of the flak for it, and people said I wanted to run the show myself. I didn't. I am a performer, not an administrator. But I was the political person.'

As so often in such circumstances, the 'last straw' was a comparatively trivial, even farcical, incident. In June 1966 the orchestra played a Viennese evening of waltzes and polkas as an end-of-season divertissement under Kertész. There was, by all accounts, a lot of larking about – not unusual in these sorts of programmes. Kertész delayed some of the downbeats in a Strauss waltz to try and catch the players out. The players began the *Radetzky March* while Kertész was off the platform, and so on. It was harmless stuff. Whether it was also funny was a matter of opinion.

Fleischmann, however, was not amused: he professed fury that the jokes had not been rehearsed and the audience not warned. Worse still, he made his anger known in public. This, most LSO members thought, overreached his authority. He was, after all, not their feudal baron but their paid 'Secretary', though the term had long seemed anachronistic and would soon be abandoned.

All through the following autumn and winter the atmosphere grew increasingly poisonous. Tuckwell encouraged his board to instigate a far-reaching overhaul of the LSO's administration. This brought to light (as was probably intended) a certain sketchiness in the orchestra's accounting systems and paperwork. Even the minutes of its own board meetings were months late in being written up. In friendlier times, such sins would have led to a reprimand and some good-humoured banter. Indeed, since the minutes of LSO board meetings now had to be scrutinised by Goodman's new

London Orchestral Concerts Board, and thus made public to rival orchestras, there might have been excellent tactical reasons for not writing them up immediately.

But these were not friendly times. Paperwork was the Secretary's responsibility, and Fleischmann had failed in this basic responsibility. The rumour swirling round the orchestra was that he had also lost his Midas touch in the matter of winning the orchestra vital recording work. In particular, the LSO's long-standing relationship with Decca seemed to be running out of steam. There were also questions about the complex formula (a mixture of 'basic pay' and 'bonuses' depending on the LSO's workload) on which Fleischmann's salary was based. Most damning of all, his enemies accused him of assuming powers that properly belonged to the board.

Again, Fleischmann possessed an obvious defence. Did his original contract not stipulate that he should exercise 'considerable initiative' in acting 'as a salesman for the Orchestra'? Surely using initiative meant acting quickly and without continuous consultation. But the board preferred to point to the clause which decreed that 'except where decisions follow an accepted pattern already applied over a period, the Secretary's decisions must be submitted to and be the responsibility of the Directors'. Not for the first or last time in its hundred-year history, the LSO players were asserting their right to govern their own affairs.

A great horn player must not only have nerves of steel; he must also positively relish making high-risk, high-altitude interventions into the symphonic maelstrom. He must revel in the limelight, feed off the drama. To play the first-horn parts in Mahler's colossal symphonies or Richard Strauss's epic tone-poems would otherwise be impossible. At this point in the LSO's affairs, Barry Tuckwell deployed all those attributes – in the boardroom. On 30 March 1967, he resigned as chairman. It was a brilliant tactical move. He had recently been re-elected with virtually a hundred per cent of the vote. He knew that practically every player was behind him, so he probably calculated that his resignation letter would resonate round the rehearsal halls and recording studios like a thunderbolt.

He explained himself in the letter:

The real reason for my resignation is that I cannot for another day associate myself with the General Secretary. I do not think the Board of Directors is any longer in a position to control the affairs of the company, that is, not while Mr Ernest Fleischmann is General Secretary. And while I must admire his almost unequalled flair for presentation and advertising, I find it too undignified and embarrassing trying to justify his inability to accept or apportion blame, which results in frequent rows and recriminations, his constant evasiveness, and the impossibility of getting a plain and accurate explanation from him. In short I do not wish it to be thought that his methods are my methods.

An emergency meeting of all the LSO players was immediately called in Bishopsgate Hall, near Liverpool Street Station. In a charged atmosphere, member after member expressed the view that the 'wrong man had resigned'. Neither at this meeting, nor at the subsequent board meeting where the directors voted (though not unanimously) to ask the orchestra's Secretary to resign, was Fleischmann permitted to speak in his own defence.

Was he even aware of his impending execution before the guillotine came down? Fleischmann later professed himself 'shocked' at the plotting against him. He had apparently entertained Tuckwell and his wife into the early hours at his house only three nights earlier. But if he was entirely ignorant of the undercurrents that were about to pull him under, he must have been either naive or stupid. Neither option strikes one as very likely.

In the event, Fleischmann departed – first to a job with the CBS record label, and then to run the Los Angeles Philharmonic, which he did with much distinction for many years. Within a year of his departure, a faction in the LSO would be begging him to return, so great had been the disarray in the intervening months. Cannily, Fleischmann replied that he would need a formal request signed by every member of the orchestra. He must surely have been aware that he had made enough enemies for that never to happen. The Fleischmann era was truly over.

What was his legacy to the orchestra? He had repositioned it on the world map, establishing a glamorous reputation that the LSO happily continued to trade off for at least another decade. He attuned the orchestra to the 'Swinging Sixties' mood, dispelling much of the fusty atmosphere that surrounded orchestral concerts. And, not least, he gave the orchestra a taste for the high life and high drama. There was never a dull moment when Ernest was around, and that suited the strong-willed characters that dominated the orchestra at that time.

But was there too much glitter and not enough substance? 'I used to keep a note in the back of my parts for *Leonora* No. 3 and the Tchaikovsky First Piano Concerto, of how frequently we performed them in the Fleischmann years,' says the bassoonist William Waterhouse. 'Sometimes weekly! When I subsequently left to join the BBC Symphony Orchestra, I had the benefit of the Boulez, William Glock, and Hans Keller years, which were the antithesis of that. There were no potboilers, but also, I'm afraid, no world-ranking soloists either.'

'Fleischmann certainly wasn't a Walter Legge or a William Glock,' says Hugh Maguire. 'Both of them made a massive difference to British music after the war. Ernest wasn't in that class. He was a much smaller individual. But I liked him; he was very approachable. You couldn't say Legge was approachable.'

*

After Fleischmann's departure, Tuckwell swiftly withdrew his resignation and resumed as chairman. But the fallout from the Fleischmann affair began almost immediately. The nastiest jolt was delivered in a letter from Decca:

Dear Mr Tuckwell,

I am in receipt of a letter from you saying that Mr Ernest Fleischmann has 'relinquished' his position . . . and that you are dealing with all correspondence pro tem. I must tell you in all honesty that our artists . . . and the company as a whole are so shocked by the turn of events that there may be no need for further correspondence. We doubt somehow that there is a reasonable explanation for this unhappy step that you have taken.

At other times, this high-handed attempt by a record company to intervene in the LSO's internal administrative affairs (and, after all, Fleischmann was only an administrator, not a conductor or player) would have infuriated the players. But in mid-1967 the orchestra had no liquid reserves and a deficit that would grow to £18,000 by the end of the year. The sense of crisis within the orchestra grew by the day, and other casualties became inevitable. On 3 August – in Daytona Beach, of all unlikely places – Tuckwell presented the board with his grandly named Comprehensive LSO Administration Plan, under which he would become managing director of the orchestra (a role he was effectively filling anyway), and another board member, Alan Jenkins, would become Company Secretary. Tuckwell's proposal was that he and Jenkins would represent the orchestra at all negotiations with the outside world.

The board was horrified. Tuckwell, it seemed, had out-Fleischmanned Fleischmann in his lust for power! In any case, with both Philips and Decca cancelling recording work, there was no evidence that he could keep the orchestra in business. The Comprehensive LSO Administration Plan was comprehensively booted out of play. Shortly afterwards, Tuckwell resigned from the board, this time for ever. He left the orchestra the following year.

Many years later, he would recall:

I left for a lot of reasons. The published version – and it is mostly the real reason – is that I was getting offered a lot of solo engagements, and I had to turn a lot down because I had obligations with the LSO. But things had gone sour; there's no question of that – the personal and political things. The funny thing was that it was never my intention to give up orchestral playing. But I found myself on another road after that. After I left, though, I realised what a hot seat I had been in, playing first horn in the LSO, and what a relief it was not to have to do that any more. People say: 'Don't you get nervous playing solos?' I say: 'Yes, but not as nervous as playing first horn in the LSO. Because if you don't play it right in rehearsals, your 'equal' – perhaps someone at the back of the violins, because we were a democracy, remember – might let you know what he thought.

It's odd that the LSO was virtually created by one charismatic foreign horn player, Adolf Borsdorf, and then virtually recreated by another fifty years later. And it's not only odd, but also sad, that both left the band in unhappy circumstances. But at least Tuckwell went on to even greater glory as a soloist and conductor.

*

If the orchestra had been enjoying a strong and happy relationship with its principal conductor while all these backstage shenanigans had been going on, the pain would have been a lot easier to bear. But at this very moment Kertész and the LSO, or a sizeable proportion of its members, fell badly out of love with each other.

Perhaps it was no coincidence. Having fought off attempts by first Fleischmann and then Tuckwell to run their affairs, the players were now faced with a maestro who, horrifically, wanted to act like a maestro. True, the players had few problems with the sort of performances that Kertész was producing in concert, though his apparent inability to draw large crowds was a continual worry, and his personality grated on some in the orchestra. 'Wonderful sense of rhythm, great sense of line and phrasing, but incredibly immature as a person,' says Denis Wick, the trombonist. 'Once, when we were in Daytona Beach, he picked up this Florida girl who was only seventeen. Imagine what the British tabloids would have made of that. Serious words had to be said.'

However, the tension in the orchestra was created not by Kertész's taste in young women, but by his increasingly strident demands to be allowed more say in the LSO's affairs. What he wanted, in effect, was a continental or American-style music directorship – hands-on, full authority, no opposition. What he had, unfortunately for him, was the proudly independent LSO. Tuckwell recalls:

Kertész wasn't difficult to get along with. He was strong, but that's not the same thing. He had great integrity, and he had humility – a recognition of where other people did things better. The problem started with a BBC TV documentary that was made about the orchestra at that time. In it he is quoted saying, rather naively, in front of the cameras, to Stuart Knussen, the chairman: 'But what power will I have?' Now, I don't think Kertész meant power in any sense other than 'what are my responsibilities?' But of course the anti-Kertész people jumped on this like a politician's gaffe.

The first shots in the 'power' battle were fired when Kertész was conducting the LSO at the Edinburgh Festival in August 1967, only a few days after Tuckwell had resigned as chairman. His contract was up for renewal, and Kertész used this as a lever, or so he imagined, to demand wider powers, more options to appear with the orchestra, and a more fulsome public acknowledgement by the LSO of his principal-conductor status. He must have been disconcerted when the LSO board's first reaction was to say that, if those were his conditions, his contract would not be renewed at all. Both sides subsequently softened their stance, and withdrew to lick their wounds.

Four months later, Kertész presented his 'final conditions' (his contract would expire the following summer). These, he said, would provide a 'completely new basis of collaboration'. They certainly would have done. He demanded the 'right of final decision on all artistic questions, without exception', the 'right to participate in all Directors' meetings, and meetings of shareholders in the Orchestra', the right 'to veto all decisions which, in his opinion, do not serve the standard, quality and reputation of the Orchestra', and the right to be furnished with 'every kind of confidential information regarding all artistic and administrative problems'.

Taken as a whole, Kertész's conditions were little short of a charter for him to become a kind of Herbert von Karajan. There was no chance that the LSO – or any of the self-governing London orchestras – would accept them. (Eleven years later Bernard Haitink would resign as artistic director of the London Philharmonic because he objected to a player being dismissed and had no power to intervene.) Consequently, Kertész's contract was allowed to expire the following summer. Happily, he did return to guest-conduct the orchestra several times after that, but five years later he drowned in an swimming accident near Tel Aviv. He was just forty-three. 'His death was one of the great musical tragedies of the twentieth century,' Tuckwell says.

Howard Snell, the trumpeter who had joined the LSO board that year, admits:

To be honest, the decision for Kertész and the LSO to part company was bad for him and bad for us. There followed a very bloody interregnum period which resembled nothing so much as an episode from the history of the Roman Empire. Bodies everywhere. The position was that we had very high standards, because Kertész had been extremely good for us. But at the same time we were in dire straits. No manager, no principal conductor. Great orchestra, no work.

In the history of the LSO there are several candidates for the epithet of *annus horribilis*. With Sargent and Beecham plotting to bring about the orchestra's demise, 1932 must come close. Or what about 1955, when every LSO principal but one resigned to form a new band? Still to come was the disaster of 1983, which was not unrelated to the fiasco of 1982 and closely followed by the misery of 1984. But for sheer, self-inflicted catastrophe, 1967 must be awarded this dubious accolade. The tragedy for the LSO was not just to have lost three such talented leaders: the flamboyant manager, the great player-chairman and the inspirational conductor. It was to have lost them at a time when the orchestra should have been riding the crest of a wave.

Across Europe, 1968 would be the year of violent street protests, student revolts, demos and disruption. But the LSO players had been through their patch of anarchy and madness twelve months earlier. What they needed from 1968 was a period of calm, stability and work – lots of it. What they stumbled upon was something rather better than that. André Previn arrived.

8 Years of living glamorously
1967–80

André Previn and British composers: Richard Rodney Bennett, Thea Musgrave, William Walton, Robert Simpson, Peter Maxwell Davies, Nicholas Maw, Malcolm Arnold; Walton's 70th Birthday Concert, 1972

previous page Conducting informal – André Previn at Daytona, 1969

Exactly how Previn was appointed is a matter of some dispute, but there is little doubt that an urbane American called Harold Lawrence played a big part. Lawrence was the LSO's largely unsung hero: the man who rescued the orchestra's administration from the turmoil of 1967.

For a while after Fleischmann's departure the player–directors had struggled to run the LSO's affairs with the help of a temporary administrator, Alan Jefferson, whose powers were strictly controlled. It was a recipe for muddle. The orchestra was almost broke, it had nobody chasing work, the board had to cope with crisis financial meetings in breaks between rehearsals, and looming visits to Japan and New York – for which virtually no sponsorship had been secured – seemed certain to topple the organisation into the chasm of receivership. (In the event, the LSO wriggled out of its Japan engagements, but had to undertake the Carnegie Hall concerts, bearing the full loss itself.)

In short, a steady hand was needed on the rudder, and a cool head to appraise the books. Various names were put forward; all deemed unsuitable. The board was probably in a state of psychological paralysis. On the one hand, it needed a go-getting impresario type who could generate work. On the other hand, it didn't want another Fleischmann. Then Neville Marriner, always the sharpest tool in the box, languidly drawled: 'Well, how about Harold Lawrence?'

Lawrence was already well known to the orchestra. As an executive with the prolific Mercury record label he had produced eighty recordings with the orchestra in the previous ten years. He knew the business inside out, and had contacts all over the British and American music and broadcasting worlds. He was also unflappable, which was probably just as well, given the state of the LSO's order book and finances when he arrived in the newly created role of General Manager in January 1968. Its deficit had lurched from £18,000 towards £40,000. He proved to be a superbly steadying influence. By the time he departed in July 1973 to run the New York Philharmonic, he had delivered five consecutive years of profit, increased the orchestra's turnover by sixty per cent, organised sixteen foreign tours, and netted enormous quantities of film, recording and TV work.

Back in that dark winter of 1967–8, however, by far the most important priority was to find a new principal conductor. A list of possible candidates, ideal or otherwise, was drawn up, and the board duly debated the merits and availability of each. Then Lawrence spoke. According to the minutes, he 'outlined the type of conductor the LSO needed: someone who was a serious musician, who was easy to work with, who would bring business (though this was not a prime consideration), who was good for publicity and who was forward-looking'. Having done that, he uttered the name which he felt best fitted the bill: André Previn.

There must have been a fairly prolonged silence at that point. The thirty-nine-year-old conductor, born in Berlin as Ludwig Andreas Priwin but long since Americanised, had worked in the studio with the LSO. His name had already been mentioned by another LSO director in connection with the principal-conductor job, but was dismissed by apparently incredulous colleagues.

Now, though, there was a much more serious discussion of his merits and weaknesses. He was undoubtedly a breath of fresh air. He had won four Oscars for supervising the soundtracks to such classic film musicals as *My Fair Lady*, *Gigi*, *Porgy and Bess* and *Irma la Douce*. He had sold hundreds of thousands of records as a solo jazz pianist. He was a born raconteur and had a brilliant sense of humour, honed on making dozens of Hollywood soundtracks (starting with a *Lassie* film in 1949) with some of Los Angeles's most grizzled session players. The public was intrigued by his new 'classical' conducting role. The LSO liked working with him. And he had a solid recording contract with RCA, then one of the giants.

On the other hand? Only in recent years had he started conducting top-rank symphonic ensembles in the concert hall. Consequently, his experience of the 'meat-and-drink' Austro-German repertoire – the Beethoven and Brahms symphonies, for instance – seemed dangerously shallow, especially when compared with the seasoned European maestros then appearing with other London orchestras: the likes of Solti, Jochum, Boult, Haitink, Kempe and Giulini. The critics would almost certainly declare him a lightweight. It was a gamble, no doubt about it, but in the end the board came down in his favour, almost unanimously.

Howard Snell recalls:

It was actually my first meeting as a board member. And I think I'm right in saying that I was the only one there who demurred. I said that I thought the orchestra needed more time to see him. He was a first-rate musician and regular sort of guy, he got on well with the orchestra and gave some good concerts. But I thought there was more to the job than that. Yet everyone else's view was that he was the man for the job, so that was what went ahead.

Another brass player, the first trombonist Denis Wick, also had reservations:

I remember Harold Lawrence coming to a general meeting of the orchestra and saying: 'I have eleven points I would like to make about why you should make Mr Previn your principal conductor.' All his points seemed to be about recording contracts. So I stood up and said: 'It seems to me that there's only one reason for him to come, and that is because the orchestra is broke.' After that there was a bit of an uproar. But Stuart Knussen, who was then the chairman, said: 'Well, I can only agree.'

In the end, though, it was a classic case of the right person being appointed for the wrong reasons, because after that we had eleven wonderful years with him. He had probably the worst stick technique any international conductor has ever had, and he was massively insecure, but what a superb musician.

Previn was overwhelmed to be asked. Or at least, that is how this most courteous of conductors liked to tell the tale, more than thirty years later:

In my wildest dreams I had never expected it. True, I had recorded with the LSO already. At the instigation of Roger Hall at RCA, I had come over to Kingsway Hall, and recorded Walton's First Symphony, Shostakovich's Fifth, Tchaikovsky's Second and something else I don't remember. By then I had not been in Hollywood for four years. I was running around the States conducting as much as they would let me.

Then in 1967 I was made music director of the Houston Symphony. I shouldn't have done it; I wasn't ready to be music director of an American orchestra. And I'm still not ready to be music director of one in Texas, but that's for different reasons. But I was overwhelmed by working with the LSO; I thought it was a most wonderful ensemble. And for whatever combination of reasons – musical, personal – we got along like a house on fire.

Then I went on *Desert Island Discs*, and Roy Plomley said to me: 'All conductors have their end-of-the-rainbow orchestra, be it Philadelphia, Berlin, Vienna, whatever; so what would yours be?' I replied, without being aware of what was going on inside the orchestra at the time: 'One day I would like to be conductor of the LSO.' Well, within a month a little delegation headed by Stuart Knussen had come to ask me if I wanted the job. No one quite believes the chronology, but it's true. So I bought a place in England and didn't go away for twenty-one years.

The vast majority of the LSO players welcomed the appointment. Perhaps, as Wick suggests, their desperation for work might have played a part. They must have felt that Previn's contacts in films and TV were potent tools that could be exploited. Besides which, his youthful, showbizzy image somehow seemed a perfect match with the groovy Carnaby Street era. He sported a

Beatles-style mop of straight black hair. He didn't wear ties. He was recognisably not Otto Klemperer.

And then there was his marriage to the Hollywood star Mia Farrow, the gamine embodiment of mid-1960s sexuality. The LSO players were dazzled to be in the presence of such allure, though it wasn't in the nature of this blasé generation of players to admit to star-struck feelings. 'Don't be silly,' one player told a journalist who had asked whether Ms Farrow impinged much on the all-male orchestra's thoughts. 'Half the time we don't even talk about her.'

'It's true,' Previn recalls, 'that I was in a lot of magazines that Reggie Goodall would not have been in. But the orchestra itself mirrored the Swinging Sixties in many ways. The players were a real presence, they had real personality. They were edge-of-the-seat performers.'

What also delighted the LSO players, however, was Previn's lightning wit – a complete contrast to the self-absorbed Kertész and the venerable Monteux. 'He's got a way with him, André,' Gervase de Peyer once recalled. 'With all orchestras there are difficult moments, and he's very good at using the moment for the witty remark that puts things in perspective.'

'He lightened the atmosphere up,' Roger Lord agrees. 'Some would say he wasn't a great classical conductor. But my goodness, when it came to Rachmaninov and the Romantics, he was wonderful. He had this great sense of colour.'

The 'not a great classical conductor' tag clung to Previn throughout his eleven years at the LSO, though the accusation was most loudly made at three specific periods in his tenure. The first was right at the beginning, when the critics were sniffy and Previn still, by his own admission, 'shaky' about handling his new band. The second was in 1975, when a vociferous minority within the orchestra decided it was time to 'oust André'. And the last period was right at the end, when the orchestra was not so much fed up with Previn as dazzled by the very different qualities of Claudio Abbado.

Yet the fact that Previn did last eleven years – longer than any LSO principal conductor before or since, in an age when principal-conductor appointments were tending to become shorter and shorter – attests not to this perceived weakness in his armoury, but to two huge strengths. One was the breadth of repertoire he brought to the orchestra, and the infectious enthusiasm with which he conducted it. Under his guidance, the LSO suddenly became a twentieth-century orchestra. The other was his astonishingly cosy rapport with the TV cameras – a gift that brought the LSO an unprecedented degree of fame and fortune.

The dramatic expansion of the LSO's repertoire is something of which Previn himself is proud. 'A lot of stuff, especially the English stuff, Vaughan Williams's nine symphonies, Walton, Britten, Tippett – I learnt on the job with the LSO. But some of it, funnily enough, they hadn't played either. So for much of the time it was a discovery for all of us.'

Previn's affinity with twentieth-century English music was a revelation. Nor was it confined to the famous names. He recorded the ripely Romantic music of the tragic George Butterworth (killed in the First World War) and the sharp, witty output of Constant Lambert. He also eased the path of rising young composers such as Nicholas Maw, Richard Rodney Bennett and, most remarkable of all, the teenage Oliver Knussen (son of the LSO's chairman and double-bass player Stuart Knussen), whose First Symphony was premièred when he was fourteen.

He was equally at home championing the big, colourful scores of the Russians: Stravinsky, Shostakovich, Rachmaninov and Prokofiev were regular names on his programmes, and with the LSO he recorded the complete music for the big three Tchaikovsky ballets. The orchestra's style of playing changed, too, as Previn recalls:

The sound got very brilliant, and people started to say: 'Oh, it's very American.' No it wasn't. I don't know what 'very American' means anyway. But the LSO was then, as it is now, capable of making an extremely hard-edged, diamond-like sound. The only thing that I might have contributed is that I used to be absolutely relentless about rhythmic accuracy, and insist that certain things had to be very angularly accented. They liked that, and dealt with it very quickly. A piece like the scherzo in Walton's First Symphony – they took to that like lightning.

Yet it wasn't just Previn's own programmes that expanded the LSO's vision in the late 1960s and early 1970s. A happy relationship was struck up with the oil company Shell UK, which began sponsoring not only a biennial LSO national tour in 1976, but also the Shell LSO Music Scholarship, awarded (in rotation) to the outstanding young woodwind, string, brass or percussion player who won an annual competition. Both the Shell tour and the scholarships continued until very recently.

It was also a time when visiting conductors developed interesting new approaches with the orchestra. One was Colin Davis, who single-handedly championed the music of Tippett at a time when the composer's fortunes seemed at a low ebb. Back in 1958, on a infamous night, the BBC Symphony Orchestra's première of his Second Symphony had broken down – and although the conductor, Boult, shouldered the blame with characteristic gallantry, Tippett became something of a figure of fun in smart musical circles.

Davis decided to remedy this, and persuaded the LSO to 'adopt' the same symphony – rehearsing it, polishing it, and repeatedly performing it until its manifest qualities shone for all to hear. Davis later remarked that it had been 'the biggest effort on behalf of Tippett that anyone had ever made, and it marked a turning point in the LSO's relationship with him – and the public's'.

As a result of that, the LSO commissioned Tippett's Third Symphony – a remarkably bold act for an orchestra that was so reliant on the box office for its income. What's more, the players prepared it so thoroughly, both in general and sectional rehearsals, that by the time of the première in June 1972, they could put it over to the public as if it was as familiar to them as the 'Eroica' or the 'New World' Symphony. The following year, Davis and the LSO wanted to take the work to the Salzburg Festival, but Salzburg (then an even stuffier place than it is now) refused to contemplate such a shockingly modern English offering, so Davis refused to go at all.

Pierre Boulez's impact on the orchestra in the late 1960s was, if anything, even greater. He had risen to fame as a composer of highly complex but superbly calculated and often mesmerising scores that took the serial techniques of Anton Webern to new levels of organisation. But he had also emerged as an abrasive champion of the avant-garde, who once called for opera houses to be burnt down. By the mid-1960s, when he turned forty, he was also greatly in demand as a conductor. His batonless style, resembling something between a karate lesson and a railway signal box, was much derided by some players, but produced immaculately clear and precise performances.

Later he would become the chief conductor of the BBC Symphony Orchestra and then the New York Philharmonic, but in 1966 he struck up a close rapport with the LSO that remained firm for the next four decades. The scheme that first brought the Frenchman to the orchestra was astonishing in its scope, boldness and ambition. Encouraged by Ernest Fleischmann, Boulez devised nothing less than a grand musical tour of the Second Viennese School, then regarded as being the most 'unapproachable' style of music ever written. Fleischmann recalls, a trifle wryly:

It was planned for 1969, but we put it together before I was sacked by the LSO. It would be the first attempt by anybody to give London audiences an overview of the Second Viennese School from Mahler to Schoenberg, Webern and Berg. And in persuading Boulez to do them, we managed to get the best man in the world to teach this music to the orchestra. That kind of teaching sticks. A lot of this music had never been given a proper chance with the public, because it needs to be rehearsed and played superbly. Boulez did that. The result was a watershed.

This was not least because the concerts in May and June 1969 (five in London, two at the Vienna Festival) required a degree of commitment and preparation that was unprecedented in LSO history. No fewer than thirty-two rehearsals were needed for the series (given the grandiose title of 'The Crossroads of Twentieth Century Music'), and behind the scenes a huge fundraising effort was required. Even so, by March 1969 it was apparent that the income generated would fall well short of the costs, and a crisis board meeting was called. By one vote the LSO directors decided to put it on anyway – one of the most heroic and admirable decisions in LSO history. In the end, despite contributions from the LSO Trust and the Peter Stuyvesant Foundation, and sizeable fees from CBS (which issued recordings of the performances), the orchestra lost £10,000 on the project. But in terms of the education that Boulez had given the orchestra, the younger audiences attracted to the concerts, and the glowing press coverage for a series that put musical idealism before commercial calculation (something the LSO of that era was not always credited with doing), it was a price well worth paying.

Despite this success, the Previn era won't primarily be remembered for the LSO's forays into serial music. In the minds of most music-lovers who recall that heady period, it will for ever be characterised as the decade in which the LSO entered the television age with such spectacular panache that, by the mid-1970s, the name of the orchestra and its suave principal conductor would be known to most households in Britain. Never before had classical musicians managed to establish such a powerful presence on the most powerful medium of the late twentieth century. Never again would they do so.

Of course, by the time of Previn's arrival, the LSO had enjoyed more than half a century of working in studios of one sort or another. The title of 'most recorded orchestra in the world' is much disputed, but if the LSO's thousands of gramophone and CD recordings since 1913 are added to the hundreds of film soundtracks made since the 1930s, and the numerous TV shows taped in the Previn years, it has as good a claim to the epithet as any. Indeed, any history of this orchestra must, in part, mirror the history of mass entertainment in the twentieth century.

The LSO's film work began in the days of silent cinema, and at a rather surprising venue – Covent Garden. In 1922 the opera house (which had been ignominiously reduced to use as a warehouse in 1914) was turned into a cinema for a season of silent 'super-films' – most notably *The Three Musketeers* with Douglas Fairbanks, the prime female heart-throb of the era – by an impresario from the fledgling Hollywood studio United Artists. The LSO was engaged to supply the backing music (live, of course), and Eugene Goossens was employed to find and conduct appropriate pieces, which he culled from more or less the entire orchestral heritage.

Goossens' memoirs, *Overture and Beginners*, record:

My sixty-five players, the flower of the LSO, produced a noble, well-rehearsed sound from the pit, providing in the process a miniature anthology of much of the world's great music. Special racks had to be provided to accommodate the mass of music performed during the show. My happiest and most useful discovery was one August Enna, a prolific and soporific nineteenth-century composer whose music provided an inexhaustible repertoire of tedious but appropriately varied symphonic accompaniments. It fitted anything and also conveyed a spurious impression of great emotional depth.

Cynics might observe that the genre of film music was pretty well defined for all time by that last sentence. Nor can it be said that the LSO players greeted this, their first contact with 'Hollywood', with unbridled enthusiasm. During the film season the deputy system 'flourished untrammelled', Goossens noted wryly. 'It is safe to assume that, by the end of the run, very few orchestral players in London had not seen Douglas Fairbanks in *The Three Musketeers*.'

Sound came to film in 1927, and in 1929 the LSO recorded its first real soundtrack, appropriately enough to a film based on the life of Beethoven. For British orchestral musicians, however, the real breakthrough came not with the introduction of sound to film, but with the arrival of 'quotas'. An Act of Parliament decreed that twenty-five per cent of all films shown in British cinemas had to be British-made, and this triggered a boom in native film-making – from thirty-four in 1926 to a hundred and twenty-eight in 1927. Suddenly, the magic words 'film sessions' became the happiest phrase a working musician could hope to hear, and the LSO players were quick to cash in on it.

It was not until 1935, however, with Arthur Bliss's score for Alexander Korda's magnificent futuristic epic, *Things to Come* (based on H. G. Wells's story), that artistry caught up with mercenary instinct. Bliss's score was the first truly symphonic composition specifically written for film. Fortunately for the LSO – then reeling under competition from the LPO and the BBC Symphony Orchestra – the twenty-four year-old conductor chosen to supervise the music, Muir Mathieson, had been a pupil of W. H. Reed at the Royal College of Music, so he naturally turned to his mentor's old orchestra, the LSO, to supply the musicians.

Bliss's score – a seminal classic of the genre, later turned into a concert suite – was recorded over fourteen sessions at the Scala Theatre in London. 'The LSO soon became a very quick and impressive recording orchestra,' Mathieson later recalled, 'because the players were interested in the performance.' Both Mathieson and the LSO went on to record hundreds of soundtracks. Very few of them, sadly, bear comparison with *Things to Come*.

Over the next few years the burgeoning British film industry provided plentiful work for the London orchestral fraternity – and all sorts of dodges, too. Orchestrators were in league with fixers, who were similarly in league with players. An orchestrator might slip in a couple of completely unnecessary notes on, say, the bass clarinet, so that the clarinettist could claim a 'doubling fee'. Or the musical director would spin out two or three minutes of recorded music over four hours of recording time, so that the players could claim two whole session fees from the film company. To the majority of London's musicians, film companies were nothing but cash cows, to be milked twice daily if possible. And why not? Everybody else was getting rich out of the movies.

Occasionally the LSO board felt that the orchestra itself had been the victim of sharp practice. Between 1935 and 1937, the directors had to clamp down no fewer than seven times on unauthorised use of the LSO's name by film companies who were employing moonlighting LSO players. A great deal of 'private enterprise' was clearly going on, and in 1935 the subsequent row led to the resignation of the orchestra's Secretary, Arthur Maney. For the orchestra generally, however, the real boom came with the war, when the LSO was contracted to record a string of stirring British films with scores by distinguished composers. They included *49th Parallel* (music by Vaughan Williams) *Malta GC* (Arnold Bax), *Western Approaches* (Clifford Parker) and of course Laurence Olivier's cinematic version of Shakespeare's *Henry V*, with music by Walton.

It was the 1941 thriller *Dangerous Moonlight*, however, that really revealed to the orchestra, and the film world, the commercial potential of a soundtrack that catches the public's imagination. At one point the plot involved the performance of a pastiche Romantic piano concerto, and for this the British composer Richard Addinsell supplied a brilliant little piece called the *Warsaw Concerto* which was played on the soundtrack by Louis

Kentner. 'The film company had wanted to use a real Rachmaninov concerto, I believe,' says the trumpeter Bram Wiggins, who played on the sessions as a very young extra. 'But they couldn't get the rights. So Richard Addinsell more or less knocked off the *Warsaw Concerto* overnight.'

If Wiggins's recollection is correct, Addinsell's work is even more remarkable. Something about it caught the dark, defiant mood of the times, and the film company was swamped with requests for recordings or sheet music. There was no time to re-record the work, so the LSO's performance was swiftly issued on 78s. Thus, more by accident than design, was the 'soundtrack album' born.

In the immediate post-war years the film work brought tensions, as well as income, to the orchestra. The problem was that film studios required full brass and woodwind, but usually only a few desks of strings. The LSO chairman, Gordon Walker, took on the dual task of touting for film work and then organising a rota of string players to carry it out. But the music directors employed by the studios – Muir Matheson and his colleagues – weren't fools. They were paying good money; they didn't want back-desk violins on a 'Buggins' turn' principle. They wanted the front-desk players, all the time. Consequently, Walker became something of a controversial figure, regarded more as a 'fixer' for the studios than as the LSO chairman. It was muttered that players had to 'keep in with Gordon' if they wanted the lucrative film work. In the end he overstepped the mark, fixing a film session for his select band when the LSO was supposed to be playing a concert. He had to resign. But the tension did not end there. As related in chapter 5, it was a perceived inequality in the way that film work was allocated that led to the LSO's internal upheavals in 1955.

By the time that Previn arrived in 1968, then, the LSO thought of itself as being the film orchestra *sans pareil*. The tradition would continue, as the trumpeter Maurice Murphy recalls:

I started with the LSO on 6 March 1977. They had sent a work schedule for that month, and I could see a large block of time covered by something called *Star Wars*. I thought: what on earth is that? I soon found out. The very first sound I produced as first trumpet with the LSO was the opening note of John Williams's score, which he was recording. Wonderful way to begin, actually.

The story of how the *Star Wars* sessions were won says much about the astute business instincts of Anthony Camden, the LSO's chairman for eleven years from 1976. On the 1978 American tour Previn and the LSO found themselves in a small town in Iowa with a spare afternoon and nothing to do.

Camden suggested that he and Previn talk business, and proceeded to ask Previn to write another film score so that the LSO could record it. Previn said he was too busy, so Camden quizzed him about other Hollywood composers.

'His favourite was John Williams,' Camden recalls. 'So I asked André to ring him immediately in Los Angeles. John answered the call, and André passed the phone over to me. He told me he had just started writing the music for a film, but that it wouldn't interest the LSO because it was all "up in the universe". In fact, he said, they were thinking of calling it *Star Wars*.' Camden immediately suggested to the composer that the LSO could record it, but Williams said that the recordings had to start within a month, and eighteen sessions were needed. 'I told him I would ring him back the next day,' Camden says. Within twenty-four hours, from a hotel phone in the American Midwest, the LSO chairman had fixed eighteen sessions in London, some starting late at night at Denham Studios, often after the orchestra had played a concert in the Festival Hall. It was a highly lucrative coup. From that time on, the LSO became John Williams's orchestra of choice.

*

Television was a much tougher nut for the LSO, or any symphony orchestra, to crack. That was the case in the early 1950s, when there was one channel to watch (the LSO's TV début, conducted by Sargent, in 1952, proved to be a false dawn). And it is just as true today, when there are five hundred channels available. The problem was, and remains, acutely irritating. Television is undoubtedly the most powerful tool of mass-communication in the modern world. If orchestras could gain even a tiny foothold inside this magic kingdom, their potential for marketing themselves and the masterpieces they play would be exponentially increased.

Unfortunately, television has an inbuilt abhorrence of orchestras, for the obvious reason that they are, on the whole, static and visually boring beasts. Only once, so far, has this objection been boldly and gloriously tossed aside. And that was when the BBC took the decision to make a series called *André Previn's Music Night*.

'I'm damned if I can remember exactly how it started,' Previn says. 'I think John Culshaw [the former Decca record producer who had gone on to run BBC TV's music and arts programmes] had seen me do a couple of masterclass things, and he thought it might make reasonable television. So he devised this programme called *Music Night*. We wound up doing endless numbers of them.'

Some critics sniffed at the casual presentation, in which Previn would speak direct to camera, and then turn and conduct the waiting LSO – dressed not in tails, but casual sweaters or shirts. 'A Strauss-and-Rachmaninov sandwich, perhaps, stuffed with a little Vaughan Williams and garnished with a loose-lipped lowbrow introduction,' the *New Statesman* sniffed in December 1973. But a vast public became hooked. More British people heard the LSO play on *Music Night* in one week than in sixty-five years of LSO concerts.

The knock-on effect was a huge surge in Festival Hall attendances: Previn's concerts rarely failed to attract full houses, even when he programmed comparatively little-known repertoire. As Leonard Bernstein had done in his Harvard Lectures, Previn had revealed himself to be a born TV performer. 'He was a joy to watch in the TV studio,' says Roger Lord. 'You just had to shine a light on him, and off he went. Absolutely natural.'

'I took to it,' Previn says. 'As this was a medium that went into people's living rooms, I felt I should talk to them as if I were in their homes.' Nor were his subjects as 'lowbrow' as the *New Statesman* claimed:

I did one show about Rachmaninov's letters. And I found that Beethoven had written three different tunes for the finale of the Ninth Symphony, so I orchestrated them to show viewers what might have been. This was not playing to the gallery: they were good subjects. Which is not only something that pleased me then, but also something that makes me sad now, because there is no one around doing it, and no one in television who seems to want it. The failure today is international. There is no such thing as classical music on TV in America.

Eventually, the *Music Night* format was deemed by BBC executives to have run out of steam:

They said to me: 'We have to stop doing those shows, because the last series only got a two million audience each week.' I thought: 'Hang about, that's an awful lot of Festival Halls!' They said: 'Yes, but *Bill Cosby* and *On the Buses* get twenty million.' So I said: 'Oh great! The lowest common denominator is more important than pleasing two million people?' They said: 'Yup, that's right.' Well, when you come up against that attitude, there isn't a lot you can do. The people who run television, with very few exceptions, do not care about the arts.

As Previn cheerfully admits, however, he did not become a hero in his local village until he appeared on the most popular British light-entertainment show of the 1970s: the *Morecambe and Wise Christmas Special*, where he was immortally dubbed 'Mr Preview' by Eric and Ernie.

I went to my local the next day: the reception was unbelievable. But my oldest son, a lawyer, only saw that show for the first time many years later, when I was given my knighthood. The British Ambassador in Washington put on a party for me, and played a tape of the programme. Well, afterwards my son turned to me and said: 'Actually, Dad, you were quite funny.'

Francis Saunders had joined the LSO as a young cellist a couple of years before Previn arrived. 'I may be wrong, but I got the impression that a lot of principals were really upset when Kertész left, because he was such a wonderful conductor; no question. So it was a difficult transition. But what can you say about André? What he did for classical music was amazing. In a sense, he copyrighted it.'

*

While Previn won the hearts and ears of the nation on the box, the LSO's new management team had to deal with some tough little problems behind the scenes. One was the LSO Chorus. To start such a body must have seemed like a good idea at the time. In the early 1950s the Philharmonia had founded a wonderful chorus to service the choral needs of the repertoire that Legge wished to record with such conductors as Giulini, Klemperer and Fruhbeck de Burgos. Comprising mostly highly skilled and fanatically keen amateurs, and trained by the legendary Wilhelm Pitz, the chorus master of Bayreuth, the Philharmonia Chorus cost very little to run and delivered a series of stunning recordings and concerts.

The LSO looked on enviously. Either it had to perform the choral repertoire with choral societies over which it had no artistic or quality control, or it had to pay Equity rates and hire the ubiquitous professional choristers of John McCarthy's Ambrosian Singers (motto: 'We perform under any name suitable either to the conductor or promoter'). It decided to form an LSO Chorus on Philharmonia lines, and such a body made its début in 1966 for Solti's performance of Mahler's 'Resurrection' Symphony.

Immediately there were tensions. The chorus master, a Cambridge-educated vocal coach called John Alldis, selected the singers mostly from London music colleges, particularly the Guildhall, and then sprinkled professionals among them. The students felt exploited. In any case, many of them couldn't do performances outside term time. So the LSO board tinkered with the structure, and tried to phase out the professionals.

Then, only eighteen months later, the 'chorus problem' erupted again. Kertész who, by this time, was already on his way out of the LSO, told the board that he was withdrawing from a performance of Janáček's *Glagolitic*

Mass because of his 'complete divergence in musical views to those of John Alldis'. He had talked over his interpretation with the chorus master, he said, and discovered that 'we disagreed on every single point'. Quite an achievement.

Kertész was persuaded to do the show, but then his record company, Decca – never slow to weigh into LSO affairs – declared that it would no longer work with a chorus trained by Alldis. The LSO management, rather weakly, duly engaged a professional chorus for its next Kertész choral recording. But that only made matters worse. Two other record companies gleefully poured fat on the fire by announcing that they rather enjoyed working with Alldis; indeed, one announced that it would only work with an LSO Chorus trained by him.

Ultimately, however, Alldis did move on – first to the Bath Festival, then to the London Philharmonic Choir, which he directed with great distinction. Arthur Oldham replaced him, and established the foundations for the superb, totally amateur LSO Chorus of today.

The second problem was even more complex. Since its foundation in 1904 the LSO, in common with every other independent London orchestra, had lacked any place to call its home. It had no official status in any of the halls in which it performed, though in the mid-1960s it began a series of prolonged discussions with the Corporation of London aimed at putting that right. Even worse, in a way, was the lack of a permanent rehearsal hall. The Festival Hall was the busiest garage in London, and orchestras could usually only rehearse a programme there on the day of the concert. So if a concert needed three or four rehearsals, the LSO frequently found itself rehearsing in as many different venues.

Not only was that artistically detrimental, since the balance and sound of the orchestra was constantly shifting; it was also draining on the players' time and energy. What the orchestra needed was a large, empty and sonorous venue, preferably near the Festival Hall – a redundant church, for instance – that could be snapped up for next to nothing and converted into a proper rehearsal and recording hall.

As it happened, a redundant church did exist in Southwark. Holy Trinity was an 1824 Georgian building, badly damaged during the war but still handsome and capacious, standing in a conservation area close to Borough High Street, barely a mile eastwards along the south bank of the Thames from the Festival Hall. It was discovered by Mary Lawrence, the LSO manager's wife, and quickly deemed to have every desirable quality for a band of wandering minstrels in need of a roof over their heads.

Nothing in the London property market is ever simple, however. The Diocese of Southwark had originally wanted to demolish the church and build offices. The lighthouse charity Trinity House, which owned the surrounding square and had originally donated the land for the church, objected. The Diocese then proposed to convert the church into luxury flats, with a swimming pool in the nave. Various petitions to Parliament were lodged.

Then the LSO appeared on the scene. Trinity House supported the orchestra's scheme, but the Diocese didn't approve. Neither, at first, did the local council, which refused planning permission. Dispirited, the LSO backed off. The trumpeter Howard Snell, who was on the board, recalls:

Quite suddenly, one or two directors turned against it. And as one of those was the chairman, Stuart Knussen, the project came to a grinding halt. I think they were worried about the cost implications. So Mary Lawrence, who was a very spirited lady, said that she wasn't going to allow this good idea to die, and went to the LPO. Of course they were interested; they were well run at the time by Eric Bravington, and had a healthy financial situation. So the LSO was out of it. Harold Lawrence couldn't really understand why the orchestra wasn't interested, but he had to accept the fact because it was the board's combined view.

As it turned out, the LSO wasn't out of it. The LPO was finding it difficult to raise the large capital sum needed, and quietly sounded out its arch-rival to see whether the two orchestras might co-operate on the venture. The LSO was on tour in North Carolina when Snell, by then the orchestra's chairman, received a call from the LSO's solicitor. 'He said: "This is really the last chance for the orchestra to come back into this project. Otherwise the LPO is going to take it and you will be left on the sidelines."'

Nothing galvanises the LSO like the prospect of being sidelined by a rival London orchestra. Snell called an emergency board meeting and wrangled with his fellow directors all night.

In the end, out of desperation, I actually said to the board: 'Look, if I can get financial support for this project, without the orchestra having any responsibility if it fails, will you allow me to go ahead?' They replied: 'But you can't get the money.' I said: 'But if I can get it, will you accept it if there are no strings?' We went on like this for several hours.

Snell finally convinced the other directors to let him try:

As soon as the board meeting was over, I phoned Jack Lyons, back in England. I explained the situation, with a bit of embellishment. I said: 'The board is now absolutely in favour of this project, so will you stand as guarantor for the LSO's share of this project?' I think it was about £125,000 then, though of course it ended up a lot more. There was a silence of about five seconds, and he said 'Yes.'

For possibly the first and last time in London orchestral history, then, two rival orchestras agreed to co-operate, wholeheartedly and harmoniously, on a single project. But the difficulties didn't end there. The Diocese persisted in its development plan. The LSO and LPO appealed over the Diocese's head, to the Church Commissioners, which ruled in their favour. Then Trinity House became alarmed at having no say in the future of the site, and counter-petitioned the Church Commissioners.

On and on the knotty negotiations went, right through 1972. Finally, the orchestras jointly received a ninety-nine-year lease, and on 19 December the LSO – absurdly kitted out in hard hats – went into the bare hall to do an acoustic test, and contractors were engaged to do the necessary conversion work.

There was one last hitch. On the night before the contractors were to start work, vandals broke in, and the church was gutted by fire. More expense, more delay. In June 1975 the church was finally ready for its new use. The orchestras named their new rehearsal venue the Henry Wood Hall, a pleasant if slightly ironic tribute to the conductor who struggled all his life to get London orchestras to rehearse properly.

*

In some ways the 1970s were even better years for the LSO than the 1960s. Previn provided continuity, glamour, instant public recognition and panache. The orchestra was filled with star players. The finances had stabilised. The order book was full to bursting. Outwardly, the LSO was one of the most successful orchestras in the world.

Why, then, did the wheels come off this bus so dramatically and suddenly in the early 1980s? Why was the management of the orchestra again in such turmoil by 1975? And why, throughout the 1970s, were the antics and back-stage plottings of the LSO featured almost as regularly in the pages of the satirical magazine *Private Eye* as its performances were reviewed on the august arts pages of the broadsheets?

One explanation, perhaps, is that the players grew blasé about success, greedy about money, contemptuous about conductors and cynical about music-making itself. Symptomatic of the era were the enormously lucrative but artistically demeaning 'Classic Rock' projects in which the LSO players undertook recordings and tours of classical arrangements of rock songs. The success of the 1960s and early 1970s had accustomed the players to a level of fame, income and glamour which they may then have felt was theirs by right. Clive Gillinson, who joined the LSO as a young cellist virtually straight out of the Royal Academy of Music, certainly sensed this mood:

In some ways the orchestra of André's era was brilliant, but the players were also very prone to fly by the seat of their pants. Sometimes it could be terrific; sometimes there were disasters. Everybody was very happy with the inspiration and the verve of the moment. But they weren't eager to take their playing to a new level. The orchestra didn't grow and didn't develop. There was something self-limiting about what the possibilities were.

Gillinson puts this down to arrogance, an endemic self-satisfaction:

The arrogance grew out of success, because the orchestra was successful in those days, and of course on the television every week. But it was also partly a function of the personalities leading the LSO then. There were a lot of people who were very full of themselves, and thought they were wonderful.

That self-satisfaction in turn bred thoughtlessness, even callousness, towards colleagues, conductors, certainly management, even audiences and the music itself. The level of indiscipline – of extravagant tantrums, wild behaviour on tour, stroppiness towards conductors, unprofessional conduct on and off the platform – crept up and up.

Of course, the LSO, by virtue of its constitution and independent traditions, had always tended to attract free spirits, strong-willed personalities, mavericks rather than mice. Back in 1922, the orchestra's platform discipline was so bad that during concerts, the wind players came and went from the stage at will if they weren't playing, even if the piece hadn't finished! A few years later a player was requested to resign for habitually reading newspapers during rehearsals. Also in the mid-1920s, a player was fined ten shillings and sixpence – quite a stiff penalty then – for showing his contempt of an engagement at the Three Choirs Festival by appearing not in morning-dress, but a 'brown coat'.

Even Neville Marriner had his wild moments when he was a young fiddler in the LSO:

I used to travel to concerts with a violinist called Peter Gibbs, who had been an RAF pilot and owned a Tiger Moth. One day we took a lot of flour-bags up with us and bombed the LSO bus on the road from Brussels to Ostend. I don't think I could tolerate players like that in my orchestra now.

What was increasingly happening during the 1970s, however, was not larkiness but wilful and persistent irresponsibility. 'The LSO was very macho,' recalls the cellist Bob Truman, who went on to be principal cello of the LPO. 'A lot of drinking, a whole lot of butching it up with the boys.' And of course, they were all boys – even in the early 1970s. In retrospect, it could be argued, the absence of women from the LSO's ranks was a large part of the orchestra's problem.

How had this all-male LSO come about? By circumstances, rather than decree, it seems. Women musicians, particularly composers, were surprisingly evident in British musical life during the early twentieth century. One thinks of the formidable Dame Ethel Smyth, lesbian and militant suffragette, conducting her *March of the Women* with her toothbrush in Holloway Prison; or Edith Swepstone, whose symphony was premièred by Dan Godfrey in Bournemouth; or Dora Bright, who played her own piano concertos very successfully; or Liza Lehmann, whose song-cycle *In a Persian Garden* is still done. And there were numerous women instrumental soloists around the concert halls of Europe.

Women had a much harder time establishing themselves in London's orchestras, however, though there was no outright prohibition on their presence. The fact that much of the 'fixing' was done in pubs such as the 'Glue Pot' was not the least of their difficulties. As a matter of necessity they were admitted into orchestras during the First World War; in fact the Queen's Hall Orchestra was led by a woman, Dora Garland, at the wartime Proms. In peacetime, however, you could count the women who played in the LSO on the fingers of one hand.

True, the orchestra had distinguished female harpists – Miriam Timothy and Marie Goossens – from its earliest days. And the great oboist Evelyn Rothwell (later to marry Barbirolli) joined the LSO in 1936 – oddly, after she had already played with the orchestra as a soloist. But her experience was hardly an encouraging one to others of her sex. She had been engaged in the first place after Busch refused to use the LSO's oboists for Glyndebourne (he thought their tone too thin and cold), hiring instead Rothwell and another woman, Natalie James. As a consequence, Rothwell had to endure a miserable first rehearsal in which, she wrote, she could feel the LSO players observing her 'critically and unkindly'. Even when she was subsequently accepted into the orchestra, she was never given the plum engagements: the lucrative film sessions. 'Gordon Walker [LSO chairman and first flute] was the fixer,' she later wrote, 'and he and others concerned preferred to engage men. At the time, there were hardly any women in the profession at all.'

That remained true at the LSO right into modern times. As late as 1970 Dougie Cummings, the wonderfully gifted principal cellist, remarked in a journalist's hearing that not having women in the LSO was the orchestra's 'best point'. And he was one of the younger and trendier members. 'For some reason women players become very hard in one way or another,' he continued. 'I don't think it is worthwhile having them in.'

Clive Gillinson confirms that this was a widespread attitude:

It was an all-male orchestra when I came in. It must have been about 1976 when the change was discussed, and there was a lot of resistance. There were a group of us that were absolutely adamant that the orchestra had to be open to women, and another group who were absolutely adamant that it shouldn't be – that it would change the culture, the sound. They liked the club. Well, we changed it. But it took a long time for it to filter through. For a while, apart from the inevitable female harpist, there was only one woman around: a violinist called Gillian Findlay. I think she found it quite tough, because there were people who resented her presence.

Today, some twenty per cent of LSO members are women, and the proportion is increasing all the time. 'I think everyone believes that it's been for the better,' Gillinson says. Whereas the older generation of conductors might have blanched to see women in principal chairs (Beecham made some notoriously vicious remarks), today such discrimination has almost entirely died out – except in Vienna, of course. 'The women have made a real difference to the LSO's string playing,' says Colin Davis. 'They don't make such a meal of it, they are much more flexible and supple, whereas men tend to give themselves a good deal of agony.'

Back in the late 1960s and early 1970s, however, the LSO was still an enclave of lads – in every sense, as Maurice Murphy testifies:

It was a real party band in those days. And I think that comes out in the playing. That first *Star Wars* soundtrack has a raw quality that's very exciting: there's a real feeling of 'give it one!' Now the strings have improved so much, the playing is fantastic, but it has lost some of its gung-ho quality.

Colin Davis acknowledges this change, but takes the opposite point of view.

The LSO was a very virtuoso orchestra when I first conducted it, but it was all-male, and very 'male male' at that. I was listening to an old Doráti recording made at that time. The playing is very accurate, but the sound is very hard, not seductive – which, I hope, it has now become.

That 1960s LSO could be obstinate as well. It was difficult for a young conductor to face such an atmosphere. I used to quarrel with them regularly, because they didn't want to rehearse, really. They didn't want you to take too much trouble. The attitude was: 'We play like this, and that's that.'

The trombonist Denis Wick confirms this: 'Our attitude was a typical English compromise. We did what the conductor wanted in rehearsal, and then what we wanted in the concert.' And that arrogance went hand-in-hand with some lamentable off-platform behaviour as well, particularly on tour, as Previn recalls:

Sometimes we would go on tour without anybody from management. 'This meant that I was not only the conductor, I was also Mr Chips. I remember being awakened at 3 a.m. in Bucharest to get a trumpet player out of jail. Another time one of the brass players, who had evidently led a sheltered life, appeared never to have come across a hotel-room mini-bar before, because he had thought it was free and drunk all the contents. And I mean all the contents. That was the only time I have ever seen a man actually catatonic. We had a concert that night. He made it backstage, but he couldn't possibly stand up because his knees wouldn't lock. Those were just two isolated instances of at least a dozen I remember.

The LSO was not, of course, the only British orchestra to misbehave abroad during that period. Regrettably, it became something of a national trait during the 1970s, like football hooliganism and wild-cat strikes. Indeed, there is one famous case of the LSO being barred from a hotel in Mexico during its 1976 tour simply because the Philharmonia has been there a few weeks earlier and devastated the place.

Colin Davis remembers:

In those days all the London orchestras were full of rapscallions of one sort or another. There were all sorts of stories about how they wrecked hotel rooms on tour. Dreadful. They would get drunk, and misbehave awfully. The worst situation, I think, was not at the LSO but at the BBC Symphony Orchestra, where players at one time were coming onto the platform completely drunk. Then I think managements realised that this couldn't go on, and people started to get dismissed if they were drunk. After that the women started to come into orchestras, which helped matters. And finally, of course, we had all the severe laws against drinking and driving. So all that culture has completely disappeared.

Drinking might have been a widespread problem throughout the London orchestral world of the 1970s. But the LSO players had developed other traits that were unique to themselves. One was a complacent belief that their orchestra would always rise to the top, and that the good times would continue to roll without too much effort, as Gillinson recalls:

The 1970s was an era of decline, basically. We had been on a high. Ernest came in after there had been that huge turnaround. Lots of people had left. The Barry Tuckwells and Neville Marriners had come in. So in a way the late 1960s and early

1970s was a real peak, a very youthful, energetic time. But then, bit by bit, all the weaknesses became exposed. All the disadvantages came back again: people being off too much, too many extras on the platform, the workload being impossible because everyone wanted to take home as much money as possible.

I remember Harold Lawrence saying, when he was manager, that 'as long as the players work from morning till night, nobody will complain and I won't lose my job.' That was how he defined the role of management.

And indeed, that's exactly what David Whelton, the present managing director of the Philharmonia, says today.

Lawrence did indeed fill the order books very successfully while he was at the LSO. But after he left, in 1973, the job of running the LSO became about as stable and secure as that of managing a top football club. If an incumbent handled all the administrative, financial and marketing pressures badly, he was removed for being not up to the job. If he handled it too well, on the other hand, he was removed for being 'uppity' and usurping the LSO players' ancient right to 'run their own affairs'. It was an impossible situation, and the attrition rate at the LSO was fearfully high. Stephen Reiss came from Aldeburgh after Lawrence left for New York, but didn't last long. John Boyden, a record producer, came and went in six traumatic months in the middle of 1975. 'Some of the managers had come and gone before I even met them,' says Osian Ellis, the harpist.

Michael Kaye, who had worked for the Peter Stuyvesant Foundation and therefore knew the LSO inside out, had a much longer and more successful run as LSO manager in the late 1970s. But his successor, Peter Hemmings – who had come from the opera world – inherited all the grief of dealing with the LSO's entry into the Barbican, and had a dreadful time.

Of course, other London orchestras were notoriously beastly to their managers as well. 'A characteristic of all London orchestras,' Antal Doráti once observed, 'is that they engage managers from the outside whose life they make utterly miserable by interfering in matters that should be none of their business.' Thus, he continued, 'to be the manager of one of the London orchestras has become the most dreaded appointment in that rather thinly manned profession, and it happens very rarely that it is held for any length of time by anyone.'

Clive Gillinson, who should know better than anyone, confirms Doráti's view:

In a player-owned orchestra the manager is in a weak position. The chairman and the board are talking to the shareholders – the players – day in and day out. Whereas the manager, up in the office, has much less contact. If a chairman is ambitious, and really wants to manage the orchestra himself, it's very easy for him to undermine the manager by talking to the shareholders. That's one of the fundamental vulnerabilities of the system.

In one or two cases, the managers hardly helped their own cause by allowing themselves to be fatally drawn into the LSO's internal conflicts. Such was the case, arguably, with John Boyden, whose tenure as LSO manager coincided with one of the orchestra's perennial disputes about the merits or otherwise of having Previn as principal conductor. Seen from a distance of thirty years, such squabbles seem rather mean-spirited. Previn, whose contract (it was announced in 1972) was to be renewed 'indefinitely', had not only brought the orchestra spectacular success on TV, at the box office and in record sales. He had also scored some notable artistic triumphs, not least in 1973 when, under his direction, the LSO became the first British orchestra to appear at the Salzburg Festival, giving the Austrian première of Shostakovich's magnificently gloomy Eighth Symphony.

Back at home, however, critics were comparing Previn's 'lightweight' interpretations with Haitink's seasoned readings with the London Philharmonic and, more tellingly, with those of the rising young Italian firebrand, Riccardo Muti, who had been appointed principal conductor of the Philharmonia. In 1975 a significant minority of LSO board members felt sufficiently distressed by these comparisons, or by their own observations of Previn at work, to demand his removal. They lost their battle, and were replaced by directors loyal to Previn. But Boyden, rightly or wrongly, became too closely identified with the anti-Previn lobby, and found himself out of a job in October that year.

That calmed down the orchestra for a while. But as far as Previn's long-term future was concerned, the writing was probably on the wall. Two years later the orchestra returned to Salzburg, this time playing under not only Previn but also Rozhdestvensky, the eighty-three year-old Austrian veteran Karl Böhm (appointed the orchestra's president in that year), and – most significantly of all – a sophisticated and highly intellectual forty-four-year-old Italian called Claudio Abbado, who was already the artistic director of La Scala, Milan, and had become the LSO's principal guest conductor a few years earlier. *The Times*'s account of the visit was ecstatic, even allowing for a certain amount of patriotic drum-beating:

British musicianship can rarely have stormed any of the jealously guarded European citadels with such proud triumphs as that which the London Symphony Orchestra achieved on their third visit to the Salzburg Festival. It has even eclipsed the success of their first visit in 1973, when they showed they had little to fear by comparison with the home teams of Vienna and Berlin.

Yet the experience of working with Abbado and Böhm, in particular, renewed doubts in the orchestra about the shortcomings of the Previn relationship. So there was little surprise in the orchestral world when the announcement came that in 1979 Abbado would succeed Previn as the twelfth principal conductor of the LSO.

That season also marked the seventy-fifth anniversary of the orchestra's formation. It was in many ways a vintage year. To cap a memorable year, in November 1979 the LSO was invited formally to become resident orchestra at the Barbican Centre in the City of London. The prospects had never seemed brighter. Few could have anticipated that within three years the LSO would be facing a catastrophe that would very nearly kill it.

9 High stakes and low cunning: the struggle for the Barbican 1980–2003

Henry Wrong (Barbican Administrator), Anthony Camden (LSO Chairman),
Claudio Abbado (LSO Principal Conductor), Sue Mallet (LSO Administrator);
Barbican as a building site, 1979

previous page Michael Tilson Thomas, Principal Conductor 1988–95

Back in 1964, when the lugubrious Lord Goodman was compiling his exhaustive if ultimately pointless report on the state of the London orchestras, Ernest Fleischmann (who supervised the LSO's submission) penned some of the most visionary words in the history of British music:

A great orchestra needs a home. It needs regular acoustic conditions to develop its own style and sound, its personality. Its members should not, as now, be required to rush from one end of London to another – often to three different halls in the course of a single day – in order to carry out their duties. . .

How can even one of today's great conductors realise an orchestra's potential, particularly in regard to quality and balance of sound, when every one of four rehearsals for a concert takes place in a different hall? How can an orchestra really build up its audience with an intelligent artistic policy when it has to share an anonymous hall with four or more other orchestras?

Fleischmann was only applying a characteristic rhetorical flourish to questions that must have occurred to LSO players practically every day during the previous sixty years. But little did he or the orchestra know that, just one year later, they would get a once-in-a-lifetime opportunity to acquire a home of their own. That opportunity was called the Barbican.

Today, forty years on, the place must be one of the two or three best-run and most inspiring arts centres in the world. Its music, dance, theatre and film programmes consistently break new ground. Its foyers and performing spaces buzz with expectation.

It attracts large, diverse audiences. Its landlord and chief paymaster – the Corporation of London – is regarded as a model of enlightened local-authority support. Headlines are made by the quality of the art created within its bush-hammered concrete walls, not by backstage discord. Aside, perhaps, from a few lingering doubts about the acoustics of the concert hall, Fleischmann could not have imagined a better home for his orchestra in his most rose-tinted dreams.

All of this will strike anyone who has followed the London arts scene over the past few decades as nothing short of miraculous. The Barbican was one of the great public building fiascos of post-war Britain. By the time the arts centre opened in March 1982 it was an astonishing ten years behind schedule and had cost more than two hundred times its original estimate. Set beside this dismal building site, even the notoriously late 'new' British Library seemed relatively prompt and the Millennium Dome excellent value for money. For years it was a byword for strikes, rows and failure on an epic scale. Yes, it gave the LSO a home for the first time in its history. But this Valhalla all but led the orchestra to its own *Götterdämmerung*. If the Barbican has hosted some of the LSO's greatest nights, it has also been the site, and the cause, of the orchestra's darkest hours. The story of its creation is also one of British determination at its best and British bungling at its worst. Luckily, the former prevailed – in the end. But it was a close-run thing.

*

Like the Royal Festival Hall, on the other side of the Thames, the Barbican came about as a result of the Blitz and post-war idealism. The Blitz left thirty-five bomb craters right in the heart of the Square Mile, just to the north of St Paul's Cathedral. Reconstructing the area was the responsibility of the Corporation of London: the ancient and immensely wealthy 'local council' for the City of London. Years passed before the task was even contemplated. But in the mid-1950s Duncan Sandys, then the Minister for Housing, chided the Corporation for delay, and advised it to create 'a genuine residential neighbourhood incorporating schools, shops, open spaces and amenities'.

The City Aldermen did just that. The Barbican Estate, with its broad walkways and piazzas, artificial lakes and fountains, is one of inner London's most strikingly unified post-war redevelopments. But being mostly money men, they left the 'amenities' bit right to the end. 'An arts centre was the last thing that the City fathers wanted, in their heart of hearts,' says Henry Wrong, the Canadian festivals director appointed in 1970 to run the Barbican Centre. They certainly never intended to start giving grants to performers. Sir Edward Howard, a former Lord Mayor of London, led the opposition. He called the plan to add an arts centre to the project 'the worst decision' taken in the City's eight-hundred-year history. Given what followed, he had a point.

At first, this arts centre was supposed to be nothing more than a 'village hall' and library, serving the community of residents who would live in or around the Barbican. Amateur dramatics, Women's Institute meetings: that was what was envisaged. The first seeds of something grander were sown in the early 1960s by the theatre director Anthony Besch. Commissioned to assess the Barbican's cultural possibilities, he suggested that an existing drama company and orchestra be invited to be resident in the new arts centre.

Peter Hall's recently launched Royal Shakespeare Company, then using the Aldwych as its London home, leapt at the chance to establish a thespian powerhouse to rival the new National Theatre on the South Bank. And in the summer of 1965 three London orchestras, including the LSO, were asked to compete in a kind of beauty contest for the right to become the Barbican's resident orchestra.

The challenge brought out the very best in Fleischmann: his competitive spirit, his panache, his genius for promotion, his eye for the main chance. He heard about the Barbican residency on a Friday afternoon and called Barry Tuckwell, the LSO's chairman, into the office. By Monday morning, after a weekend of brainstorming in a proverbial smoke-filled room, the two had cooked up a brilliantly optimistic, not to say pie-in-the-sky dossier about the orchestra, stressing its manifold artistic achievements, its long tradition, its glamorous international connections – but above all, its ambition. This, of course, was the year of Tuckwell's 'grand inquest' into the orchestra's playing standards, personnel and future organisation. Talk of 'permanent contracts' and 'consolidation' was all around the bandroom, and both Tuckwell and Fleischmann could see how having a proper home concert hall could help to bring these changes about.

What Fleischmann proposed to the Corporation, however, was something even more brazen – considering that the LSO had virtually no assets to its name at the time. The orchestra, he wrote, would assume complete artistic and financial control of the new hall. In return, it would pay the Corporation a rent that was somehow to be related to the construction costs of the hall – which at that stage, had not even been designed.

Howard Snell, the trumpeter who was on the LSO board at that time, recalls:

With his unique form of chutzpah, Ernest presented this proposal which the Corporation found irresistible, because it meant the orchestra paying the City of London large sums of money for the privilege of being in the Barbican. I don't think any other orchestra had the nerve to do this. So of course the Corporation people thought that Ernest was sent from heaven. They accepted the proposal absolutely at face value.

Fleischmann, and Peter Hall for the RSC, started to have regular meetings with City officials, and in March 1966 some basic agreements were signed.

But then the atmosphere started to sour. The British economy was in turmoil, sterling was plunging, wages were out of control. By the turbulent summer of 1968 the original estimate of the Barbican's building costs had to be revised upwards by a massive fifty-one per cent. That destroyed the basis of Fleischmann's 'rent related to construction costs' proposal. What's more, the LSO had commissioned a consultant to analyse its own financial prospects, and he came up with the gloomy (though surely not unexpected) forecast that the LSO would be running a deficit anyway by the time it moved to the Barbican. Far from paying rent to the Corporation, it seemed the orchestra would need a subsidy from the City.

To say that the Corporation was irked by this 'adjustment' in the LSO's plans would be an understatement. 'Gradually,' Snell recalls, 'these financial innocents in the City of London began to realise that the LSO's proposals were not quite as they seemed, or as they had been told they were. At that point their attitude became very glum and antagonistic towards the orchestra.'

To make matters worse, Fleischmann and Tuckwell chose this very summer to have their own private version of the *Gunfight at the OK Corral*. Every time a Corporation official picked up the phone to talk to the LSO, it seemed, a different voice was 'speaking for the orchestra'. The whole situation played into the hands of the many City councillors – such as Lord Mayor Howard – who considered that spending Corporation funds on arts organisations was a monstrous waste of ratepayers' money.

Not surprisingly, all negotiation ceased – for years and years. 'I remember that when I joined the LSO in 1970 people were always talking about how we were going to move to the Barbican,' Clive Gillinson says. 'But it was like a mirage. No one believed it was actually going to happen.'

At that point, it wasn't. The Corporation had taken such umbrage at the prospect of dealing with the whingeing arty types of the LSO and RSC that it had abandoned the resident-companies idea, and appointed Henry Wrong to run the arts centre on an 'Albert Hall' basis: this essentially meant renting it out to all comers, as much for business conferences as for arts events. Howard Snell, by then the LSO's chairman, realised that if he didn't act quickly, the dream of a home for the orchestra would die. 'I ferreted around, and found out that the City people had never ever discussed the project with the Arts Council. Which was very bizarre. After all, they were building an arts centre.'

Snell and Harold Lawrence, then the LSO manager, wrote a new proposal. This suggested that, rather than the Corporation bearing the entire brunt of subsidising the LSO to play in the Barbican, a revolutionary new tripartite funding formula be drummed out by the Corporation, the Arts Council and the Greater London Council. Snell recalls:

We made lots of comparisons, particularly with how continental orchestras such as the Berlin Philharmonic were funded. When we presented this report to the City and the Arts Council it prompted, for the very first time, a meeting between the two to decide what to do about the Barbican. But of course they left out the LSO, though we had proposed the thing. We were mere musicians, you see, and they don't count in England. However the ball was rolling again, and from that point the City became more friendly to us.

Meanwhile, the Corporation had appointed as architects a company – Chamberlin, Powell and Bon – that had never designed anything remotely arts-oriented before. Now they were to be entrusted with a showcase venue in the centre of London that included a two-thousand-seat concert hall, two theatres, an art gallery, cinemas, a conservatoire (for the Guildhall School of Music and Drama) and a library. 'Gilbert Inglefield, the Lord Mayor, was chiefly responsible for letting his old friend Peter Chamberlin in by the back door to do the architecture,' Henry Wrong claims.

Whether that was the case or not, the approach of Chamberlin and his colleagues to the concert-hall design soon set alarm bells ringing at the LSO. 'All the classic errors that architects can make, and they can make many, were being made,' Snell says. 'For instance, they hadn't considered how to get a piano on stage. And there was no proper provision for a choir – which is still the case, because it was too big an item to redesign into the scheme.' Nor was there provision for an organ. But most worrying of all was the sprawling width of the hall: fine for shareholders' meetings; absolutely crazy for orchestral concerts.

Henry Wrong, too, had his doubts about the architects' plans. 'They never told us how much it would cost to run the centre,' he says. 'And they made the idiotic decision not to give it a proper street entrance. 'People will walk,' they said. Peter Chamberlin once told me that "in five years' time, nobody will be using cars in London."'

Whatever qualms there may have been about the design were quickly overshadowed by the trauma of actually building the Barbican. The 1970s were the heyday of militant trade unionism in Britain, culminating in the 'winter of discontent' in 1979, which in turn triggered the election of Margaret Thatcher as Prime Minister. The Barbican, perceived as being bankrolled by the 'fat cats' of the Square Mile, was a classic target for industrial action, and its construction was continually halted by long and cripplingly expensive strikes. Intervention by such baroque bodies as the London Regional Joint Emergency Reconciliation Panel proved unhelpful. Costs soared by the month. The Corporation sued the builders. The builders sued the Corporation. The architects sued the *Sunday Times*, and threatened to sue Wrong for scuppering their pet notion of designing a cinema where people lay flat on their backs and watched a screen on the ceiling. There were even more bizarre setbacks. In 1975 a fish-wise saboteur secretly introduced pike into the Barbican's prized artificial lakes. By the time the dastardly act was discovered, eight and a half thousand goldfish had been devoured.

When the Queen finally opened the Barbican Arts Centre, on 3 March 1982, the cost had risen to £187 million. The original estimate had been £8 million. 'Still less than the price of a second-hand aircraft carrier,' said *The Times* soothingly, in a supportive editorial. But many in the City were horrified at their own profligacy. Little did they know that the Rake's Progress had barely begun.

*

Virtually anything that could go wrong in that first season did go wrong. To begin with, the Barbican Centre had 123 separate entrances, but no recognisable front door. It was right in the heart of the City of London, yet somehow concealed in a vast estate of windy walkways and service roads that seemed to baffle even London's usually infallible cabbies. Satirical newspaper columnists such as Bernard Levin had weeks of fun propagating urban myths about concertgoers lost for days in this concrete maze.

The Barbican management attempted to remedy the situation by painting yellow lines on the walkways, leading audience members from the nearest Tube stations to the concert hall. But this public-relations disaster only got worse when people finally reached the building. The arts centre was constructed on a dozen different levels – some connected by grand staircases, some not. It had five different box offices, each covering a different series of events. To add pain to bemusement, many concertgoers also received electric shocks from the static in the new carpets.

Then there were the technical problems specifically affecting the LSO and RSC. The actors found the heat and claustrophobic atmosphere of the aptly named Pit – a theatre several levels beneath the ground – intolerable, and lost no time in making their feelings public. The musicians, to their intense disappointment, found that the Barbican acoustics were as poor, if not worse, than those of the despised Festival Hall – dry and unresponsive on the platform; alarmingly patchy in the hall.

At first Peter Hemmings, the LSO's managing director, put on a brave face. 'We've given a lot of concerts during the past year, first as acoustic tests, later as previews,' he told the trade magazine *Classical Music*, a week before the Barbican's gala opening. 'Acousticians were present at each one and adjustments subsequently made. We have noticed a steady improvement. I don't think the acoustics will be any problem.'

The blithe public front was soon to be shattered. Word leaked out that Claudio Abbado was particularly critical of the hall's acoustics, and worse followed. Abbado's friend, the great Italian pianist Maurizio Pollini, refused to play in the Barbican until two thousand plastic balls, bizarrely placed high up on the ceiling (doubtless for some arcane aesthetic purpose), had been removed. Pollini was right to insist, perhaps – but the débâcle did nothing to improve morale at the Barbican. Eventually Derek Sugden, an acoustician with the engineers Ove Arup, was called in to tinker as best he could with the sound of the hall. But the fundamental flaws in the hall's designs could not be easily remedied by what were, essentially, sticking-plaster solutions, and it was to be nearly twenty years before radical architectural changes produced significant improvements.

When the disastrous box-office receipts of the Barbican's opening weeks became apparent, some LSO players seized on all these factors – plus the outset of the Falklands War, which kept people glued to their television sets and killed off several durable West End shows – as evidence that the orchestra should never have moved from the Festival Hall. 'The orchestra began a whispering campaign against the Barbican,' says Henry Wrong, the Barbican's managing director. 'There were certain Viennese players who didn't want to like it. Claudio Abbado was not particularly constructive in his criticisms. The LSO was desperate to find a scapegoat. It didn't seem to occur to them that they had planned foolish programmes.'

The LSO's programmes for those opening months were indeed naively idealistic and foolhardy, if not foolish. Rather than presenting a couple of concerts a week through most of the year, as had been the pattern in London for decades, the orchestra decided to mount three intensive, month-long 'festivals' each season – each one a complex mesh of repeated programmes, as Gillinson recalls:

The orchestra basically bought off the peg a sort of all-purpose subscription package from an American marketing guru called Danny Newman. So we did these three one-month seasons, and it was a total catastrophe. It was completely unprofessional – though fairly typical of how the arts were run in Britain in those days. It made absolutely no reference to our own marketplace. The bizarre thinking was: because we are now a resident orchestra, we ought to do what resident orchestras do in other cities. But no other resident orchestra faces the competition that there is in London, where there is a huge choice for concertgoers every night. We were repeating concerts several times and doing lunchtime partial repeats – to almost nobody. The orchestra would look out at all those empty seats, and get so depressed. You could almost see the money pouring out of the building.

If the public was hopelessly bamboozled by the format, it was undeniably turned off by the uncompromising or quirky repertoire – a Berlioz and Tippett series, for instance, conducted by Colin Davis. 'Colin felt really depressed about that,' Clive Gillinson recalls. 'You can understand why. They were two of his favourite composers, and he was turning round to take his bow and finding virtually nobody in the hall.' But it wasn't just Berlioz and Tippett that drove the crowds away. Abbado mounted a brave but financially ruinous performance of Stockhausen's *Gruppen* for three orchestras. Five concerts of Hans Werner Henze's music were scheduled. Acres of Webern were planned. The entire first year's programming read like the orchestral equivalent of a suicide note.

Had the orchestra's finances been healthy before the move to the Barbican, the shock of such poor attendances might have been easier to bear. But the early 1980s were grim years of economic recession in Britain. People had less money to spend on leisure pursuits; the LSO's Festival Hall audiences had slumped by twelve per cent in a single season between 1979 and 1980. At the same time, artists' fees and other overheads were relentlessly rising. An Arts Council secretary-general announced that 'inflation in the arts' was running at twenty per cent a year. Even before it moved into the Barbican, the LSO was anticipating a £117,000 deficit by the end of that season. 'Within a year that deficit had gone up to £430,000,' says Gillinson. 'And that was in an organisation which turned over about £3 million a year at that time, and had never made a loss of more than about £20,000 or £30,000 on an annual season.'

The players were horrified. So were the LSO's bankers. The orchestra was losing £2,000 each time it played at the Barbican. In June 1982 – just three months after the 'triumphant' opening gala at the Barbican, a debenture in favour of Lloyds Bank was drawn up over all the LSO's assets. At the same time the orchestra's directors undertook to clear the deficit within two years. But how?

One way was by raising money through increased sponsorship and private patronage. The orchestra's chairman through that traumatic period was Anthony Camden, a brilliant first oboist (he was the scion of a famous wind-playing dynasty), and a spirited 'operator' behind the scenes. He was nick-named 'Ayatollah' by the satirical magazine *Private Eye*, which pilloried him and his leadership to such a relentless extent that Camden and the orchestra subsequently sued for defamatory libel. '*Private Eye* published scandalous comments which it had received from musicians in other orchestras who were jealous that we were receiving larger grants than they were,' Camden says. 'Finally we sued and received money from the magazine, plus a printed apology. The amount of money I personally received enabled me to buy a nice apartment in Spain.'

In the dark days of 1982 and 1983 Camden's fundraising efforts were prodigious. He estimated that he devoted seventy-five per cent of his waking hours to the task (at one point he even took an entire month off playing in the orchestra to concentrate on its finances), and as a result the LSO's sponsorship total increased from £360,000 to £580,000 in a year. 'Peripheral' concerts, such as the regular seasons at the Fairfield Halls in Croydon, were unceremoniously dumped. Meanwhile the players – who had increased their workload of nakedly commercial work to more than six hundred sessions a year – each agreed to chip £43 a week into an emergency fund to keep their own orchestra afloat.

It was not enough. After a letter from Lloyds Bank had expressed 'grave concern about the present accumulated deficit and cash-flow problems', Hemmings and Camden secured an interest-free loan of £100,000 from the Musicians Union to 'tide the orchestra over'. Yet the deficit continued to rise inexorably while the relationship between the LSO and the Barbican got steadily worse. Henry Wrong and his Barbican colleagues were particularly incensed when the LSO decided to perform a prestigious Beethoven cycle of symphonies and concertos with Abbado and Pollini in the Festival Hall, where nearly a thousand more people could be accommodated for each concert. But the LSO could, and did retort that the Corporation seemed more concerned in 1982 and 1983 to promote the Barbican as a conference venue than as a concert hall: indeed, the Centre took out imposing newspaper advertisements to trumpet its achievement in bagging such exciting gatherings as the World Petroleum Congress, the Annual Conference of the European Dialysis and Transplant Nurses Association, and the National Convention of the Life Assurance Association. Not surprisingly, the orchestra felt neglected and slighted. Its Barbican residency, which had been years in the making, seemed on the verge of collapse after a few months.

Inevitably, somebody had to carry the can. Back in the heady days of February 1982 the affable Peter Hemmings had told the press that 'if we can't get the audience to the Barbican then I don't think there's much hope for the LSO anywhere.' Such remarks invariably return to haunt the speaker! A year later, when it was quite apparent that the programmes and marketing tactics devised under Hemmings' management had manifestly failed to get an audience to the Barbican, his contract was not renewed and he was asked to leave early. (He returned, with much success, to the world of opera.)

The orchestra advertised for a replacement, but didn't receive a single application from suitably qualified music administrators – not surprisingly, since it was technically bankrupt, it owed hundreds of thousands of pounds, its prospects were virtually nil, its financial controls non-existent, it had fallen out with its landlords at the Corporation, it was widely known to be on the Arts Council's 'hit list', and its stroppy and arrogant players had a terrible reputation for making life miserable for their own administrators. Managing the LSO was the job from hell.

Yet someone had to do it. In the autumn of 1984 Camden and his board turned in desperation to a young cellist in the orchestra's ranks, who was known to run an antiques business with his wife as a sideline, and therefore presumed to have a 'head for figures'. 'Luckily,' Clive Gillinson recalls, 'when I accepted the job I didn't know enough about the LSO's finances to know how bad things were.' He was soon to find out.

*

Born in Bangalore and brought up on a farm in Kenya, Gillinson was in many ways typical of the new breed of musician who came onto the scene in the 1960 and 1970s. He had read maths at university before going to the Royal Academy of Music to complete his cello studies. He was cosmopolitan in outlook, numerate, well read and well connected. He inhabited a different universe from the old military bandsmen and theatre-orchestra veterans who still made up the bulk of the LSO's rank-and-file when he joined in 1970.

Inevitably, his intellect and his background drew him towards the LSO board, to which he was elected in 1975. So he was steeped in 'LSO culture', yet somehow he had remained detached from its more Neanderthal aspects. Unlike Fleischmann or Hemmings or any other manager brought in from outside, he had the advantage of knowing the orchestra literally inside out. Yet the experience had not soured or hardened him. One of nature's born idealists, he had retained a vision of how orchestras might operate in a perfect world, and how much of the LSO's funny little ways would have to change if it was to develop as an artistic entity.

In 1984, such highfalutin notions were distant daydreams. All that mattered then was survival, and Gillinson (quickly nicknamed 'Gullible' by the cruel wits of *Private Eye*) seemed to have a snowflake's chance in hell of securing that. 'I walked into the office that first morning with the intention of analysing where we were as a business,' he says. 'I couldn't. The figures simply weren't there. I had to sit down with the accountant and try and bash out a method of financial reporting which at least helped us to understand where the problems lay.'

Wherever the problems did lie, they were quickly compounded, as Gillinson remembers:

I had only been in the office for a few weeks when Neil Duncan came to see me. He was writing a report for the Arts Council about whether there were too many London orchestras – the usual thing. Well, I tried to sell him the notion that we were sorting ourselves out, though at that stage I had no idea how. I was bullshitting like mad. In the end he gave us three years to get rid of the deficit, otherwise we would lose our Arts Council funding. Only several years later did I discover what he wrote in his report – that there was no way the LSO would achieve this. That's how the Arts Council thought they would solve the problem of too many London orchestras. Well, we actually eliminated the deficit in two years.

Some decisions were virtually dictated by circumstances. Out went the concept of the three month-long festivals. Out went the confusing tangle of repeated programmes at odd times of the day and night. Out, for the time being, went adventure. In came endless numbers of film sessions, tacky tours backing pop bands or 'classic rock' shows, and low-grade programmes of lollipop classics. Gillinson recalls:

We had to do an awful lot of things that I wasn't proud of. The orchestra was working morning, noon and night to earn management fees, and there were a lot of concerts where we basically did popular programmes on nominal rehearsal with conductors who weren't very expensive, just to balance the books and get things back on course. I was genuinely depressed some nights, sitting in the audience and thinking: 'My God, I hope there are no critics here.' To feel ashamed of your own orchestra because things weren't properly rehearsed is awful. It was total survival-first policy.

And it would have been impossible to achieve without the support of the stalwarts who were in the LSO office then – people like our administrator Sue Mallet, PR consultant Dvora Lewis and Libby Rice, who was at that time our head of development. I'm thrilled to say they are all still here.

Measured by the yardstick of survival at all costs, the policy worked. Within a year the £437,000 accumulated deficit had been reduced by a quarter. A year later it was wiped out. But the stress of working those six hundred sessions a year, sometimes in three different venues each day, produced casualties. One was Mike Davis, who resigned as the LSO's leader in the summer of 1987, after eight years in the hot seat, in order to return to his previous job as leader of the Hallé in Manchester. 'You don't work for a London orchestra, you give your life to it,' he told the *Sunday Times*. 'There is no time for your family, recreation or even practising. In the end, you are not a musician but a musical zombie.'

Years later, Davis (who subsequently became leader of the BBC Symphony Orchestra) elaborated on his reasons for leaving the LSO. 'I was scared that I was using up what little credit I had left in the bank, in terms of my fiddle playing. The LSO work then was really tough: physically, mentally, spiritually. I sometimes felt like a piece of driftwood. I didn't know where I was. Just to stay one step ahead of the game was about as much as you could do. But you can't get by on adrenalin and determination for ever.'

It must have been tempting for Gillinson and the board to have responded to these complaints (which were widespread in the LSO at that time) by doing what the LSO principals had suggested thirty years earlier: turning the orchestra into a full-time 'session band', and dumping all the 'quality' concert work that took so much rehearsal and lost so much money. But in his first months as managing director Gillinson had persuaded the LSO board to make one crucial decision that affected the entire future history of the orchestra. Abbado wanted the orchestra to mount an enormous 'themed' festival of concerts and related events called 'Mahler, Vienna and the Twentieth Century', which would examine the notion of Vienna as the crucible of modernism in art and music, psychoanalytical thought, fascism, and a lot more besides. It was intellectually and musically ambitious, it was conceived as a showcase for some of the most glamorous musical talents in Europe, and it would undoubtedly put the LSO and the Barbican at the centre of international attention. It was to dream up projects such as this that the LSO had chosen Abbado as its music director. But it was also hugely expensive. And late in 1984, with a mountain of debt still to clear, the LSO board suffered a collective failure of nerve, and told Gillinson to scrap the whole event, as he recalls:

One of the first things I had to do as managing director was tell Claudio that the orchestra wasn't going to proceed with his pet project. But Claudio said to me: 'If you don't do this, what are you in music for?' And of course he was right. These are the sort of events for which an orchestra exists. So I went back to the board and said: 'I'm sure we can raise the money.' Of course, I had no real idea whether we could or couldn't. But because I believed in the project, I genuinely thought the money would be found.

Gillinson persuaded Abbado to break the Mahler/Vienna project into two parts, with the second part proceeding only if the first hadn't already bankrupted the orchestra. 'It could have gone disastrously wrong,' he says. 'I could have been back in the cello section or, more likely, there wouldn't have been an LSO cello section for me to go back to.' But £135,000 was raised in sponsorship (an unprecedented achievement for any British orchestral series in 1985), both halves of the festival were performed, the crowds flocked to Abbado's sensational Mahler performances, the critics raved, and the LSO's relationship with the Barbican and the Corporation of London suddenly seemed much less frosty. 'In a way, that festival was the saving of us,' Gillinson says. 'It meant that we retained some artistic credibility, even though we were still doing some really bad things at the same time.'

At the halfway point in the festival, Gillinson gave a remarkable press interview. 'Financially we're sound and artistically we're in a position to pursue the goals we ought to be pursuing,' he told *Classical Music*. 'There could be a real blossoming here now.'

To cynical music-business observers in the mid-1980s, especially those who knew their LSO history, such cheery words must have seemed naive, perhaps even ludicrous. But the man who spoke them truly believed them. And within five years this mild-mannered figure had stealthily wrought a revolution at the LSO.

*

'With Clive, it's personal,' a top London music agent once astutely remarked. 'Or rather, it's all about family.' That's true. Few managers in musical history can have talked so much about their organisations as a musical family. This family consists of the LSO players, obviously, but also long-standing patrons and sponsors, trusted PRs and backroom administrators – and, not least, the circle of illustrious soloists and conductors such as Rostropovich and Boulez who have returned to the LSO time and again over the past twenty years.

The family might be large, but it is also tightly knit, mutually supportive, intensely loyal, and utterly discreet. The phrase 'soul of discretion' might have been invented for Gillinson himself, and his style quickly percolated through the LSO administration. From being the most gossipy, leaky and combustible orchestral outfit on the planet (no lightly contested epithet) the

LSO was transformed within a couple of years into an organisation from which nothing but good news was allowed to emanate. That might have been irritating for journalists in search of a juicy story, but it was undoubtedly beneficial to music-making and morale within the LSO.

That was one of Gillinson's first noticeable achievements. At the same time, and with similar quiet purpose, he defused one of the fatal tensions at the heart of the LSO: the relationship between the manager hired by the orchestra, and the board and chairman elected by the players. The issue had been simmering since Fleischmann's era, twenty years earlier, but never properly resolved. 'One of the last things I did as chairman was to circulate a paper which suggested that certain areas of the orchestra's management be taken out of the players' hands,' Howard Snell recalls. 'Not the big decisions, but a lot of the day-to-day stuff which the board quite liked doing but were frankly no good at. Well, as soon as the paper had been read by a couple of the older directors I was told to burn it, because the suggestion was so explosive.'

Just a decade later, however, Gillinson was able to make the historic change:

As soon as I took on the job I found there were some really uncomfortable and bizarre things about the way the orchestra was run. One was the fact that there was no definition of who was managing the orchestra. For instance, the manager would go off to Japan, perhaps, and fix up a tour. But at the same time the chairman would be fixing up a tour in America for the same period. It was ludicrous and incredibly messy. They were all treading on each other's toes. I said: 'I can't be the manager if someone else is also managing.' We had that discussion, and Tony Camden, who was chairman, was perfectly happy to step back.

The deal they worked out was that the chairman and board would retain their responsibility for internal matters – appointments to the orchestra, auditions, discipline, and so on – but that Gillinson would be allowed to 'run the business' and handle all outside relationships. It was a radical and historic change for such a proudly self-governing orchestra as the LSO. But Gillinson characteristically (or tactfully) prefers to regard it as the inevitable product of changes in the musical world, rather than as an epic victory in some sort of eternal power struggle. 'This business has become more and more complex,' he says. 'I think it would have been increasingly hard for a chairman to handle all that, as well as playing in the orchestra. In any case, the most important relationship of my life within this orchestra is still with the chairman. If we don't back each other, and talk everything through together, then the whole thing falls apart.' The fact that Gillinson was him-self an LSO player – an 'insider', utterly committed to the long-term welfare of fellow musicians – undoubtedly enabled him to gain a degree of trust from his colleagues, and an autonomy in his decision-making, that would always be denied to the likes of Ernest Fleischmann.

That trust became a crucial element in the next phase of Gillinson's quiet revolution. Having sat in the orchestra and watched the turmoil and artistic mediocrity caused by the greed of some players in the 1970s, he was deter-mined to change the fundamental culture of the LSO, once and for all. But that couldn't be done by decree. He had to persuade the players slowly to think in terms of substantial artistic goals, rather than quick money-spinners. Such a policy may seem obvious enough to outsiders, but London's orches-tral musicians viewed it with the most beady-eyed suspicion, as Gillinson remembers:

The players' view during my early days in the LSO was: the orchestra exists to serve us. I said: 'OK, but if you are going to do well personally you have to serve the music, because if you don't put the music first there is no way that the orchestra will be suc-cessful.' I had to get people to see that there's a monumental difference between long-term self-interest and short-term self-interest, and that if you adopt the latter then ultimately you lose.

What this entailed, initially, was getting the players to agree that Gillinson should have the right to turn down work which might be considered harm-ful to the orchestra's playing standards or prestige – even if it paid hand-somely. Such an idealistic policy was unthinkable in the mid-1980s, when the LSO needed to grab every session it could. But by late 1987 the deficit had been wiped out. And in the autumn of that year Gillinson's hand was strengthened by the publication of some trenchant comments about the London orchestral scene made by Simon Rattle. 'The problem,' the conduc-tor told his biographer, Nicholas Kenyon, 'is that the London orchestras have some great players and that's about it. They don't have the halls to rehearse in and they don't have the time to rehearse, so they don't have the repertory. It's just not good enough.'

Gillinson wanted to create the time to rehearse properly, but he also wanted to create an atmosphere within the LSO that was conducive to good rehearsing. He abhorred the rudeness with which the orchestra treated (and alienated) so many conductors in the 1960s and 1970s. 'It's not just a ques-tion of not upsetting conductors because they might be useful to you in ten years' time,' he says. 'It's also to do with not treating people badly simply because you feel superior. That all reflects the sort of person or orchestra you are. You should treat everybody with respect.'

The fact that such a statement of basic decency needed to be articulated at all speaks volumes for the boorish depths to which the London orchestral world could, and did, occasionally stoop. Slowly, and sometimes painfully, Gillinson erased the LSO's rough edges, its reputation for surliness and arrogance. 'I think he had quite a few battles, but he certainly won them,' says Colin Davis. 'Just look at the orchestra now, compared with then. It's an altogether different of breed of players. Everything today is about making music, which it wasn't in the old days. And as a result the standard has gone up astonishingly.'

None of that would have been possible if Gillinson hadn't delivered something to the players in return. What he brought were two vital ingredients that lifted the LSO, for the first time in its history, clear of all its London competitors. The first was a regular stream of starry performers. Inspired by the Mahler/Vienna series, Gillinson negotiated a dazzling series of megaprojects, each built round the personal enthusiasms of a 'star' conductor or soloist who would work with the orchestra for a substantial period of time, in a way that the 1985 series had been built round Abbado.

A Leonard Bernstein festival in 1986 produced sell-out houses and an even closer relationship with the ebullient American during the final few years of his life, culminating in him becoming the orchestra's president and conducting the LSO in memorable concerts and recordings of his opera *Candide*. Rostropovich's unique personal associations with Shostakovich, Prokofiev and Britten were exploited in a succession of revelatory series. The young American conductor Michael Tilson Thomas devised an ingenious exploration of earlier Russian repertoire in a festival called 'The Flight of the Firebird'. Colin Davis presided over a magisterial cycle of the Sibelius symphonies. The young German violin sensation, Anne-Sophie Mutter, 'did a Rostropovich' and played half a dozen violin concertos with the LSO in a single week. And so on. Rival orchestral managers shook their heads in disbelief and wondered how on earth the LSO could afford to hire the most expensive musical talent on earth. Gillinson's attitude was always: 'If you believe in a project, you find a way to pay for it.' And big sponsorship deals did indeed follow, as hard-nosed captains of industry found themselves as enthused by the LSO's programmes, and star attractions as the visionary manager who was selling the concept to them.

Gillinson's other great achievement was, in some ways, even more far-reaching. As Rattle had pointed out, the players of the top London orchestras

15 Leopold Stokowski, 1960s

16 LSO with conductor Sir Edward Elgar, *The Apostles*, Civic Hall, Croydon, 1932
17 George Stratton, Leader, 1937–52
18 Hamilton Harty, LSO Principal Conductor, 1932–5

19 LSO Board of Directors 1950, *l to r*: James Soutter (violin), Francis Drake (violin), Gordon Walker (flute), Reginald Mouat (violin), Harry Dugarde (cello and Chairman), John Cruft (cor anglais and Secretary), George Stratton (Leader)

20 LSO Board of Directors 1963, *l to r*: Max Weber (violin), Arthur Griffiths (double bass), Alexander Murray (flute), Jack Steadman (violin), Lowry Sanders (piccolo), Barry Tuckwell (horn and Chairman), Ernest Fleischmann (General Secretary), Michael Winfield (oboe/cor anglais), Stanley Castle (violin), Stuart Knussen (double bass)

21 LSO with conductor Josef Krips and Claudio Arrau, piano, 1950
22 Pierre Monteux (LSO Principal Conductor 1961–4) visiting the London Fire Department, 1963
23 Igor Stravinsky and Pierre Monteux; 50th Anniversary Performance of *Rite of Spring*, Royal Albert Hall, 1963

24 Antal Doráti, 1960s
25 István Kertész, LSO Principal Conductor, 1965–8
26 Howard Snell, Principal Trumpet (1960–76) and Chairman (1971–5)

27 Mstislav Rostropovich and LSO Principal Conductor André Previn
in rehearsal, 1970s
28 Pierre Boulez and John Georgiadis, in rehearsal for 'The Crossroads of
20th Century Music Series', 1969

29 Mstislav Rostropovich and Clive Gillinson on the Lakeside Terrace,
Barbican Centre, 1990s
30 LSO recording a film soundtrack, 2001

31 LSO Members with LSO Principal Conductor Sir Colin Davis

had less job security, less time to practise or recharge their batteries, and probably less job satisfaction than their counterparts virtually anywhere in the Western world. The working week somehow had to be reduced; often it ran to six and a half days out of seven. That meant a considerable increase in the players' basic engagement fee. More rehearsal time had to be freed up for the main Barbican concerts. The orchestra had to have fixed holiday periods, so that its ranks weren't constantly depleted by players having time off. And if the LSO was to attract the really top string players, it had to instigate a 'joint principals' system, so that such high-fliers could continue with their solo or chamber work without a conductor being faced with inferior deputies.

Many of these ideas, of course, had been knocking round the London orchestral world for decades; indeed, Fleischmann and Tuckwell had included most of them in the LSO's submission to the Goodman Committee, more than twenty years earlier. The problem was finding the considerable funds to put them into practice. But in 1988, Gillinson saw a way to make that happen. The LSO was receiving public subsidy from both the Arts Council and the Corporation of London, the Greater London Council having been unceremoniously abolished by Margaret Thatcher in 1986. Now the Arts Council was proposing to offer certain clients 'enhancement funding' so that they could make substantial improvements to their performing standards. 'We made a bid for enhancement money to the Arts Council,' he says, 'but we did it on the basis that they would then challenge the Corporation of London to match it pound for pound.' The strategy succeeded. Impressed by Gillinson's vision, by the artistic consistency of the LSO's programmes, and by the orchestra's new-found financial prudence, both bodies increased their grants to the LSO by £200,000 a year. When added to the £700,000 that the orchestra was raising annually in corporate sponsorship by the end of the decade, it meant that Gillinson had around £2 million to spend, even before box-office and other earned income was taken into account.

It still amounted to peanuts by the lavish standards of the Berlin Philharmonic or some of the fabulously endowed East Coast American orchestras. But by London standards, it was a breathtaking breakthrough – particularly as it was achieved with almost no fuss or fanfare, at a time when, on the other side of the Thames, the other three London orchestras seemed locked in a perpetual war of attrition, with each other and the power-hungry South Bank Board, who had run the Festival Hall since the GLC's demise. 'Players, managers and bureaucrats are always talking about "breaking the mould" of London music-making,' *The Times* observed in January 1989. 'Has the London Symphony Orchestra quietly succeeded at the Barbican, while the other London orchestras noisily jostle for position on the South Bank?' It was a blindingly rhetorical question. Nearly every numerate music-business insider could work out that the answer was yes.

The 'double cast' of string principals was duly initiated, though the system of bringing in top soloists who, in some cases, had not played in an orchestra since their schooldays, was not without its initial pitfalls. One of those recruited was the viola player Paul Silverthorne. 'We were playing *The Rite of Spring* at the Barbican the other day,' he told me shortly after he arrived, 'and I looked round and suddenly realised that three principal string players, including the leader, had never done it before in their lives.'

But Silverthorne – a formidable soloist and contemporary music specialist – quickly adapted to the big-orchestra life and became one of the pillars of the LSO in the 1990s. 'Until I came here,' he said, 'I thought of a symphony orchestra as a hard slog – soulless, nothing you could put your personality into. Then I discovered that the LSO itself has an enormous personality. And it thrives on accommodating players with big personalities.'

That much, at least, has never changed.

*

Through all the traumas of the LSO's move to the Barbican, its subsequent near-terminal financial crisis, and its gradual, painful recovery, one figure had been constantly, if enigmatically, present. Claudio Abbado was appointed principal conductor in a blaze of excitement and anticipation at the end of the 1970s, and was expected to supply the LSO with all the things that Previn was perceived to lack: continental sophistication, heavyweight intellectual ideas, finesse and depth in the great symphonic warhorses, Italianate fire and Mediterranean pin-up looks to woo those susceptible to such things.

In a way, he fulfilled all those expectations. The best concerts that the LSO gave under Abbado's direction were stupendous occasions for players and audience alike. 'The work with Claudio was the most satisfying and important I have ever done,' says Mike Davis, the LSO's leader for most of the 'Claudio Years'. That opinion is echoed by many who played under him. Yet it's hard to think of another conductor who has perplexed and, at times, infuriated the LSO as much as the monosyllabic and aloof Abbado sometimes did.

Clive Gillinson says:

Claudio is odd because he's so verbally uncommunicative. When I went to speak with him about whether we should proceed with the Mahler/Vienna project, he really didn't want to talk about what the LSO's problems were. It wasn't that he didn't care, I don't think. It was more that Claudio exists in a world that is totally about music. The rest is irrelevant. And he couldn't understand why an orchestra would think any differently.

Denis Wick, the LSO's principal trombonist at the time, detected something of this detachment on another occasion:

We had been recording *Star Wars* with John Williams all day, having a whale of a time, and then went to the Henry Wood Hall in the evening to rehearse Mahler with Claudio. He was imparting what he thought was absolutely essential information about bowing, and people were clearly getting very bored. Well, Claudio gave Warwick Hill [the principal second violinist] a bad time, and Warwick said words to the effect of: 'What do you expect? We've been working hard all day.' Claudio was horrified. He had absolutely no idea what his orchestra did when they weren't with him.

When this distanced attitude was projected into the way that Abbado rehearsed the music, there were bound to be tensions. Abbado, like Colin Davis, abhorred displays of power or histrionics on the podium. Perhaps this repugnance can be traced to an incident in his wartime childhood; his mother was imprisoned by the Nazis for harbouring a Jewish child. He once told me that he hated Toscanini because 'he was horrible to his orchestras; all that shouting!' But Abbado himself could also be stubbornly perfectionist, and his rehearsals could get very static if the sound in his imagination wasn't precisely matched by reality.

It was this trait of rehearsing a passage again and again without explaining what he wanted that so irritated many of the musicians. 'When he first came to the LSO,' Ernest Fleischmann recalls, 'he hardly said anything at rehearsal. Just "Letter C" or "Figure 14", and I thought there was a language problem. When I came to Los Angeles about eight years later, there he was again, and again he said just "Letter C" and "Figure 14". Musicians didn't know quite what to make of it.'

Denis Wick endorses this view:

He was clearly brilliant. But his remarks were completely unintelligible. They always sounded like broken Japanese. Nobody understood what he wanted. We just smiled and did it again. He smiled back, and it seemed to be all right. He was also one of the most disorganised conductors I have come across – the sort who would spend three quarters of the rehearsal on the overture, then wonder why he hadn't got enough time to finish the symphony.

Mike Davis shared Wick's bewilderment at Abbado's rehearsal manner, but has far more positive memories of the end results:

The first concert I did with him was Mahler Three at the Edinburgh Festival. At the first rehearsal I couldn't for the life of me get my head around it. It was so cerebral. There was no ball of fire, no tension, no explosion. It was like a workshop. Then at the concert we went up about fifteen divisions in terms of mental energy. The tension was unbelievable, and I suddenly realised that this was music-making at a very serious level. Over the years I saw a pattern emerge. You realised that he never stopped digging forensically into a score, refining it, polishing it, making it ever more sophisticated. He had a musical understanding of the highest order.

But a principal conductor needs more than musical understanding if he is to form a stable relationship with an orchestra as disinclined to meek compliance as the LSO. An acute understanding of human nature, and a rapport with the players, also helps. Abbado began well. He bought the LSO table-tennis equipment for its bandroom, and promptly beat all comers. At the Edinburgh Festival in the late 1970s there was a famous football match when Abbado played for the LSO against the LPO. 'Claudio was really committed,' recalls Lennie Mackenzie, the LSO's sub-leader. 'And when he went for a tackle on an LPO horn player he virtually knocked him out. The referee went for his red card, but he told me afterwards that he got such a look from Claudio that he was too petrified to take it out of his pocket. I said: "Yes, that's what we get on the stage."'

As the years went by, however, a feeling grew within the orchestra that Abbado was using the LSO as a stepping stone to grander things, notably the top jobs in Vienna and Berlin (both of which he subsequently got). The writing was on the wall as early as 1983, when Deutsche Grammophon, Abbado's record company, offered him the chance to record all the Beethoven symphonies. Fine, except that the orchestra selected was the Vienna Philharmonic, not the LSO. The scenario would be repeated several times over the following years, sometimes with the Vienna Phil, sometimes with the Chicago Symphony Orchestra, where Abbado was principal guest conductor.

Quite apart from the snub to the LSO's pride, and the loss of substantial recording fees, many in the orchestra felt that an issue of loyalty was involved. Abbado would later claim that DG decided which orchestra to use, not him. But that explanation hardly bolstered his authority inside the LSO, and incidents of backchat and sometimes open insolence at his rehearsals grew dangerously commonplace. The attitude of the orchestra, or a vociferous section of it, was summed up in 1988 by Maurice Murphy, the trumpeter, in a notorious feature in the *Sunday Times*. 'Although we were sweating our guts playing those vast Mahler symphonies for Abbado,' Murphy told the journalist, 'he would go and record them with other orchestras, which made us feel like second, maybe even third choice.'

By then the whole issue was academic. In 1986 Abbado, as expected, had been confirmed as Generalmusikdirektor of the city of Vienna and music director of the Vienna State Opera. He subsequently decided not to renew his LSO contract. His eight years as principal conductor and then music director had incorporated the most turbulent period in the LSO's history, when the orchestra came as close to destruction as it had ever been. Yet Abbado floated serenely over it all, like a beautiful bird surveying a train crash from on high. It was an Olympian performance.

*

It's odd how, when great cultural organisations are choosing their leaders, they tend to recoil from one extreme to another. Previn had bought a dash of urbane, all-American wit and charm after the inspired petulence of Kertész. Abbado's appointment marked a return to Old World reticence and breeding. He was succeeded in 1987 by Michael Tilson Thomas – a Bernstein protégé who oozed laid-back charm, was never short of words, and loved to dazzle in the 'firework' repertoire of the late Romantics.

Perhaps nobody was better at describing Tilson Thomas's style of music-making than the man himself. Even in 1986, the year before his appointment to the LSO, he offered this dazzling piece of self-analysis in an interview with *The Times*:

I come from a family of romantic Russian theatre people, very experimental and ardent in their outlook. Superimposed on this was a highly rationalist education. [He originally studied science at the University of Southern California.] For years the balance of my musical judgements was affected by this rational training. Now I am learning to trust my instincts again. I look for those moments of recognition a performer has when he hears a measure of music and says: 'My gosh, this measure, it's me. I know exactly what this experience is; I have lived it.' From the performer's ability to re-create this experience – and from his willingness to put his personality on the line in public – comes the performance's strength.

All that was apparent from the start of his relationship with the LSO. On his best days Tilson Thomas displayed a Maazel-like ability to galvanise, even mesmerise, orchestral musicians – but with a far less abrasive personality than his older compatriot sometimes disclosed. His music-making had fizz and wit, and he was exceptionally alive to orchestral colouring, particularly in the late Romantic repertoire. True, the cruel wags of the London orchestral world quickly transmuted his middle name into 'Tinsel' in sardonic homage to his Californian mannerisms, but that hardly did justice to his finesse, his intellect or his astonishingly thorough preparation of works. Whereas Abbado communicated almost nothing in rehearsal, Tilson Thomas piled on the information, supplying the players with his own, specially edited parts that gave them far more details about the surrounding texture, the importance of their line and relative dynamics than the composer had done.

He was a brilliant deviser of thematic series, too; they ranged from 'The Gershwin Years' and 'The Flight of the Firebird' (exploring the music of Rimsky-Korsakov and his circle) to surveys of Takemitsu's exquisite scores and Steve Reich's orchestral output. And, again unlike the taciturn Abbado, he was only too pleased to talk at length to journalists or the public about the philosophy behind his choice of repertoire, or about the music itself. In an age when fewer and fewer people have a musical education or a grasp of music history, such easy and intelligent communicators are increasingly valuable – and Tilson Thomas's 'Discovery' concert-lectures with the LSO were soon taken up by BBC TV. On the small screen he eloquently extolled the virtues of such comparatively esoteric pieces as Sibelius's Symphony No. 6 and Mahler's *Das klagende Lied*, as well as fronting programmes that celebrated more predictable musical heroes, like Gershwin and Bernstein.

His links with Bernstein produced other benefits for the LSO as well, notably a two-week residency in the summer of 1990 at the Pacific Music Festival in Sapporo, Japan. This was a new venture, involving hundreds of talented young instrumentalists, which Bernstein and Tilson Thomas had modelled on the Tanglewood Summer School in America. The experience of giving masterclasses and taking sectional rehearsals in Sapporo fed, in turn, into the LSO's new educational programme back in London, which had been set up that year, and which was soon to assume a significance in the orchestra's life that few players might have anticipated in 1990.

Like Previn, Tilson Thomas sometimes took a critical mauling for allegedly not displaying enough depth in the Austro-Germanic repertoire. It is undeniable that, when compared with other conductors regularly working in London at that time – such profoundly Eurocentric figures as Haitink, Tennstedt, Dohnányi and Solti – Tilson Thomas's interpretations of Beethoven or Brahms sometimes seemed a little strident and gimmicky. Perhaps, too, the LSO in the 1980s had not yet found a way of sounding anything other than punchy and pungent in the hard, unyielding acoustics of the Barbican – and this overall sonic 'trademark' affected the way that Tilson Thomas's approach to the classics was perceived.

Even so, his era as principal conductor was a relaxed, largely successful and progressive one. But when he left in 1995 (he subsequently became principal conductor in San Francisco, which was probably his spiritual home), the LSO abruptly changed tack yet again – from a genial American extrovert back to a buttoned-up, intense European. This time the orchestra's choice was the man rejected for the same post thirty years earlier – Colin Davis.

*

In the intervening three decades the Englishman had enjoyed both tremendous acclaim, mostly abroad – and wounding disdain, mostly in his native land. He had rebounded from the disappointment of not landing the LSO job in 1965 by taking up the chief-conductor post with the BBC Symphony Orchestra. He fulfilled that role with distinction, though he never seemed entirely at ease presiding over the jingoistic shenanigans of the Last Night of the Proms (he once declared that the mandatory performance of 'Land of Hope and Glory' 'smacked of Earl Haig' – a reference to the First World War general whose bull-headed tactics contributed to the slaughter on the Somme).

It was his fifteen-year tenure as music director at the Royal Opera House that gave Davis his finest and his worst hours. His predecessor had been the bustling, bruising Georg Solti – a man whose entire physical and mental attitude embodied the words 'I'm in charge'. By contrast, the mystical and circumspect Davis, who had come to hate displays of podium arrogance, seemed to many critics to be a pallid presence – even though he conducted neglected masterpieces such as Mozart's *La clemenza di Tito* and Berlioz's *Benvenuto Cellini* with a mastery that can rarely have been surpassed. He was accused of being too weak to stand up to the wiles and whims of star singers and directors, and he bore the brunt of the London critics' anger when the opera house started to experiment with radical new styles of production, especially in Götz Friedrich's staging of *The Ring*.

Yet even as he was pilloried in his native land, he was fêted abroad. The French adored him for championing Berlioz. The Germans loved his Wagner, and invited him to conduct the *Ring* at Bayreuth – the first British conductor ever to raise a baton in that hallowed theatre. American orchestras fell over themselves to engage him. Davis was offered the principal conductorships of Cleveland before Dohnányi, and New York before Masur. Characteristically, he declined them both, and plumped instead for long-term relationships with the Bavarian Radio Symphony Orchestra and the Dresden Staatskapelle – fine ensembles both, steeped in tradition, but hardly at the centre of international attention.

His appointment in 1995 as the LSO's principal conductor must have unlocked a tangle of contradictory emotions in this most complex of musicians: pride and perhaps a small feeling of vindication, but also possibly trepidation about whether the sniping of the 1970s would be revisited all over again. In the event, that never became an issue. The British have a disturbing attitude to their native talent. It is first exalted to the skies, then mercilessly reviled, and finally – if the talent has survived to attain the status of 'grand old man' or 'national treasure' – exalted again. By 1995, Davis had passed painfully through the first two conditions, and was now safely embedded in the pantheon of national treasures. Even the most jaundiced of critics was prepared to admit that his Sibelius, Elgar and Berlioz cycles were among the most thrilling musical events heard in London's concert halls for decades.

What Davis brought to the orchestra, however, was a good deal more than an expertise with certain composers. Slowly but perceptibly, the basic sound of the LSO was transformed under his direction. A conductor conveys a great deal by instruction and gesture, of course – but perhaps even more by that indefinable thing called 'charisma'. Davis detests that word, as he frequently says. Nevertheless, this very hatred of unnecessary showmanship, of histrionics, of displays of power, in itself adds up to a highly influential form of charisma. It encourages orchestras to pursue truth through beauty and gentleness rather than forcefulness and stridency. It does not rule out passion, but the passion must be properly generated through profound engagement with the essence of the composer's intentions, rather than ladled onto the music like cream onto strawberries.

All this had a marked effect on the LSO's sound. Its strings developed what some critics perceived as a 'Germanic' warmth, perhaps for the first time in the LSO's modern history; while Davis's collegiate, ego-free, first-among-equals approach to the conductor–orchestra relationship gave the wind principals the freedom, the space and (most importantly) the responsibility to phrase their solos with individualistic flair. More than that, Davis's own unflagging love of music-making helped to dispel, once and for all, any lingering remnants of the bad old cynical traits evident in the LSO even in the 1980s.

All that was to the good. But did the very congeniality of Davis's approach have the side-effect of dampening down the sizzle in the LSO's playing? In certain moods and repertoires, Davis's interpretations could seem resolutely 'steady' – glowing rather than incandescent, the work of a mellow, mature master, rather than the temperamental firebrand that Davis once was.

Against that should be set the power and majesty of his great Brahms centenary cycle, his epic Bruckner interpretations, his award-winning recordings of Berlioz's *Les Troyens*, and his wonderfully idiomatic and affectionate forays into Czech and Slavonic music. At a time when orchestras around the world were bemoaning the scarcity of truly magisterial conducting talents, the LSO was universally envied for establishing what appeared to be (and astonishingly, actually was) a trouble-free and creatively rewarding relationship with a great maestro living in a typically modest Highbury terraced house just three miles from its own concert hall. In the end, Davis's homecoming was a triumph.

*

Securing Davis as principal conductor was one vital plank of the LSO's expansive plans in the 1990s. But just as important was securing the orchestra's future at the Barbican. By 1994, the LSO's ninetieth anniversary year, that should have been easy. The attitude of the Corporation of London towards the LSO had warmed a good deal since the *annus horribilis* of 1983. Gillinson had secured additional funding from the City. And audiences had learnt to find their way through the windy walkways to the concert hall. All should have been sweetness and light at the Barbican.

In fact it was anything but. Four years earlier, Henry Wrong had been succeeded as managing director by Baroness Detta O'Cathain, an Irish economist whose only previous claim to cultural fame had been running the Milk Marketing Board. A Thatcherite free-marketeer, she was high-handed with staff (fifty senior managers resigned from the Barbican during her four years in charge) and contemptuous of the 'whinges' of people she habitually referred to as 'arty-farty types' – insults that seemed clearly directed at the Royal Shakespeare Company and the LSO. She told the House of Lords in a debate in January 1994:

In my experience of four years' standing, I can assure your Lordships that many projects are put on by the arts sector for the enjoyment, entertainment, education and enlightenment of those who work in the sector. Not too often do you hear the question asked, 'Will the man or woman in the street benefit from this?'

The slur was not only unjustified but also monstrously disloyal to the Barbican's prime cultural residents, including the LSO – which had embarked on its series of 'discovery' concerts and its educational programmes precisely in order to benefit 'the man or woman in the street'. But there was little that either the orchestra or the RSC could do by way of rebuttal. O'Cathain appeared to have the support of the Corporation, and her strident views about 'profligacy' in the arts world chimed with many in the Tory Government of the early 1990s.

Luckily, however, the newspapers got wind of what was going on. 'Such is the climate of fear inside the Barbican,' *The Times* wrote in October 1994, 'that no insider will say publicly what all say daily in private: that there must be a change of management if twelve years of achievement are not to be cut to shreds.' The repercussions of such adverse publicity were swift and brutal. O'Cathain demanded a public expression of confidence in her management from the Barbican's landlords (the Corporation) and from all the resident companies at the Centre. This was not forthcoming. She resigned immediately.

The 'Detta Affair', as it became known, was grim for all involved, but in a strange way it was also beneficial for the Barbican, and thus for the LSO. It brought to a head the issue of whether the Barbican was going to be a pioneering and enlightened cultural centre, or a 'garage' for commercial entertainment and conferences. Had O'Cathain stayed, the latter would probably have been the case – and the LSO's position would, sooner or later, have become untenable, because the underlying philosophy was that subsidy was 'wasted' on such 'profligate' organisations.

Instead, and greatly to its credit, the Corporation opted for the other route. O'Cathain's replacement was John Tusa, the former head of the BBC World Service – and a man so steeped in culture that he rarely seemed to miss a first night or exhibition opening in any sphere of the arts. He and his chief lieutenant, a gifted arts programmer called Graham Sheffield, soon had to cope with the withdrawal of the RSC from the Barbican (for reasons best known to the managers of that company). That could have been a disaster for the centre; instead, Tusa and Sheffield treated it as an opportunity to open up the theatre to the best and most radical performing-arts companies from around the world. It was a brilliant notion. At the start of the twenty-first century the Barbican was buzzing in a way that scarcely seemed possible ten or fifteen years earlier.

For the LSO, too, the new regime brought big gains. Tusa shared Gillinson's gift of being able to sweet-talk the usually sceptical 'money men' in the City into investing extra subsidy in the arts, confident in the belief that it would be spent wisely. In the nine years after he arrived at the helm, the Corporation poured upwards of £10 million into redesigning the foyers and the bizarre signposting – 'clearing away the crud', Tusa called it. Most important of all, from the LSO's point of view, significant improvements were made to the acoustics of the Barbican Hall. Under the supervision of the Chicago acoustics guru, Larry Kirkegaard, a spectacular new canopy was installed over the platform, and reflectors placed in the ceiling of the auditorium – all done in an extraordinary, psychedelic purple that changed its hue as the onlooker moved around the hall. The visual merits of these additions divided opinion, but they certainly made a measurable improvement to the hall's acoustics. 'There's much more chance now of producing a nice string sound,' says Colin Davis.

You could argue that, in the 1990s, the LSO and the Barbican reaped the benefits of changes and pressures within the 'Square Mile' that were entirely out of their hands. The City of London, for so long the undisputed financial capital of Europe, suddenly found that it had intense competition not just from foreign financial markets such as Frankfurt, but on its own doorstep from the towering skyscrapers of Canary Wharf, in the old Docklands of East London – to where many of the biggest finance houses defected. According to Gillinson, 'the City realised that if it wanted all these top merchant banks to keep their headquarters in the Square Mile, the cultural benefits of the Barbican are a really big plus point.'

Yet there can be little doubt that if figures like Gillinson and Tusa had not been in place – exuding competence, a sense of vision, and wise judgement – the City would have been far more reluctant to pour yet more funds into an arts centre that was already receiving over £20 million a year in subsidy. Whatever the reason, the long and tortuous saga of the Barbican now appears to have turned into one of Britain's more improbable success stories. And after a hundred years, the LSO has a home where it can blossom and shine.

LSO St Luke's

previous page Sir Colin Davis, LSO Principal Conductor

Does the symphony orchestra have a future? Will there always be a market for a large ensemble of musicians, quaintly attired as if for some sedate nineteenth-century ball, playing music that was mostly written more than a hundred years ago to connoisseurs who sit in rapt and contemplative silence? Can this ritual continue in an age when a thousand different varieties of entertainment are beamed or cabled into our houses at the flick of a remote-control?

The prospects may not seem good, yet art forms do have a habit of lingering long after their obituaries have been penned and published by gloom-mongering hacks. Many declared the theatre to be doomed when 'talkies' first appeared in the cinema. Eight decades later, London still has forty play-houses open, even if they don't all flourish at the same time. As we saw in chapter 4, the coming of radio was similarly – and wrongly – expected to signal the demise of live concerts. And when television came along, it was predicted to be the death-knell for cinema. 'Why should people pay good money to see bad films, when they can see bad television for nothing?' the great film producer Sam Goldwyn asked in 1956. Yet, nearly fifty years on, bad films and bad television flourish side by side.

So one has to weigh the regular newspaper jeremiads announcing the imminent death of the symphony orchestra against the knowledge that this particular combination of musical possibilities has proved remarkably resilient thus far. When the LSO was founded, a hundred years ago, the symphony orchestra was already nearly a century old. Beethoven had introduced trombones, piccolo and double-bassoon into his Fifth Symphony in 1808, and the modern 'standard orchestra' was completed by the appearance of the tuba in the 1830s. Although various exotic extras – Wagner tubas, saxophones – made guest appearances in later years, there was little radical change in the constitution of the symphonic ensemble thereafter, only modest expansion. If Schumann or Brahms were to return to a concert hall today, only the huge size and variety of the percussion department employed by a modern composer might surprise them.

The similarity between today's symphony orchestra and that of the early nineteenth century would surely have astonished Beethoven. Perhaps it should astonish us too. Just consider how vast the changes in instrumental sonorities had been in the two hundred years before 1800 – from the lutes, viols, sackbuts and wooden cornetts of the late Renaissance consort to the sound world of the 'Eroica' Symphony and *The Creation*. Consider too the vast array of instruments, invented in the years since 1800, that haven't made it into the symphony orchestra, at least not as permanent fixtures.

Perhaps the biggest surprise of all is how limited the effect of the electronic revolution of the twentieth century has been on the symphony orchestra. As early as the 1930s, Messiaen and others had started to use comparatively primitive electronic instruments such as the ondes martenot. By the 1950s Stockhausen, Boulez and Xenakis were pioneering the use of primitive computers to generate sound in concerts. The venerable symphony orchestra might, one feels, easily have keeled over and yielded supremacy to the paraphernalia of sine waves and frequency modulators. But somehow, this never quite happened. Fashions in electronic instruments have proved fickle. The technology is fiddly. Even specialist contemporary-music ensembles such as the London Sinfonietta or the Ensemble Modern appear to have settled for a set-menu of sounds that would hardly have surprised Elgar. And the young or middle-aged composers who are setting the pace internationally in the LSO's centenary year – figures such as John Adams, Thomas Adès, Heiner Goebbels, Mark-Anthony Turnage, George Benjamin, Poul Ruders – seem as wedded to the symphony orchestra as Mahler and his contemporaries were.

Is this inertia or perfection? Is the institution of the symphony orchestra now so indelibly bound into the fabric of classical music life that it is effectively the only choice for a composer wishing to reach a substantial audience with a new instrumental work? Or is the constitution of the symphony orchestra a kind of miracle that was arrived upon by historical accident but magically embodies the best possible combination for all time?

To me, the latter seems unlikely. I don't think it is mere coincidence that the rise of the fixed symphony orchestra in the early nineteenth century coincided with the rise of the concept of 'repertoire' – of a concert life predominantly concerned with continually reviving the work of deceased composers, rather than premièring contemporary music. Mendelssohn's brave decision to revive Bach's *St Matthew Passion*, after a century in which it went entirely unplayed, is often said to have heralded that change. The practical effect of this shift from 'contemporary' to 'historical' repertoire was to ossify the symphony orchestra's instrumental constitution for all time. If its main function was to play the music of earlier eras, it had to have available the instruments of those times. But this, in turn, meant that – for economic and logistical reasons – contemporary composers generally needed to conform to this time-honoured format, whatever their personal inclinations.

This tension between the need to revisit 'traditional' repertoire and the desire of present-day composers to experiment with new sounds is neatly summed up by Pierre Boulez, one of the greatest of composer-conductors:

The difficulty for the symphony orchestras is that they have to be at the same time a museum and a gallery. They must be a museum to old music, which is important because new people discover the riches of museums every day. But at the same time they have to offer some daring new experiences. It's very difficult to combine the two roles. Just look at the situation in London. The British Museum and Tate Modern are two very separate things, serving very different purposes. But the London Symphony Orchestra must try to be both things at once.

*

At many points in the orchestra's history – from its long associations with Elgar, Vaughan Williams and Britten to its more recent links with Boulez, Colin Matthews and George Benjamin – the LSO has played an honourable role in promoting the new, rather than playing safe by programming the old. The four-year-old *Enigma Variations* was on the programme for the LSO's first concert. A year later, Vaughan Williams – then hardly known outside academic and folksong-collecting circles – successfully persuaded the orchestra to run through one of his pieces in rehearsal. Shortly afterwards the LSO board agreed to a British Composers Association proposal that, at one specially convened public rehearsal each year, it would give an airing to six new works by young British composers. Whilst not being as satisfactory as a fully rehearsed public performance, the scheme at least allowed composers to hear the music they had written performed by experienced players who, by all accounts, were not slow to make their own suggestions for improvement.

Even in its early years, however, the LSO found that the dictates of financial circumstance and conservative audiences sometimes forced it to ditch its idealistic notions of programming pieces by living composers. When the orchestra was losing money in 1913, for instance, its immediate response was to drop all semblance of adventure and play nothing but tried and trusted repertoire. Thus, in the twelve-month period that saw the première of Stravinsky's *Rite of Spring* and Schoenberg's *Pierrot lunaire* elsewhere – in effect the birth of 'modern music' – the LSO's season consisted of four Beethoven symphonies, three Brahms symphonies and dollops of Tchaikovsky, Dvořák and Wagner. When the music critics moaned that the programmes weren't daring enough, the LSO retorted, no doubt accurately, that the majority of its subscribers had no wish to hear 'modern music'. *Plus ça change!* You could have heard the same debate in London in 1933, 1963 or 1993 – and doubtless the same old arguments and counter-arguments will still be knocking around in 2033 as well.

To pile all the blame for the 'museum culture' of symphony concerts on conservative audiences is to miss an essential point, however. Vibrant and confident artists and arts organisations don't slavishly follow public taste. They lead it. Boulez acknowledges that the LSO is 'one of the few orchestras that has shown a desire to move into new fields'. But there are many others, he contends, that are constrained by complacent soloists and conductors.

Musical life remains what it is because of the laziness of the artists themselves. Too many feel comfortable with what already exists. They have their repertoire, and they don't have any curiosity about what lies beyond it. They don't ask themselves any questions. They don't have any imagination. In our musical world too much unadventurousness is blamed on lack of rehearsal time or on union constraints, or the economic conditions of orchestras. But look at the average progamme of a piano recital or a violin recital – programmes decided by individuals who are under no such constraints. All you generally find is music written between 1800 and 1914. That is terrifying! It is a sign that the culture of these artists is dead.

Perhaps Boulez overstates the problem. And of course he also takes a famously narrow view of what constitutes 'proper' new music. (He once told me that he considered crowd-pleasing tonal compositions written by living composers to be 'whore's music'.) Even so, his criticisms have resonance. Nearly everybody accepts that, if orchestras are going to stay culturally and socially relevant in the twenty-first century, they simply have to nurture a generation of composers with the passion and the panache to excite big audiences, rather than coteries.

A comparison with the visual arts is revealing. The astonishing surge in the popularity of British modern-art galleries during the 1990s was fuelled almost entirely by the public's fascination with a bunch of young artists – Damien Hirst, Antony Gormley, Rachel Whiteread, Tracey Emin, Anish Kapoor – who proved consistently startling and stimulating. Once curious art-lovers were lured into the gallery by the current 'sensation', they could make their own discoveries.

It is surely time that orchestras learnt to flaunt adventurous young composers in the same way – as provocateurs who will grab headlines and attract new audiences, rather than as disruptive embarrassments who will shock and repel hallowed blue-rinse patrons unless their products are carefully concealed within the stultifying folds of Brahms. Such a bold attitude towards the music of today was clearly in Sir Simon Rattle's mind in September 2002, when he launched his tenure as music director of the Berlin Philharmonic not with some warhorse from the mighty fortress of the Austro-German symphonic repertoire, but with the techno-inspired *Asyla* by the young British composer, Thomas Adès – a choice which, to the surprise of some pessimistic critics, had the Berlin public on their feet cheering.

*

Rediscovering the courage to flaunt provocative new music is not the only or even the most pressing challenge facing the twenty-first-century symphony orchestra. It must also fight to protect its own traditional repertoire from the avaricious advances of the period-instrument orchestras that made such spectacular leaps forward in the last two decades of the twentieth century. Fifty years ago, even a far-sighted music critic would have toppled into the Festival Hall aisles in disbelief if someone had suggested that, by 2000, symphony orchestras would feel squeamish about playing Bach or Handel, and would even entertain doubts about whether they had any right, in strict stylistic terms, to play Haydn, Mozart and Beethoven. Yet so far-reaching has been the revolution wrought by these fashionable ensembles with their flowery, pseudo-historical names – the Orchestra of the Age of Enlightenment, the Orchestre Révolutionaire et Romantique, Les Arts Florissants, the Academy of Ancient Music – that this is indeed the case.

The danger for a non-specialist symphony orchestra such as the LSO is obvious. Its 'legitimate' repertoire might soon be swallowed up altogether. If audiences start to crave the period-instrument sound in Haydn and Beethoven, and then in Schubert and Berlioz, why not also in Brahms, Tchaikovsky, Mahler . . .? It makes just as much sense in historical terms. As Robert Philip convincingly demonstrated in *Early Recordings and Musical Style*, a Russian orchestra of Tchaikovsky's day would probably have played his music very differently from a twenty-first-century British or American orchestra.

The symphony orchestras' response to this intellectual assault has been canny. On the hallowed principle that if you can't beat 'em you should poach 'em, they have wooed the pioneers of the period-instrument movement to cross the great divide. Gurus of authenticity such as Nikolaus Harnoncourt, John Eliot Gardiner, Roger Norrington and William Christie now seem to work as often with 'modern instrument' orchestras – the very organisations which they sought to supplant in their more radical days – as with their own period-instrument ensembles.

The cynics jibe that they have put their careers before their musical princi-ples – unfairly, because such conductors have had a beneficial effect on the symphony orchestras they have directed. Players have been forced to open their minds to different musical approaches, and to reconsider some of the most basic tenets of their technique and style. Most obvious has been the change in string playing, particularly the move away from the blanket appli-cation of vibrato. But the 'authentic brigade', as they are disparagingly known in some quarters, also brought fresh ideas about everything from basic tempos to seating arrangements within the orchestra.

Their views have largely been welcomed in the symphonic world as a liber-ating alternative approach to repertoire that orchestral musicians have played dozens or hundreds of times. 'Quite often the early-music specialists are not technically the best conductors, but they have the best brains,' says Tim Lines, the LSO's former chairman and co-principal clarinettist. 'When we work with John Eliot Gardiner, for instance, rehearsals can sometimes be a bit slow. He wants you to play differently, but he has to explain verbally because he can't do it just with his hands. Yet the results he gets at the end are fascinating.'

*

The Norringtons and Harnoncourts of the musical world are not the only ones spurring the symphony orchestras towards greater flexibility. At the other end of the repertoire, conductors such as Boulez argue that the very rigidity of the symphony orchestra – its fixed membership and (especially in America) its fixed working patterns – discourages adventure in programming and acts as a disincentive to young composers. Boulez comments:

A body of a hundred or a hundred and twenty musicians can be divided for repertoire purposes into ten here, twenty there, sixty there, and so on. Of course, the musicians must be open-minded about this. They cannot expect to work as if in a factory, with set hours and set days every week. When I first came to the New York Philharmonic in 1969 it was shortly after the 1968 Consequences [the student uprisings in Europe and America], and there was a desire to explore and experiment. Unfortunately, after a while there was a return to normality. But at that time I did split the orchestra into two chamber groups, doing different repertoire, for some weeks.

Of course at first the musicians jumped into the ceiling! They would say: 'He is cut-ting the lemon and expecting to get twice the juice.' But after a few weeks they saw that they had days free while the other half rehearsed, and they got to play music they had never done before. Now with the LSO I often start with a smaller piece involv-ing a few players, then move on to a bigger piece. It is all a question of strategy and organisation.

Of course, such a policy also requires the presence of a live-wire mind like Boulez to do the creative thinking which such radical programming requires. Sadly, many eminent maestros today seem too intellectually lazy or incurious to tamper more than minimally with the overture/concerto/symphony format that has been the staple of symphonic concert-giving for more than a century.

*

If flexibility is desirable in planning concerts, it is absolutely crucial to an aspect of the symphony orchestra's work that has exploded in the last twenty-five years or so: education, or 'outreach', or 'audience development'. The terms vary, but they all reflect the same sense of gnawing unease: a disquieting perception that symphonic music's 'traditional' audience is getting older and smaller, and that the orchestra's place in modern society is becoming more and more tenuous and peripheral by the year.

The crisis is not entirely of the orchestras' making, at least not in the United Kingdom. Various changes in the British educational system – notably the introduction of a National Curriculum in 1988 which resulted in much less time for subjects such as music, drama and art – have conspired to squeeze the study of music out of children's lives. In 1997 the trend was accelerated by the incoming Labour Government, whose Education Secretary, David Blunkett, initially removed music and art altogether from the mandatory primary-school curriculum. Under intense pressure from Simon Rattle and others, Blunkett later reversed his ruling, but a dangerous signal about the unimportance of music had already been sent out to thousands of state schools.

At the same time, the trend towards 'local management of schools' turned out to have unforeseen and disastrous consequences for music. Now head teachers controlled a large part of their own budgets, many felt that a subscription to a local-authority music centre that only a minority of their pupils used was at best a luxury they couldn't afford, and at worst, élitism. Dozens of borough- or county-wide music services that had painstakingly built up superb youth orchestras, bands and choirs over many years were undermined. To make matters worse, the provision of peripatetic instrumental teaching in state schools became a postcode lottery: some local councils were enlightened and generous, others seemed to regard music provision as inherently élitist.

The dangers were recognised by leading musical figures, and a vigorous campaign to demonstrate the importance and proven success of Britain's youth music tradition resulted. But in 2004 the outlook remains uncertain, the provision patchy, and the consequences of these music-less years of state education are now all too apparent. A whole generation, perhaps two, has passed through British schools without ever having heard an orchestra live, without having had the opportunity to learn a musical instrument, and without learning more than the very basics of musical notation or history. It is not surprising that to most of them, symphonic music is a closed book, or that they are no more likely to enter a concert hall later in life than they are to fly to the moon.

*

To their credit, British orchestras have been quick to wake up to the bleak implications of this cultural tragedy. Between 1980 and 1995 nearly every professional British orchestra established its own in-house education department, in order to make links with local schools and communities and dispel some of the enervating clouds of mystique and prejudice surrounding classical music. Pioneers such as Gillian Moore (for the London Sinfonietta and later the South Bank Centre) and Richard McNicol, who established the LSO's scheme discussed below, devised admirable and often ingenious methods for enthusing and engaging children with little prior knowledge of music. However, the two dozen or so full-time symphony, opera and chamber orchestras in Britain could not possibly hope to make contact with more than a tiny percentage of British schools. Moreover, some orchestras gave the impression that they regarded their education departments as peripheral: an add-on extra, perhaps undertaken in order to gain extra Arts Council subsidy, rather than a commitment at the heart of their work. In summer 2002, when the Arts Council issued what appeared to be damning statistics showing that the percentage of young people at symphony concerts was still falling, some sceptics began to question whether the orchestra's education schemes were having any effect at all.

At the start of the twenty-first century, several leading lights in the music-college and orchestral world started to advance a much more radical blueprint for the survival of classical music. They envisaged the orchestra more as a musical 'resource bank', and its members as multi-skilled animateurs and missionaries for music in the wider community, rather than as skilled performers narrowly focused on providing exemplary performances to a narrow circle of connoisseurs. They wanted to see students at music colleges trained as much in communication, education and community skills as in the techniques and mystiques of their instrument; and they argued that orchestras should be spending as much, if not more, of their energies and resources working outside the concert hall – in schools and unconventional venues such as shopping malls or rock arenas – as within it.

Even as late as 1990, such suggestions would have been dismissed as an insulting waste of time by most orchestral musicians, especially those who regarded themselves as belonging to world-class ensembles. 'Education work comes hard to some players who have been in orchestras for twenty or twenty-five years,' Tim Lines admits. 'For them, there had always been the concerts, the tours, the film sessions. That way of life seemed a bit like the Church of England: established, always there.'

By the end of the twentieth century, however, even the proudest of the world's orchestras was gripped by a desperate sense of siege. It wasn't simply the fact that their audiences were, on the whole, getting smaller and greyer. A more alarming factor was the virtual collapse of the classical recording industry between 1990 and 2000. For an orchestra such as the LSO, recording had been a steady and substantial source of income since the mid-1920s. Of course the process whereby new CDs of the same old symphonies could be churned out again and again was recognised to be unsustainable. Nevertheless, many orchestral musicians were startled to see just how swiftly and brutally a major, long-established record label such as EMI or Decca could reduce its classical operation to a mere trickle of predominantly 'crossover' or populist albums, mostly featuring photogenic young violinists or string quartets who seemed more interested in *Top of the Pops* than the Proms. The effect of this abrupt change of direction on the economics of the orchestral business was devastating, and the problem was compounded by the virtual disappearance of the symphony orchestra from mainstream television.

All this contributed to the orchestras' sense of crisis, and to their gradual realisation that, whether they liked it or not, they had been plunged into a fight for their very lives. Even the most complacent and ostensibly secure ensemble suddenly felt very vulnerable. And consequently the orchestral profession began to feel much less hostile towards the hitherto shocking idea that players should spend almost as much of their working lives enthusing children in classrooms as rehearsing and playing concerts.

That realisation was, as all parties admitted, one of the most compelling reasons behind the Berlin Philharmonic's decision to ask Sir Simon Rattle to be its music director in succession to Claudio Abbado in September 2002. Rattle promised not only electrifying concerts but the instigation of a far-reaching programme of education and community work – extending into poor suburbs in the former East Berlin – on a scale never before attempted by any German orchestra, let alone one as haughty as the Berlin Phil. To watch 'Karajan's orchestra' undergoing this astonishing volte-face was a true sign of the times.

*

But even if orchestras do succeed in introducing a new generation of school-children to the excitement and power of live orchestral music, what then? There is no guarantee that these briefly enthused youngsters will somehow be converted into the orchestral audiences of the future. Indeed, the success of the British radio station Classic FM suggests that it is the arcane rigmarole and rigidity of the concert hall that deters the uninitiated from attending orchestral events, rather than any lack of appreciation for the music itself. The station's spectacular listening figures – seven million and rising – and particular success with teenagers and young adults raised the uncomfortable question of why those who regularly tuned to the station for their daily 'fix' of invariably tuneful classical music were rarely tempted to buy a ticket for a live concert.

Were they concerned that they would not know when to clap, when to cough, when to breathe? Were they put off by the absence of any familiar voice or face to welcome them from the stage and guide them through the music? Did the prospect of sitting silent and still through two hours of com-munal music-making prove unappealing? With the average price of a London orchestral concert ticket creeping above £20 (three times the price of cinema admission), was cost a deterrent?

At the beginning of the twenty-first century, all these questions suddenly became very hot issues. The general consensus – in London and New York at least, if not in the more comfortably subsidised orchestral strongholds of continental Europe – was that the orchestras had pulled off a minor miracle to get through the twentieth century without fundamental changes to their constitution, marketing, presentation or (for the most part) repertoire, but that it was virtually impossible for survival to continue long into the twenty-first century without some radical upheavals in their way of doing business.

The growing importance of the internet in disseminating information and changing people's leisure habits, the vast proliferation of 'home entertain-ment' options ranging from satellite television to video games, and the devas-tating negative impact that the September 11 atrocity had on the box-office figures of all kinds of live entertainment – all these factors also helped to rein-force the perception that a post-war era of relative stability for the orchestral profession had been rudely terminated, as Clive Gillinson admits:

Compared with when I started in orchestral management, twenty years ago, the whole music business has become so much harder. There's so much less recording work around. International touring is much harder to organise and negotiate. Revenues from the box office haven't kept pace with costs. And, if you look at the sort of places where we customarily toured, their grants are being eroded too. Look at Germany. Huge sums of money used to be available in that country for promoting touring orchestras. We find everybody is being tougher and tougher on budgets. Everybody argues over every penny. Now you often get promoters saying: 'Can you change the repertoire, because we want to pay for fewer players?'

As if that wasn't bad enough, cultural organisations also had to contend with the new breed of politicians who came to the fore in Europe during the late 1990s. Even if they belonged to parties that were theoretically socialist by tradition or belief, and therefore instinctively more sympathetic towards the notion of state support for the arts, they took a hard-nosed and unsentimental attitude towards the subsidy of 'high culture'. The old notion of 'art for art's sake' cut no ice with them. If the arts were to be supported by taxpayers' money at all, they argued, then the organisations concerned had to demonstrate that they were improving the quality of life for people in all economic and social categories, not just for the relatively small band of mostly well-educated and prosperous people who traditionally attended arts events.

Not everybody is convinced by such arguments, to put it mildly. Sir Colin Davis, the LSO's principal conductor, believes that the attitude is merely a smokescreen: a diversionary tactic to deflect attention away from the failure of the current political élite, particularly in Britain, to support culture properly:

They don't believe in it. There isn't a great lobby for the arts in Westminster at the moment. MPs on the whole are genuinely philistine, which wasn't the case when I was young. Sorry, that sounds like Yeats. But it's what I feel. Those old Labour people – Crossman and Cripps and Jennie Lee and Nye Bevan – were cultivated, idealistic and determined to do something about the quality of life. Politics is even more imperfect now than it ever was, because the idealism has gone. Now, as far as the politicians are concerned, everything is just a question of money.

Some would argue that such blanket condemnation is unfair. But there is no doubt that an atmosphere of general political indifference or even scepticism towards the value of the arts, when combined with all the other adverse factors of recent years, has caused orchestras across the world to flounder. Many at the extreme ends of the funding spectrum – those in Eastern Europe that had relied solely on public subsidy, and those in the United States utterly at the mercy of the box office, sponsorship and private donors – found the pressures too much, and folded in the final years of the twentieth century and at the start of the twenty-first.

For the rest, it was a time when nothing was certain except uncertainty, and no tradition too sacred not to be jettisoned in the quest for renewal and, ultimately, survival. There were no easy answers. Each management had to find its own path. And it was entirely in keeping with its history that the LSO mapped out a future for itself which was so bold, so original, such a challenge to established orchestral preconceptions, that it caught the imagination of the entire musical world.

*

The date is 27 March 2003. In a disused Baroque church in half-gentrified Shoreditch, a few hundred yards north of the Barbican, are gathered Cabinet ministers past and present, bankers, millionaires, mayors, MPs and councillors of all political hues, architects, industrialists, top civil servants, headteachers, computer specialists, journalists and BBC producers. It could be one of those earnest multidisciplinary conferences to discuss 'the future of society'. And in a way, the future of society is very much what is being discussed. But this is no earnest conference. Also present are children from two nearby secondary schools, who perform their own musical compositions on a bewildering variety of instruments. Then the Scottish composer James MacMillan strides in and proceeds to pin everybody's ears back with a startling new violin concerto, its eerie modes and clangorous dissonances stunningly delivered by LSO members and Gordan Nikolitch, the orchestra's leader.

The strident and passionate twenty-first century sounds seem to rouse new energies from the time-ravaged walls of this 271-year-old building. Which is apt and symbolic – for this is the gala opening of LSO St Luke's, and if any building could be said to encapsulate the hopes, the ambitions and the dreams of not just a single orchestra but an entire profession, this is it.

Ninety-nine years earlier, Adolf Borsdorf, John Solomon and their rebellious cronies in the brass section of the Queen's Hall Orchestra would have been sitting in a pub a mile or two west of here, discussing how to break away from Henry Wood and form their revolutionary new musicians' cooperative, the London Symphony Orchestra. Had they hopped into one of the wonderful time machines evoked in the H. G. Wells novel that everyone in Edwardian London was talking about, I wonder what they might have made of the scene in LSO St Luke's on its inaugural night?

They would have been delighted, and perhaps a little surprised, to have found that, a century later, their ad hoc band of renegade instrumentalists was not only still in existence, but capable of inspiring admiration in London's smartest business, political and cultural circles. They would possibly have been perplexed by MacMillan's wild and distinctly untraditional music, but thrilled and awed beyond belief by the technical prowess of their LSO successors, three or four generations down the line. They would have nodded approvingly at learning that 'mere musicians' had become so adept at running their own affairs that they had raised £18 million to restore and convert this mighty eighteenth-century ecclesiastical ruin into a twenty-first-century musical powerhouse. After all, had Borsdorf and his confrères not had confidence in their own business acumen, the LSO would never have been founded.

But one thing would surely have astonished them. St Luke's is not primarily a concert venue or a rehearsal hall, though at times it *is* both of these things. It is an orchestral education centre: the first in the world. From here, the LSO hopes to engage the ears, hearts and minds of schoolchildren and adult learners not just in London, but (via the wonders of the digital information superhighway) around the whole of Britain, and perhaps overseas as well.

Quite apart from being baffled by the technology (H. G. Wells said nothing about the internet), Messrs Borsdorf and Solomon would have found this ambition quite incomprehensible. Educational work? They were hard-nosed musical mercenaries, the best in the business – and their job, as they saw it, was quite simple: to play concerts for the highest fees they could obtain. That was why they founded the LSO. And, for the next eighty years or so, that is basically why the LSO existed.

What has happened to the orchestra since the mid-1980s has been nothing short of a philosophical revolution. And St Luke's is both the physical expression of that revolution, and the chief tool in continuing it. It defines what the orchestra has now become, and what it hopes to become. It is not only a landmark in LSO history, but also a lantern lighting the path into the future.

Borsdorf and Solomon would certainly have recognised the building itself. For nearly three centuries it has been one of London's most distinctive landmarks – albeit, for most of that time, a rather distressed one. Nicholas Hawksmoor, the eclectic and eccentric genius of English Baroque architecture (his masterpiece was Christ Church, Spitalfields), reputedly had a hand in designing it. Certainly its strikingly peculiar obelisk tower, with its fluted stonework and golden weathervane (which the guidebooks describe as a dragon but locals describe as a louse), has the unmistakable stamp of Hawksmoor.

But whoever it was that built it, he didn't do a very good job – not surprisingly, given the circumstances of its construction. It was commissioned under the curiously named Fifty New Churches Act, passed in 1711 during a rare moment of Parliamentary piety to provide handsome places of worship for what were then London's burgeoning 'outer suburbs'. But St Luke's wasn't built until the early 1730s, by which time funds were running low and the public's interest in new churches even lower. The whole place was erected, on unstable foundations laid over marshy ground, on a budget of just £10,000, a quarter of what had been spent on Thomas Archer's contemporaneous St John's in Smith Square, Westminster.

As is usually the case, the penny-pinching proved costly in the long run. Within a year the walls of St Luke's started to subside. They were propped up twice by the diligent Victorians, and twice more in the early twentieth century. To no avail: in 1959 a hot, dry summer caused a degree of subsidence that was then regarded as untreatable. At this point, the Church of England shouted 'Abandon ship!', the roof and the internal fittings were removed (the organ on which Henry Smart composed some of his best hymn-tunes ended up in St Giles, Cripplegate), and the interior was turned over to detritus, weeds and dope-dealers for the best part of four decades.

In the 1990s, the saga of St Luke's intersected with the story of another indomitable London institution – the LSO. Clive Gillinson and the LSO's then Head of Education, Emma Chesters, came across the church, and promptly decided that it would make an ideal base from which to develop the orchestra's educational work. It was a remarkably brave decision. Looking at that roofless, derelict shell with its crumbling, unstable walls and flaky steeple, not everyone would have shared his faith in the restorative powers of the British building trade.

To understand why the LSO felt the need in the late 1990s to raise the vast sum of £18 million (nearly twice its annual turnover) to develop St Luke's, we must go back and ask how orchestras got involved in educational work in the first place.

*

The LSO's links with London's education authorities go back decades. As long ago as 1926, at the orchestra's twenty-first birthday concert, a block of seats at the Queen's Hall was handed over to the London County Council at a nominal cost so that schoolchildren could attend. But that seems to have been a one-off gesture. More substantially, in 1946 – at the height of postwar austerity – the orchestra embarked on a scheme that was revolutionary in its day and a precursor of many more recent education schemes. The Harrow Schools' Orchestral Concerts Scheme, devised by Muir Mathieson in conjunction with the Borough of Harrow in north London and the (now defunct) county of Middlesex, was a three-year syllabus of music education intended to be 'part of the normal school curriculum'. It included not only full orchestral concerts and school visits by LSO players and ensembles, but also discussions and classroom study using records and scores.

Today, the emphasis on children being educated in the passive appreciation of music, rather than learning how to make music themselves, would be regarded as hopelessly old-fashioned. But the idea of giving Harrow's schoolchildren the benefit of close and sustained contact with so famous an ensemble seems extraordinarily enlightened for 1946.

Unfortunately, Middlesex County Council (which ran what is now the northern part of Greater London) lost its nerve, and never adopted the scheme on a county-wide basis. That was a pity. Giving music such a prominent place in London schools, at the very moment when post-war secondary education was in the melting-pot, would have sent out a strong message to every local authority in the land.

Despite its limited scope, the music critic Hubert Foss, writing in the early 1950s, declared that the LSO/Harrow scheme 'sets a splendid example' in contrast to 'the widespread philistinism towards music still unfortunately shown by a large number of municipal authorities in this country'. How ironic, and slightly depressing, to find virtually the same words ('a shining beacon in an era of generally philistine educational values') used half a century later by *The Times* when it reported the opening of LSO St Luke's.

Sadly, the orchestra's association with Harrow schools ended in 1965, when the LSO board of that era decided that it would rather fill its schedule with more film sessions and glamorous foreign tours than children's concerts in north-west London. It was a short-sighted and selfish attitude, but not untypical of the way in which orchestras generally regarded such work until very recently.

Then in 1987, with the LSO emerging shakily from the worst financial crisis in its history, Clive Gillinson made a momentous decision – as his friend and fellow LSO cellist Francis Saunders recalls: 'He told me he wanted someone on the board to do research on education, and to see how we can bring that into our mainstream work.'

At the time, the notion of orchestras or any top-level performing organisations doing educational work was still fairly novel. But the huge reduction in music teaching, both at a classroom level and in the form of individual instrumental tuition, had set alarm bells ringing. It was beginning to dawn on far-sighted music administrators and managers that the music profession could no longer rely on the British educational system to teach youngsters to understand or appreciate music. If orchestras wanted to play to knowledgeable audiences in the future, or indeed any audiences at all, they would have to do a large proportion of the teaching themselves.

Saunders spent six months talking to music educationalists, and then presented his recommendations to the LSO board. This time, unlike their predecessors in 1965, the directors realised that they had to move into the teaching business. The LSO's education department began modestly enough: a composing project with Newcastle children; an expedition for some intrepid players into Wandsworth Prison (always a grim place: it has Britain's last functional gallows); an intensive two-day summer music jamboree for London children at the Barbican; and work in old people's homes and community centres.

With the appointment in 1992 of Richard McNicol as official LSO Music Animateur, the orchestra's educational work suddenly gained a new dimension and a new name – LSO Discovery. A former LPO flute player, McNicol had pioneered many new techniques to encourage children of all abilities and backgrounds to understand even quite complex pieces – *The Rite of Spring*, or other twentieth-century classics – by composing and performing pieces of their own, based on melodies, rhythms or harmonies from the original. It was a far cry from the old 'music appreciation' classes of the 1950s, and it was successful, not least because the LSO's education department (which quickly grew to become the biggest run by any British orchestra) developed packs of back-up material for hard-pressed classroom teachers who were not necessarily music specialists.

These background resources were enormously expanded when the internet arrived in schools in the late 1990s. By 2002, thirty thousand people – mostly, but not all, children – were passing through some five hundred and fifty Discovery events each year. That was an impressive achievement for one orchestra, but it still reached only a tiny fraction of the million-plus children in Greater London. If the project had a dedicated education centre, however, able to provide live sessions for hundreds of pupils each week and for thousands more connected by two-way video relay, Discovery might be able to establish links with ten times the number of schools. What's more, such a centre could become the base on which an entirely new sort of orchestra might be launched, as Gillinson comments:

Part of our thinking in the long term is to start appointing LSO players who don't actually play in the orchestra. They would be employed solely to do educational work. But they would be right at the heart of LSO culture, they would be driven by the same values of musical excellence, and they would be first-class players in their own right.

The plan is that these non-playing members of the orchestra – who would ideally be funded out of the state education budget, rather than by the usual arts funding bodies – could then enormously expand the reach of the LSO's educational activities, perhaps to the point where the orchestra could complement the school music curriculum for all the London boroughs in its vicinity.

It's an ambitious idea. But if it takes off, it would not only greatly extend the LSO's funding base, and provide what Gillinson calls 'a template for what every orchestra could do in its own region', it would also represent one of the biggest conceptual upheavals in the history of music education. For the first time, a top performing organisation would be completely integrated into the educational system. 'We could transform the way orchestras are, as well as how they are perceived,' Gillinson says.

All these grand dreams depended, in the first instance, on finding a venue for the education centre. For a London orchestra to contemplate financing and supervising the renovation of what was, bluntly, an architectural wreck – albeit a Grade 1 listed wreck – would have been unthinkable in normal times. But in the mid-1990s, with the advent of the enormously lucrative National Lottery (which originally had a mandate to spend a fifth of its proceeds on culture), the usually impoverished British arts world was temporarily awash with money, and impossible dreams suddenly seemed possible. Covent Garden, the British Museum, the Albert Hall, the Tate Gallery . . . most of London's great cultural institutions had joined the queue for lottery handouts, and had walked away with anything up to £50 million each.

The LSO put in a much more modest application for St Luke's, and was successful: over the course of the project, the Arts Council supplied a total of £5.56 million from its lottery fund, and the Heritage Lottery Fund gave £3.16 million in recognition of St Luke's architectural merits. A Swiss bank, UBS, raised a handsome £3.5 million, which enabled the LSO to go to the lottery funders with over twenty-five per cent of the funding already in place, and cultural charities such as the Jerwood and Clore Foundations also made major contributions.

Encouraged by such generosity, Gillinson and his colleagues may have felt that their new education centre was as good as in the bag. If so, they should have remembered that little in London's cultural life has ever gone to plan.

What followed was a seven-year saga that at times tested the nerve, determination and financial reserves of the LSO management to breaking point.

*

To provide all the resources required by an education centre, the LSO needed rather more space than was allowed by the nave of St Luke's, impressively wide though that was. It would also need to rescue and stabilise the almost-collapsed crypt, which would have to be extended into the surrounding graveyard in order to accommodate practice rooms, a gamelan room, a technology centre (the 'nerve centre' of the whole enterprise, allowing St Luke's to be linked to schools across Britain), a cafeteria, an instrument store, the orchestra's library of scores and parts, and offices.

That was the first challenge, and it proved to be a macabre task. A thousand corpses had to be excavated and reburied in a South London cemetery. Then the architects had to solve the problem of erecting a new roof for the main body of the church – one that would necessarily have to conform to twenty-first-century building and safety regulations – without increasing the load on the tottering eighteenth-century walls. The architects chosen, Levitt Bernstein, had already displayed their ingenuity in supplying chic modern interiors to historic buildings; the magical 'enclosed shell' of the Royal Exchange Theatre in Manchester was their most celebrated work.

Their solution to the St Luke's problem was no less resourceful. Within the existing nave they erected four massive steel 'trees', not dissimilar in concept to the internal square of columns used by Hawksmoor in, for instance, Christ Church, Spitalfields. These would bear the entire weight of the new roof. Meanwhile the old walls, with their window openings suitably multiple-glazed for sound insulation, would be left largely in their age-withered state – a decision based not only on a desire to preserve the building's architectural integrity, but also on the knowledge that rough-textured walls are acoustically preferable to hard plaster. The steel trees also supported new steel galleries. These, and the new retractable seating on the floor of the nave, allowed this new 'Jerwood Hall' to seat an audience of up to 370 people when used for concerts.

To devise all this was in itself an ingenious achievement, but at almost the end of the building process, two huge additional problems were discovered. One involved Hawksmoor's celebrated 'fluted spire', as Gillinson recalls:

When the builders put up the scaffolding to restore it, they discovered that Hawksmoor had added the fluting only as an afterthought, and that in places the original masons had virtually gone through the stone altogether. What's more, the restorers found that much of the original rubble had just been dumped inside the spire.

Huge amounts of stonework had to be replaced and strengthened, and the inside of the spire had to be sealed and bonded.

That was an expensive enough blow, but a worse one soon followed. The main walls of St Luke's appeared to be a metre thick, with the brick clad in Portland stone on the outside. It was assumed that it was a single wall, but in many places the inner and the outer parts had separated and were standing independently of each other, with the outer cladding in danger of toppling away. There was no way round the problem except to pin and grout the two parts together – an enormously costly piece of engineering.

It didn't take the LSO management long to grasp the disastrous implications. 'It could be up to a million pounds extra, just to sort out the bloody walls!' exclaimed the normally imperturbable Gillinson shortly after the bad news was broken to the orchestra, early in 2002. 'And they have only discovered that now. Nobody has been negligent; it's just one of those things.'

One of those things or not, the setback threatened to destroy the solid financial foundations so painstakingly laid by the LSO management. The problem was not so much the delay in opening St Luke's as paying for the extra building work. When approached in the spring of 2002 for additional support, the grandees of the Heritage Lottery Fund, inexplicably and inexcusably, simply washed their hands of the new problem – though the preservation of the original walls was clearly a heritage issue.

'They said: "We think this is roughly a £3 million project, so we aren't going to give any more."' Gillinson recalls. 'It was absolutely unbelievable.' That meant the whole burden of finding the extra money needed – almost £1.5 million – fell on the orchestra, at a time when London's entertainment sector was going through one of its worst depressions for years, and when big-money sponsors and patrons were reeling from the post-September 11 effects of the tumbling stock market.

There was no panic, but much anger inside the LSO camp at the way in which the orchestra was expected to jeopardise its own survival in order to bring into existence an institution that would benefit the musical education of thousands, perhaps millions, of schoolchildren across the whole country. Why should the musicians have to take such colossal risks? 'Poor Clive has had to double back and forth begging for money,' Colin Davis fumed in April 2002. 'And it's extraordinary how people just don't want to give it. How can they abandon something that is almost finished. How can they abandon such a wonderful idea, as well as a beautiful church? The orchestra can't shoulder the burden by itself – it hasn't got any money.'

In the end, though, the orchestra did shoulder much of the burden, running a sizeable deficit for two years and diverting the sponsorship department that would otherwise have subsidised the orchestra's day-to-day work towards the building project, so that St Luke's could open in a blaze of media glory and Establishment approval in March 2003. But in the summer of 2003, it became clear that, unless even more funding could be urgently found, St Luke's would never operate at its full capacity as an education centre – a terrible shame in view of its enormous potential. The whole experience has made Gillinson reflect wryly on the shortcomings of the British arts-funding system:

Everyone said St Luke's had to happen. Everyone says we are doing a fantastic job. But the nub of the matter is that, after fifteen years of achievement, we have to put the whole organisation at risk every time we want to move forward. That's completely crazy. There isn't a company in the world that can succeed with every risk it takes, especially if it is aspiring to do exceptional things. And yet we are expected to be successful every time.

Establishing an orchestral education centre has been one major plank of the LSO's strategy over the past decade. Another related aim has been to tackle the whole question of the accessibility and 'fusty' image of the symphony orchestra. How can these venerable institutions – custodians and curators of so much great music of the past, and (one hopes) catalysts for so much yet to be written – break through the psychological, social, geographical and financial barriers that seem to deter the vast majority of people in Britain and America from going to concerts or buying classical recordings?

For Gillinson, this is the question that underpins every plan – almost as much as what he calls the 'fairly obvious' notion of making the LSO play better and better:

When the players say to me, as they do from time to time, 'We aren't paid enough, it's not fair, etc, etc,' what I say to them is: the basis on which we are paid in a free society is the basis on which there is a demand in that society. What you are basically telling me is that not enough people enjoy or value what we are doing. The only way to change that is for more people to value it, and that's our responsibility. We have to put ourselves at the centre of society in a completely different way from how the arts were presented in the past. Everything we do relates to that.

This isn't just a 'youth' issue, though it is usually perceived as such. It's true that no orchestra in the world attracts enough young adults, but the

LSO's audience profile (fifty-five per cent under the age of forty-four) means that it actually has the friskiest 'fan base' in Britain. 'You could argue that our potential development is with older people,' Gillinson observes. It's more a matter of smashing the age-old assumption that only a certain class of person goes to orchestral concerts. Is that because only a certain class of person can afford to go? Gillinson clearly believes this to be part of the problem, hence the bold decision to reduce ticket prices for the LSO's centenary season, so that they run from £5 to £25, rather than from £6.50 to £35. 'It's tricky, because in Britain generally people judge quality by price,' Gillinson admits. 'If something is cheap, they think it's poor. The marketing department and I debated the new pricing policy for a long time and we now think we can turn the market on its head.'

There's a hard-nosed economic case underpinning this idealism, too. In theory, cheaper tickets require less selling, so advertising budgets can be much reduced. If demand does soar because of cheaper tickets, the LSO could then repeat more concerts, leading to savings in rehearsal costs, since each new concert programme costs £20,000 or more to rehearse.

But would moving towards the American model, where the same programme may be played four times in a week, be a good thing artistically? Opinions are divided. The LSO's own principal conductor, for one, has reservations. 'The American system traps musicians on a treadmill,' says Colin Davis. 'Because it's so regular – the same pattern of rehearsals, concerts and repeats each week through the whole season – it's numbing. Nor do I think it's true that a performance gets deeper when it is repeated three or four times.'

His predecessor, Michael Tilson Thomas, profoundly disagrees:

The hardest thing in concert life is what the LSO has to do twice or sometimes three times a week: move from one musical landscape to a completely different one – perhaps too quickly. That orchestra taught me so much about maintaining musical ardency in the face of unhelpful conditions. The biggest difference in my life now, working primarily with the San Francisco Symphony Orchestra, is that although the amount of rehearsal time I have on each programme is not dissimilar to the amount I had with the LSO, we will do each programme four or five times. By revisiting that same landscape again and again, we can discover larger possibilities. I think that is one of the greatest rewards a musician can have.

Perhaps wisely, Gillinson does not take sides in this argument. But he does point to the marketing problem that has confronted the LSO throughout its hundred-year existence, and will most likely do so for the next hundred years: how to make a sustained impact on the public's consciousness while operating in the busiest and most competitive musical marketplace in the world.

There is no city to match London for this endless supply of entertainment every night. Even New York doesn't have so many musical organisations in such direct competition. In that environment, it's almost impossible to build an identity and a loyal audience with one-off concerts. So if you can create an event – a Mahler festival, a Boulez or Rostropovich birthday, a Mutter festival – that really helps. We don't do this in a formulaic way, but we do need to make a significant number of weighty artistic statements each season, which can only be made through series of concerts.

Modern concertgoers do seem to lap up packages and 'voyages of exploration', even if they contain individual items that would normally not attract them, as Gillinson notes:

I vividly remember the Shostakovich festival in 1998. Because we did it in chronological order, the last programme contained the *Michelangelo Sonnets* and the Fifteenth Symphony. If we had put that on as a one-off programme in London, I would have been amazed if we had sold thirty-five per cent of the seats. But at the end of the Shostakovich cycle it sold out, and people simply went wild when it finished.

Pricing concerts attractively is one tactic in the LSO's drive to be accessible to all. Another has been the launch of LSO Live, its own record label. Twenty years ago, the notion of the LSO's players voluntarily foregoing their 'upfront' recording fee for the promise of 'jam tomorrow' (a slice of any future profits) would have been unthinkable. Even today, without Gillinson's persuasive qualities and rapport with the players, it is unlikely that LSO Live would be in existence. 'Actually, we call it LSO Clive,' quips Lennie Mackenzie, the orchestra's sub-leader.

Gillinson, characteristically, turns the argument on its head, and declares that the record label's foundation and continued success is a tribute to the strength of the LSO's player-owner tradition. 'The reason that most American orchestras can't set up a similar label even now,' he contends (speaking in late 2002), 'is because the players don't identify with, or feel involved in, the management of their orchestras in the way that ours do.'

With the once-powerful classical recording industry becoming a shadow of its former self in the early 1990s, and with public taste swinging away from artificially manicured studio recordings and back towards CDs that preserved memorable live performances, it was perhaps inevitable that some orchestras would begin to think of making their own recordings of their concerts. In Britain, the Royal Liverpool Philharmonic Orchestra was first in the field, launching its own label in 1998.

Gillinson's notion was altogether more radical, however. LSO Live would charge just £4.99 a CD, at a time when top-price CDs were three times that amount in Britain. The ruse was a triumph. Some quarter of a million CD sets were sold in the first three years, and the label even penetrated the hallowed shelves of the Sainsbury's supermarket chain, normally occupied only by pop CDs or 'crossover' albums. In an extraordinary coup, it also carried off both the 'Best Classical Recording' and the 'Best Opera Recording' prizes at the 2002 Grammy Awards for an epic performance of Berlioz's *Les Troyens* conducted by Colin Davis.

Such success has, not surprisingly, attracted sour comments from some of the dwindling band of classical record executives still employed by the major labels. 'I don't know how long the Musicians' Union officials will let LSO Live carry on before they step in,' said the boss of one distinguished British classical label, implying that the LSO players were being exploited by their own management. 'Why should I now book the LSO at premium rates to make recordings for us? I think Clive is underselling the orchestra and devaluing its image by making these recordings on the cheap and selling them for £4.99 a CD.'

LSO Live is undoubtedly a gamble, but it needs to be assessed in a broader context. In the future, Gillinson believes, orchestras will have to seize every available medium – visual, aural, or via some as-yet-unknown avenue of cyberspace – to get their names and performances across to the public. True, some of the new media that were considered five years ago to be 'the future' have not, as yet, fulfilled expectations. Nobody, for instance, is making money from selling music on the internet (though many are losing vast sums from internet piracy). And the digital arts TV channels launched in Britain over the past few years, both by independent companies and the BBC, have garnered so few viewers so far that their continued existence must be in question.

Yet there can be little doubt that any performing organisation which simply ignores these huge revolutions in mass communication will be, at best, marginalised from the mainstream of culture, and more likely swept away by the tide of change. The story of the LSO throughout its first century has largely been one of a band of musicians refreshingly prepared to embrace technological change as a challenge and an opportunity, not to bemoan it as a threat. The LSO was the first London orchestra to 'back' a season of silent films, the first to have a regular recording contract, the first to embrace film session work, the first to win a weekly television series, and the first to exploit the full educational and marketing potential of the internet. The decision to launch LSO Live fits into that progressive tradition, and its impressive sales have done much to dispel the fashionable myth that 'the market for classical CDs is dead'. At the right price and quality, it is very much alive.

*

What, though, of the orchestra's playing standards in the twenty-first century? In an ever-shrinking musical world, can the LSO compete as an equal with the likes of Berlin, Vienna, New York and Chicago? With the competition to grab lucrative tours and big corporate sponsors growing more intense each year, such a question is of far more than academic interest.

In financial and organisational terms, the LSO is still a small fish in an ocean of whales and sharks. Its combined Arts Council and City of London grants (standing at £3.2 million in 2003), may give it considerably more subsidy than some British orchestras, but the amount is still less than half of that enjoyed by the Berlin Philharmonic. Similarly, the initial target of £10 million set for the Endowment Fund that the orchestra will launch in its centenary year – though it will make an enormous difference to the LSO's financial security – pales beside the $150 and $200 million endowments enjoyed by some American orchestras. The LSO's annual turnover of £10 million is less than a third of an American orchestra's, and its 'back office' staff still seems skeletal when set beside the army of fundraisers, managers, clerks and volunteers apparently considered necessary to keep big orchestras running on the other side of the Atlantic.

Yet the LSO has always 'punched above its weight', both in the energy and fervour of its playing, and in the way it does business. It has forged vital and durable business and sponsorship links with the Far East, as Gillinson reports:

One of the most important decisions I have made in my time running the LSO was to invite Mr Yamataka to become our International Vice President. He has worked tirelessly to involve major Japanese companies with the LSO. These have included Nomura, Toshiba, Mikimoto, Nikon, IBJ, Itochu Fashion Systems and many more. And, the central underpinning of our international touring for the last fourteen years has been the support of Takeda Chemical Industries. Without that the LSO's international presence would have been far less important, colourful and comprehensive.

The orchestra has also maintained its regular New York residencies even when – like the fantastically plunging dresses of the starlets on Oscar night – they have appeared to have no visible means of support. And despite the fact that London traditionally pays a fraction of the fees commanded by the top conductors and soloists elsewhere, the LSO somehow continues to catch the top talent. The centenary season of 2003–4 is graced by such names as Davis, Previn, Mutter, Pletnev, Midori, Gergiev, Vengerov, Kissin, Bashmet, Brendel, Chailly, Rostropovich, Haitink and Antonio Pappano, the Italian-American music director of the Royal Opera (who became many people's favourite to succeed Colin Davis as the LSO's principal conductor after Mariss Jansons threw in his lot with the Concertgebouw Orchestra in Amsterdam).

Clive Gillinson emphasises the importance of relationships with its most regular visitors:

Over the last eighteen years, there have been a number of central relationships in the LSO's life that have stamped an indelible mark on London's musical life. We have been remarkably fortunate that, as well as Sir Colin Davis, Pierre Boulez, Slava Rostropovich and more recently Bernard Haitink and Tony Pappano have all made the LSO their London symphonic musical homes. This has resulted in some visionary musical journeys, primarily covering vast and contrasting swathes of the music of the twentieth century, the LSO's lifetime.

The orchestra's new-found stability and success has brought much generous acclaim, even from unexpected quarters. Fergus McWilliam, the ebullient Scottish horn player who has been a fixture in the Berlin Philharmonic Orchestra since the days of Karajan, says:

I'm proud of what the LSO has done over the past fifteen years with Clive. In 1984 they had not only run out of money, they had run out of air. Their corporate model didn't work any longer. They had to reinvent themselves, and they have succeeded phenomenally well. So much so that in Berlin now we are studying everything they do, and emulating it. Especially on the educational and outreach side.

Has something of the traditional LSO spirit been lost in the process of all this reinvention? The LSO of the 1960s and 1970s might have had its organisational and financial shortcomings, and its arrogant behaviour towards certain conductors may sometimes have verged on professional misconduct. But on its best nights it played with a swashbuckling verve that could be thrilling. Perhaps the very fact that the organisation was so insecure instilled an 'edge' that is difficult to recapture in calmer and more stable times.

That's a charge that Gillinson and the present LSO players would vehemently deny, of course. And anybody who has listened regularly to concerts in London over the past thirty years would find it hard to argue against the proposition that the technical quality of the orchestra, and particularly its string players, is better now than ever before. It's certainly far more consistently maintained over the course of a season. 'The other day,' Gillinson recalls, 'a wind player said to me: "In the old days I could hear the strings cocking it up, and felt, Oh well, it doesn't matter. Now I hear them playing superbly, and know I have to raise my game too."'

Nevertheless, there are those in the music business who feel that the orchestra's new-found steadiness and sense of artistic and social purpose has attracted a breed of players who are impeccably dedicated, disciplined, superbly equipped and well-balanced musicians, but perhaps lacking that element of devilry or fantasy that makes for excitement (or sometimes disaster) on the platform. 'The modern LSO is cast in the likeness of Colin Davis and Clive Gillinson,' said one top London agent. 'It's very good all of the time, but a duller place than it used to be.'

That feeling is echoed to an extent by André Previn:

It was like a sixth form with instruments in the old days. Now it's very conservative by comparison. And it's the younger people in the orchestra who are so conservative, not the old. When I was rehearsing recently someone made a pleasant and marginally filthy joke, a few people laughed, and one of the old guys said, 'Some things never change.' I replied, 'Yes they do,' because in the old days the whole orchestra would have fallen about with laughter. The players are just as wonderful today, and a lot more reliable about turning up on time. But some old-timers with the orchestra, me included, lament the disappearance of the insanity that was present in the old days.

Much more forthright in his criticism is Denis Wick, the LSO's principal trombone through most of the 1960s, 1970s and 1980s: 'The characters aren't there now. The whole thing has been so carefully contrived that there are no accidents any more, though the results are absolutely wonderful. It seems to me that the modern orchestra is both more polished and more bland.' Maurice Murphy, his colleague for many years on principal trumpet, disagrees: 'We still have players who take chances. In fact, I detest orchestras that play safe, that get the notes at any cost. Here, if someone wants to take a chance, make something sound really fantastic, they do it. When it comes off, it's stunning – and the danger is part of the fun.'

Gillinson accepts that the change in atmosphere within the LSO has affected its personnel and recruitment.

The culture of the orchestra defines the sort of people who are attracted to join. In the early days of the 1980s, when we had all those battles about cultural change, lots of people left – the people who wanted the orchestra to serve them, rather than the other way round. What's interesting now is that whereas one used to have quite difficult fights about nearly every major issue, now that almost never happens. Positive cultures are as self-perpetuating as negative ones.

But he passionately rejects the notion that the modern, strife-free, family-friendly LSO can't play with the wild exhilaration of its forerunner:

The fact that the culture has changed hasn't altered the reality that there are a lot of star players in the LSO who take just as great risks as their precedessors. The difference is that they are totally committed to demanding the best of themselves and everyone else in everything they do.

It's hard to disentangle the truth from these essentially subjective impressions – if, indeed, there is a single 'truth' to be told about any organisation as complex and volatile as an orchestra. But there is undoubtedly a simmering jealousy of the LSO's extraordinary run of success under Gillinson's management in some quarters of the London music world. The orchestra has become the Manchester United of British music: a brand so big and powerful that it has no real competitors in its own country. Even the Arts Council, it seems, is oddly determined to preserve an 'egalitarian' funding policy towards all the London orchestras, even when one of of them is clearly of a world-class standard. Gillinson acknowledges the existence of this backlash:

Back in the 1980s, when the orchestra was in a bad way, the funny thing was that this didn't create many PR problems – because in Britain people seem to accept failure more readily than success. The minute you are up there, people want to pull you down.

Jealousy undoubtedly colours, perhaps even motivates, some of the spikier talk about the present LSO. But the LSO of today is manifestly not the same orchestra as the rambunctious boys' club that swaggered around the globe thirty years ago – just as Britain is not the same country. The musical world and the record business, too, have undergone profound transformations. That the LSO could run as long as it did with a philosophy and a management system basically unchanged since Edwardian days was a miracle – a triumph of bloody-minded determination over circumstance and logic. Sooner or later, though, the orchestra would have had to reform itself, or it would have perished. The second miracle is that it has somehow reformed itself so compellingly that it is now held up as the very model of the twenty-first-century orchestra, its tactics and innovations envied and emulated through much of the orchestral world.

Can it keep its nose ahead of the opposition? After all, London still has five full-time symphony orchestras and innumerable chamber outfits, all scrabbling for the same audience, the same sponsors, and the best new playing talent as it emerges from the music conservatoires. Gillinson declares:

As far as I am concerned we are not competing with the Philharmonia, the LPO, the Berlin Philharmonic or anybody else. You mustn't let other people define you. You have to do what you believe in, go for it hell for leather, and then move on before other people catch up. For the first time in the history of music there isn't a model for the future of the orchestra, we have to define it ourselves. But it's very scary – because in Britain there is never, ever, enough money to do any of this.

That's true – but there again, there never was. In any case, it is somebody else's problem now. In August 2004, twenty years after becoming the manager of the LSO and two months after masterminding its centenary gala, Gillinson announced that he was leaving the orchestra. Headhunted to run Carnegie Hall in New York, he had brushed aside American blandishments once, but accepted when a second approach was made. Nobody, inside or outside the LSO, thought Gillinson was wrong to accept such a different challenge after so long a period of loyal service to one organisation. Nevertheless, the news sent a shockwave through the British music scene. After two decades of unprecedented stability, the LSO would have to embark on its second century with a new hand on the rudder.

Chronology

1904   Founding of the LSO as Britain's first independent, self-governing orchestra: a limited company with the players as shareholders. Thomas Busby, horn player, becomes first Managing Director and Secretary and remains so for twenty years. Hans Richter is appointed Principal Conductor (1904–11).

1905   First provincial tour – Sir Edward Elgar conducts.

1906   First British orchestra to tour abroad, to Paris.

1908   First London performance of Elgar's First Symphony (second ever performance).

1911   Sir Edward Elgar becomes Principal Conductor (1911–12).

1912   Artur Nikisch is appointed Principal Conductor (1912–14). The LSO becomes the first British orchestra to visit the United States, conducted by Nikisch, and narrowly avoiding travelling on the *Titanic*.

1913–14 LSO makes its first recordings, for HMV, conducted by Nikisch.

1915   Sir Thomas Beecham is effectively Principal Conductor, although never officially given the title.

1918   Adrian Boult makes his first London appearance with the LSO.

1919   Albert Coates is appointed Principal Conductor (1919–22).

1920   Coates conducts first complete performance of Holst's *The Planets* at the Queen's Hall. LSO signs three-year contract with Columbia Gramophone Company.

1922   Walter Wanger from United Artists promotes series of super-films in Covent Garden Opera House, accompanied by the LSO and conducted by Eugene Goossens. Richard Strauss conducts recordings of his own works, including *Don Juan*. Prokofiev gives the first UK performance of his Third Piano Concerto, conducted by Coates.

1923   Koussevitzky conducts first performance of Mussorgsky/Ravel *Pictures at an Exhibition*. LSO purchases first instrument van from Ford for £200.

1924   LSO Board becomes fully elected and the Endowment Fund is created. First radio broadcast on the BBC from Southwark Cathedral: Vaughan Williams conducting his *Pastoral Symphony*.

1925   LSO's twenty-first birthday concert conducted by Elgar and Koussevitzky. Each member of the orchestra given a bonus of £20.

1927   Barbirolli makes his London début with the LSO.

1929   The LSO becomes a contracted permanent orchestra of seventy-five players, each with the guarantee of a specified number of performances over a three-year term. End of the 'deputy system'. Elgar undertakes a series of recordings of his own works with the LSO. Yehudi Menuhin makes his London début, aged twelve, with the Brahms Violin Concerto.

1930   Willem Mengelberg assumes duties of Principal Conductor (1930–1)

1932   Sir Hamilton Harty is appointed Principal Conductor (1932–5). Opening
of Abbey Road Studios: the LSO, conducted by Elgar, make the first
recordings there, including his Violin Concerto with Menuhin as soloist.
Prokofiev records his Third Piano Concerto with LSO.

1934   LSO records Sir Arthur Bliss's score (the first specifically composed for a
film recording) for *Things to Come*, a film based on H. G. Wells's book.
LSO opens first Glyndebourne season with *Le nozze di Figaro* conducted by Busch. First performance of Walton's Symphony No. 1 (first
three movements) conducted by Harty. The complete work is recorded
in 1935.

1940   Sir Henry Wood conducts the LSO in its first Prom season at the Queen's
Hall, renewing their association, and tours with the orchestra all over the
country during the war years.

1946   LSO performs in a film called *Instruments of the Orchestra* featuring the
première of Britten's *The Young Person's Guide to the Orchestra.* Samuel
Barber conducts his *Adagio for Strings* at the Three Choirs Festival.

1947   Benjamin Britten first conducts the LSO at the Norfolk and Norwich
Festival.

1948   The LSO is reconstituted as a non-profit-distributing concern in order to
qualify for more advantageous tax relief.

1950   Josef Krips is appointed Conductor-in-Chief (1950–4). Sibelius cycle with
Anthony Collins.

1951   LSO performs as the Royal Festival Hall is formally opened by
George VI.

1952   LSO's first television appearance, conducted by Sir Malcolm Sargent.

1954   LSO Jubilee Concert at the Royal Festival Hall – a repeat of the inaugural
concert conducted by Sir Malcolm Sargent, Anthony Collins, Basil
Cameron, George Weldon and Muir Mathieson.

1955   After a major policy crisis and a mass resignation of LSO principals, the
orchestra suddenly becomes a young and enthusiastic band with an average age of around thirty. BBC TV *Music for You* series begins.

1956   LSO becomes the first British orchestra to visit South Africa when it performs at the Johannesburg Festival.

1957   Stokowski conducts the LSO, returning to London after an absence of
thirty years.

1959   Colin Davis conducts the LSO for the first time at the Royal Festival Hall.
Beethoven series features London début of Glenn Gould playing all five
concertos.

1960   LSO International Series is initiated.

1961   Pierre Monteux becomes Principal Conductor at the age of eighty-six,
stipulating a twenty-five-year contract with a renewal clause (1961–4).

1963   Fiftieth anniversary performance of *The Rite of Spring* at the Royal Albert
Hall, conducted by Monteux in the presence of Stravinsky. Board of
Trustees is set up to receive and administer funds for the well-being and
financial stability of the orchestra.

Orchestra receives first-ever commercial sponsorship, from the Peter Stuyvesant Foundation, for playing and commissioning new works or appearing in unfamiliar venues.

LSO becomes first British orchestra to visit Japan, with Monteux, Doráti and Solti, accompanied by BBC TV and David Attenborough who make a *Monitor* programme about the tour.

1964   LSO makes its first world tour, to Israel, Turkey, Iran, India, Hong Kong, Korea, Japan and the United States where they gave a concert at the United Nations HQ in New York.

1965   István Kertész is appointed Principal Conductor (1965–8). Negotiations with Corporation of London regarding Barbican residency begin. Rostropovich cycle of thirty-one cello concertos in London and New York, conducted by Rozhdestvensky.

1966   First season as resident orchestra at the Florida International Festival. Bernstein conducts Mahler Symphony No. 8 at the Royal Albert Hall. Second world tour including Far East and Australia, conducted by Kertész and Colin Davis. Performances of Berlioz's *Les Troyens* with Colin Davis. London Symphony Chorus formed with John Alldis as chorus master

1967   LSO visits Florida again, this time accompanied by J. B. Priestley who writes about his experiences in the book *Trumpets over the Sea*.

1968   Previn's first concert as Principal Conductor: gala in aid of LSO Trust with Jacqueline du Pré. Previn spent an unprecedented eleven years as LSO Principal Conductor (1968–79).

1969   'Crossroads of Twentieth-Century Music' series with Pierre Boulez, which changed public attitudes towards contemporary music in Britain.

1971   Tour to Russia and the Far East (Previn and Britten). BBC TV presents *André Previn's Music Night* – the popular television series which brings the LSO to the attention of a huge new audience.

1972   Sixtieth anniversary of Stokowski's first appearance with the LSO – he repeats the programme of 1912.

1973   LSO is first British orchestra to be invited to perform at Salzburg Festival, conducted by Previn, Ozawa, and, for the first time, Karl Böhm. Britten's sixtieth-birthday concert at the Royal Albert Hall.

1975   The LSO Trust, in conjunction with the LPO, restores Holy Trinity Church in Southwark to become a much-needed rehearsal venue, Henry Wood Hall.

1976   First Shell LSO Music Scholarship and National Tour.

1977   Walton's seventy-fifth-birthday concert.

1978   Sergiu Celibidache returns to conduct after fifteen years. LSO shares in three Grammy awards for the score to *Star Wars*. *Classic Rock* recordings become hugely popular and provide handsome royalties.

1979   Claudio Abbado is appointed Principal Conductor and then Music Director (1979–88). LSO seventy-fifth birthday: gala concert at RFH in the presence of HRH The Prince of Wales. Tour to Russia with Sir Colin Davis.

1981   Carlos Kleiber conducts the LSO in Milan and London.

1982	Barbican Centre opens. LSO takes up first-ever London orchestral residency.
1984	Clive Gillinson becomes Managing Director. American LSO Foundation is formed. BBC TV documentary series *Life of an Orchestra*, produced by Jenny Barraclough.
1985	The highly successful 'Mahler, Vienna and the Twentieth Century' festival, masterminded by Claudio Abbado, heralds a new format for the LSO's concert-giving.
	Outside Directors are admitted to the Board for the first time, including a representative of the Arts Council.
1988	LSO establishes education policy and founding of LSO Discovery. Michael Tilson Thomas takes up the position of Principal Conductor (1988–95).
1989	LSO wins first-ever Royal Philharmonic Society Orchestral Award for 'excellence in playing and playing standards'. Concert performances of *Candide* with Leonard Bernstein.
1990	LSO visits Japan with Bernstein and Michael Tilson Thomas, creating the Pacific Music Festival in Sapporo – the first of its kind.
1991	Colin Matthews appointed Associate Composer. Enhanced Funding Award from the Arts Council matched by the Corporation of London, enabling 'joint-principal players policy' to be established.
1992	LSO wins five Gramophone awards, and shares Grammy award for *Candide*.
1993	LSO records *Concerto!* with Tilson Thomas – a major TV series made for Channel 4 with Dudley Moore, which wins an Emmy Award. Richard McNicol appointed as LSO's Music Animateur.
1994	LSO receives the first ever *Evening Standard* Classical Music Award for 'Outstanding Ensemble Performance'.
1995	Sir Colin Davis takes up position as Principal Conductor.
1997	Arts Council stabilisation award for new flexible membership conditions throughout the orchestra. Annual New York residency established – the first by a British orchestra.
1995	LSO website is launched.
1998	Online booking is established on the LSO website – the first British orchestra to offer this service.
1999–2000	Berlioz Odyssey: Sir Colin Davis conducts a series of all Berlioz's major works, including *The Trojans*.
2000	LSO Live is created. LSO wins Royal Philharmonic Society Award – the first orchestra to receive this award for a second time.
2002	LSO Live wins two Grammy Awards and a Classical Brit for the recording of *The Trojans* with Sir Colin Davis.
2003	LSO St Luke's, the UBS and LSO Music Education Centre, is opened. LSO Live sales top 250,000.
2004	LSO centenary year.

Holders of office

President

Lord Howard de Walden	1920s
Sir William Walton	1948–57
Sir Arthur Bliss	1958–74
Dr Karl Böhm	1977–81
Leonard Bernstein	1987–90

Principal Conductor

Hans Richter	1904–11
Sir Edward Elgar	1911–12
Artur Nikisch	1912–14
[Sir Thomas Beecham	1915–16]
Albert Coates	1919–22
[Willem Mengelberg	1930–1]
Sir Hamilton Harty	1932–5
Josef Krips	1950–4
Pierre Monteux	1961–4
István Kertész	1965–8
André Previn	1968–79
Claudio Abbado	1979–88
Michael Tilson Thomas	1988–95
Sir Colin Davis	1995–present

Leader

Arthur W. Payne	1904–12
William H. Reed	1912–36
George Stratton	1937–52
Thomas Matthews	1953–4
Granville Jones	1954–5
Hugh Maguire	1956–61
Erich Gruenberg	1962–5
John Georgiadis	1965–72
John Brown	1973–6
John Georgiadis/Neville Taweel	1977–8
John Georgiadis/Richard Studt	1978–9
Michael Davis	1979–86
Guest leaders	1987–9

Alexander Barantschik   1989–98
Alexander Barantschik/Gordan Nikolitch   1998–2001
Gordan Nikolitch   2001–present

Chairman

Ellis Roberts (violin)   1905–9
Edwin James (bassoon)   1909–21
Henri van der Meerschen (horn)   1922–32
William H. Reed (leader)   1932–42
Gordon Walker (flute/piccolo)   1945–9
Harry Dugarde (cello)   1949–60
Lowry Sanders (principal piccolo)   1961–2
Barry Tuckwell (principal horn)   1962–7
Jack Steadman (violin)   1968–70
Stuart Knussen (principal double bass)   1970–1
Howard Snell (principal trumpet)   1971–5
Anthony Camden (principal oboe)   1976–87
Terry Morton (violin)   1987–8
Lennox Mackenzie (sub-leader)   1988–92
John Lawley (oboe)   1992–9
Jonathan Vaughan (double bass)   1999–2002
Timothy Lines (principal clarinet)   2002–3
Patrick Harrild (principal tuba)   2003–present

Managing Director/ Secretary

Thomas Busby (horn)   1904–24 (Managing Director and Secretary)
Bertram Jones (violin)   1924–9   (Secretary)
Arthur Maney (cello)   1929–35 (Secretary)
W. G. Wood (double bass)   1935–44 (Secretary)
Gordon Walker (flute/piccolo)   1945–9   (Managing Director)
John Cruft (oboe/cor anglais)   1949–59 (Secretary)
Ernest Fleischmann   1959–67 (General Secretary)
Harold Lawrence   1968–73 (General Manager)
John Boyden   1974–5   (Managing Director)
Michael Kaye   1975–9   (Managing Director)
Peter Hemmings   1980–4   (Managing Director)
Clive Gillinson (cello)   1984–2005 (Managing Director)

First Performances given by the LSO

Conductor, soloist/s and other groups performing, where known, are listed in brackets. Asterisk indicates a commission. (PSF = Peter Stuyvesant Foundation, AC = Arts Council, FIF = Florida International Festival.)

1905   Elgar, *Introduction and Allegro for String Orchestra* (Elgar)
        first performance
1905   Elgar, *Pomp and Circumstance* March No. 3 (Elgar)
        first performance
1905   Saint-Saëns, *Caprice Andalous* (Colonne/Wolff)
        first performance
1905   Stanford, *Five Songs of the Sea* (Stanford/Plunket Greene)
        first London performance
1905   Stanford, Symphony No. 5 (Stanford)
        first London performance
1906   Bowen, *New Symphonic Fantasia* (Richter)
        first performance
1906   Lohr, *Songs from the Norseland* (Lohr/Rumford)
        first performance
1906   Mozart, 'Et incarnatus est' [Mass in C minor] (Sinclair)
        first London performance
1906   Stanford, Symphony No. 6 (Stanford)
        first performance
1906   Wynne, 'If Thou be Near' (Ronald/Braine)
        first performance
1907   Bantock, *The Witch of Atlas* (Ronald)
        first London performance
1907   Mackenzie, Violin Suite (Richter/Elman)
        first performance
1907   Massenet, *L'extase de la Vièrge* (Fiedler)
        first UK performance
1907   Metzl, *The Sunken Bell* (Safonoff)
        first UK performance
1907   Rimsky-Korsakov, *Christmas Eve* Suite (Safonoff)
        first UK performance
1907   Vaughan Williams, *Norfolk Rhapsody* No. 2 (Vaughan Williams)
        first performance
1907   Vaughan Williams, *Norfolk Rhapsody* No. 3 (Vaughan Williams)
        first performance
1908   Arbos, *Noche de Arabia* (Arbos)

first performance
1908   J. D. Davis, *The Maid of Astolat* (Ronald)
first London performance
1908   Delius, *A Dance of Life* (Arbos)
first performance
1908   Elgar, Symphony No. 1 (Richter)
first London performance
1908   Stojowski, *Rhapsodie Symphonique* in D (Mlynarski)
first London performance
1909   W. H. Bell, *The Ballad of the Bird-bride* (Richter)
first performance
1909   Delius, *Dance Rhapsody* No. 1 (Delius)
first performance
1909   Karlowicz, *Odwieczne Piesni* [World-old songs] (Mlynarski)
first London performance
1909   Maclean, *The Annunciation* (Maclean)
first performance
1909   Paderewski, Symphony in B minor (Richter)
first UK performance
1909   Sinigaglia, Overture: *Le Baruffe Chiozzotte* (Nikisch)
first London performance
1909   Haydn Wood, Piano Concerto in D minor
first performance
1910   Adam von Ahn Carse, Symphony No. 2 (Nikisch)
first London performance
1910   C. P. E. Bach, orch. Steinberg, Concerto in D (Koussevitzky)
first UK performance
1910   Bantock, *Omar Khayyám* (Fagge)
first complete performance
1910   Henry Coates, *Nocturne for Orchestra* (Safonoff)
first London performance
1910   Elgar, Three Songs from a New Cycle (Elgar/Foster)
first performance
1910   Holbrooke, Piano Concerto (Holbrooke/Bauer)
first performance
1910   Hans Huber, Piano Concerto in D (Safonoff/Lochbrunner)
first performance
1910   Skryabin, *Poem of Ecstasy* (Koussevitzky)
first UK performance
1910   Vaughan Williams, *Fantasia on a Theme of Thomas Tallis*
(Vaughan Williams)
first performance
1910   Vaughan Williams, *A Sea Symphony* [Symphony No. 1] (Vaughan Williams)
first performance
1911   Cowen, *The Veil* (Cowen)
first London performance

1911	Elgar, Symphony No. 2 (Elgar) third and fourth performances
1911	Elgar, Violin Concerto (Nikisch/Kreisler) third performance
1911	Vaughan Williams, *Five Mystical Songs* (Vaughan Williams) first performance
1912	Holbrooke, *The Raven*: symphonic poem (Holbrooke) first performance of revised version
1912	Ippolitoff-Ivanoff, *Dans l'Aoul et Cortège du Sardar* (Safonoff) first London performance
1912	Rimsky-Korsakov, *Russian Easter Festival*: overture in D (Safonoff) first UK performance
1912	Vaughan Williams, *Fantasia on Christmas Carols* (Vaughan Williams) first performance
1912	Wagner, *Der Ring des Nibelungen* (Riseley) first complete British concert performance
1913	Butterworth, *A Shropshire Lad*: rhapsody for full orchestra (Nikisch) first performance
1913	Elgar, *Falstaff* (Elgar) first performance
1913	Glazunov, *Spring*; symphonic picture (Safonoff) first UK performance
1913	Henry Hadley, *Overture in Bohemia* (Hadley) first UK performance
1913	Henry Hadley, *Symphonic Fantasie* in E flat (Hadley) first UK performance
1913	Henry Hadley, Symphony No. 2 (Hadley) first UK performance
1913	Harty, *The Mystic Trumpeter* (Harty/Bates) first performance
1913	Harty, *Variations on an Irish Theme* for violin (Harty/Kochanski) first London performance
1913	Basil Harwood, *On a May Morning* (Harwood) first performance
1913	Ethel Smyth, *On the Road* (Nikisch/Heyner) first performance
1913	Somervell, Symphony in D minor, 'Thalassa' (Nikisch) first performance
1913	Stojowski, Piano Concerto No. 2 (Nikisch/Stojowski) first London performance
1914	Elgar, *Carillon* (Elgar) first performance
1914	Glazunov, *Oriental Dance* No. 6 (Camilieri) first performance
1914	Wagner, *Parsifal* (Fagge) first performance in English by English artists

1915	Delius, *North Country Sketches* (Beecham) first performance
1915	Elgar, *Polonia* (Elgar) first performance
1915	O'Neill, *Humoresque* (Mlynarski) first performance
1915	Montague Phillips, *Heroic Overture* (Mlynarski) first performance
1915	Cyril Scott, Piano Concerto (Mlynarski/Scott) first performance
1915	Donald Tovey, Symphony in D (Verbrugghen) first performance
1916	Elgar, *The Spirit of England* (Elgar) first London performance of second and third movements
1917	Bantock, *Hebridean Symphony* (Harty) first London performance
1917	De Greef, Piano Concerto (Harty/de Greef) first UK performance
1918	O. H. Gotch, Scherzo from Symphony 'In Memoriam' (Boult) first performance
1918	David Piggott, *Pavane and Morris Dance* (Boult) first London performance
1918	Ravel, *Shéhérazade* (Boult) first London performance
1918	Vaughan Williams, London Symphony (Boult) first performance of first revised version
1918	R. T. Woodman, *New Forest Rhapsody* (Boult) first London performance
1919	Elgar, Cello Concerto (Elgar/Salmond) first performance
1919	Mussorgsky, Field Marshall Death [*Songs and Dances of Death*] (Coates) first UK performance
1919	Rimsky-Korsakov, *Sadko* (Coates) first UK performance
1919	Rimsky-Korsakov, Vakoula's Air [*Christmas Eve*] (Coates) first UK performance
1920	Georges d'Orlay, *Flamma Artis* (Coates) first performance
1920	Holst, *The Planets* (Coates) first performance
1920	Cyril Jenkins, *The Magic Cauldron* (Coates) first performance
1920	Vaughan Williams, *Four Hymns* (Vaughan Williams) first performance
1920	Vaughan Williams, *A London Symphony* [Symphony No. 2] (Coates) first performance, second revised version

1921   D'Erlanger, *Concerto symphonique* for piano and orchestra (Coates/Moisewitsch)
        first performance

1921   O'Connor Morris, *Two Pieces on Irish Folk Tunes* (O'Connor Morris)
        first performance

1921   W. H. Reed, *Elegy* for organ and strings (Coates)
        first performance

1921   Szymanowski, Symphony No. 3, 'Song of the Night' (Coates)
        first UK performance

1922   Bax, Symphony No. 1 (Coates)
        first performance

1922   Bliss, *A Colour Symphony* (Bliss)
        first performance

1922   Roger-Ducasse, *Orphée* (Coates)
        first UK performance

1922   Holst, *Ode to Death* (Coates)
        first performance

1922   Prokofiev, Piano Concerto No. 3 (Coates/Prokofiev)
        first UK performance

1922   Respighi, *Ballad of the Gnomes* (Coates)
        first English performance

1923   Berners, Three Orchestral Pieces (Buesst)
        first London performance

1923   Buesst, Scherzo from Symphony: *Queen Bess* (Buesst)
        first performance

1923   Goossens, Sinfonietta (Goossens)
        first performance

1923   Holst, *Festival Te Deum* (Vaughan Williams)
        first London performance

1923   Mussorgsky/Ravel, *Pictures at an Exhibition* (Koussevitzky)
        first UK performance

1923   Warlock, Three Carols (Vaughan Williams)
        first performance

1923   Gerrard Williams, Three Preludes (Coates)
        first performance

1924   Boccherini, *Miniature Symphony* (Koussevitzky)
        first London performance

1924   Holbrooke, *The Birds of Rhiannon* (Goossens)
        first London performance

1925   Holst, *Choral Symphony* (Coates)
        first performance

1925   Respighi, *Pines of Rome* (Coates)
        first London performance

1925   Tcherepnin, Sinfonietta in C (Coates)
        first performance

1925   Whittaker, *A Lyke-Wake Dirge* (Vaughan Williams)

263

first London performance

1926 Vaughan Williams, *Sancta Civitas* (Vaughan Williams)
first London performance

1927 W. H. Reed, *Rhapsody* for viola and orchestra (Beecham/Tertis)
first performance

1927 Schelling, *A Victory Ball* (Blech)
first London performance

1928 Kurt Atterberg, Symphony (Beecham)
first London performance

1929 Bax, *Serenade*
first performance

1929 Bliss, *Serenade* for orchestra and voice (Klemperer/Henderson)
first performance

1929 Bruckner, Symphony No. 8 (Klemperer)
first London performance

1929 Rachmaninov, Piano Concerto No. 4 (Coates/Rachmaninov)
first London performance

1929 Szymanowski, Violin Concerto
first UK performance

1930 Elgar, Pomp and Circumstance March No. 5 (Elgar)
first performance

1930 Hindemith, Overture: *Neues vom Tag* (Sargent)
first UK performance

1930 Hindemith, Viola Concerto No. 2 (Sargent/Hindemith)
first UK performance

1930 Vaughan Williams, Prelude and Fugue in C (Vaughan Williams)
first performance

1930 Bernard Wagenaar, Sinfonietta (Mengelberg)
first London performance

1931 Beethoven, Sonata in B flat, orch. Weingartner (Weingartner)
first UK performance

1931 Stravinsky, *Capriccio* for piano and orchestra (Sargent/Stravinsky)
first UK performance

1931 Stravinsky, *Firebird* suite No. 2 (1919) (Stravinsky)
first UK performance

1931 Walton, *Belshazzar's Feast* (Sargent)
first performance

1932 J. S. Bach arr. Graeser, *Die Kunst der Fuge* (Weisbach)
first UK performance

1932 Bax, Overture: *A Picaresque Comedy* (Harty)
first London performance

1932 Delius, *Songs of Farewell* (Sargent/Philharmonic Choir)
first performance

1932 Stravinsky, *Symphony of Psalms* (Sargent/Bach Choir)
first UK performance

1932 Stravinsky, Violin Concerto (Sargent/Dushkin)

first UK performance

1932   Vaughan Williams, *Magnificat* (Vaughan Williams/Desmond)
first performance

1933   Gershwin, *Rhapsody* No. 2 for piano and orchestra (Harty/Solomon)
first London performance

1933   W. H. Reed, Symphony for Strings (Harty)
first London performance

1933   Respighi, Overture: *Belfagor* (Harty)
first London performance

1934   Bax, Cello Concerto (Harty/Cassadó)
first performance

1934   Glazunov, *Le Kremlin* (Harty)
first London performance

1934   Sibelius, Three Pieces for violin and orchestra (Harty/Lambert)
first UK performance

1934   Walton, Symphony No. 1 [first three movements] (Harty)
first performance

1934   Leó Weiner, *Hungarian Folk Dances*, op. 18 (Harty)
first performance

1934   Leó Weiner, *Prinz Csongor und die Kobolde* (Harty)
first UK performance

1935   Bizet, Symphony in C (Harty)
first London performance

1935   Fauré, Requiem (Boulanger/French choir)
first UK performance

1936   Albert Coates, *Pickwick* (Coates)
first performance

1936   Albert Coates, *The Defence of Guinevere* (Coates)
first UK performance

1936   Quilter, *The Wild Boar*
first performance

1936   Vaughan Williams, *Two Hymn-Tune Preludes* (Hull)
first performance

1937   Dyson, Symphony in G (Dyson)
first performance

1937   Vaughan Williams, Introduction and Scene from *The Poisoned Kiss*
first concert performance

1938   Vaughan Williams, *Serenade to Music* (Wood)
first performance

1940   Lennox Berkeley, *Introduction and Allegro* for two pianos (Wood/
Berkeley/Gluck)
first performance

1940   W. H. Harris, Overture: *Once upon a Time* (Wood)
first performance

1940   Theodore Holland, *Ellingham Marshes*, poem for viola and orchestra
(Cameron/Winifred Copperwheat)

first performance
1940 Lutyens, Three Pieces (Wood)
first performance
1940 Nettlefold, Suite for Strings (Hambourg)
first performance
1940 W. H. Reed, Overture: *Merry Andrew* (Reed)
first performance
1940 Alec Rowley, Concerto in F for harpsichord and orchestra (Wood)
first performance
1940 Vaughan Williams, *Serenade to Music* [orchestral version] (Wood)
first performance
1941 Vaughan Williams, *49th Parallel Prelude* (Mathieson)
first performance
1942 Tippett, *Fantasia on a Theme of Handel* (Goehr/Sellick)
first performance
1943 Britten, *Matinées Musicales*, Suite No. 2 (Fistoulari)
first performance
1943 Kabalevsky, Piano Concerto (Fistoulari/Cohen)
first performance
1944 Alwyn, *Concerto Grosso* (Mathieson)
first London performance
1944 Albert Coates, *Russian Suite* in five movements (Coates)
first performance
1944 Kabalevsky, Symphony No. 2 (Coates)
first UK performance
1944 Prokofiev, *Lieutenant Kijé* (Fistoulari)
first concert performance in England
1944 Shostakovich, *The Golden Age*: ballet suite (Boult)
first UK performance
1945 Alan Bush, *Fantasy on Soviet Themes* (Bush)
first performance
1945 Hindemith, *Cupid and Psyche*: ballet overture (Cameron)
first UK performance
1945 Martinů, *Memorial to Lidiče* (Cameron)
first UK performance
1945 Thomas Tertius Noble, *Introduction and Passacaglia* (Cameron)
first London performance
1945 Vaughan Williams, *Story of a Flemish Farm*: suite (Mathieson)
first performance
1946 Arnold, Divertimento No. 1
first performance
1946 Bax, *Northern Ballad* No. 2 (Cameron)
first performance
1946 Vaughan Williams, Concerto for Two Pianos and Orchestra
(Boult/Smith/Sellick)
first performance

1946   Britten, *The Young Person's Guide to the Orchestra* [for film: *Instruments of the Orchestra*] (Sargent)
first performance

1947   Bartók, *Mikrokosmos* Suite, arr. Serly
first UK performance

1948   Elizalde, Piano Concerto (Poulet/Elizalde)
first UK performance

1948   Moeran, Serenade in G (Cameron)

1949   Alwyn, Concerto for Oboe and Strings (Cameron/Rothwell)
first performance

1949   Finzi, Concerto for Clarinet and Strings (Finzi/Thurston)
first performance

1950   Alwyn, *Concerto Grosso* No. 2 (Sargent)
first performance

1950   Britten, Diversions on a Theme for Piano [left hand] (Sargent/Wittgenstein)
first London performance

1950   Ravel, *Ma mère l'oye* [complete ballet music]
first concert performance

1950   Vaughan Williams, *Fantasia on the 'Old 104th' Psalm Tune* (Vaughan Williams)
first performance

1950   Vaughan Williams, *Folk Songs of the Four Seasons* (Boult)
first performance

1951   Alwyn, *Festival March* (Sargent)
first orchestral performance

1951   Dello Joio, Suite: *New York Profiles* (Sokoloff)
first European performance

1951   Rawsthorne, Piano Concerto No. 2 (Sargent/Curzon)
first performance

1952   Bliss, Scena: *The Enchantress* (Rignold/Ferrier)
first London performance

1952   Adrian Cruft, *Interlude* (Stratton)
first London performance

1952   Fricker, Symphony No. 2 (Rignold)
first London performance

1952   Fricker, *Three Sonnets of Cecco Angiolieri* (Weldon/Fricker)
first performance

1952   Messiaen, *Turangalîla-symphonie* (Goehr)
first British performance

1952   Milhaud, Cello Concerto No. 2 (Blech/Kurtz)
first UK performance

1952   Moule-Evans, Symphony (Sargent)
first UK performance

1952   Roussel, Suite in F (Poulet)
first London performance

1952   Humphrey Searle, *The Shadow of Cain* (Searle)
first performance

1952	Stravinsky, *Circus Polka* (Weldon)
	first UK performance
1953	Walton, Coronation March: *Orb and Sceptre*
	first concert performance
1953	Alwyn, Symphony No. 1 (Barbirolli)
	first London performance
1953	Andriessen, *Ricercare* (van Beinum)
	first London performance
1953	Collins, Violin Concerto (Collins/Kaufmann)
	first English performance
1953	Elizalde, Sinfonia Concertante (Elizalde)
	first English performance
1953	Falla, *Seven Popular Spanish Songs* (Elizalde/Iriarte)
	first London performance
1953	Richard Strauss, Symphonic fragment, *The Legend of Joseph* (Goossens)
	first London performance
1954	Boccherini, Symphony No. 2 (Previtali)
	first London performance
1954	Finzi, *Grand Fantasia and Toccata* (Russell)
	first London performance
1954	Fricker, Piano Concerto (Boult/Cohen)
	first performance
1954	Havergal Brian, Symphony No. 11 (Newstone)
	first performance
1954	Serge Lancen, Concertino for Piano and Orchestra (Raybould/Iles)
	first English performance
1954	Vaughan Williams, Concerto for Bass Tuba (Barbirolli/Catelinet)
	first performance
1954	Vaughan Williams, *Hodie* (Vaughan Williams)
	first performance
1954	Veale, Clarinet Concerto (Sargent/Fell)
	first performance
1955	Alwyn, *The Magic Island* (Rignold)
	first London performance
1955	Stanley Bate, Symphony No. 3 (Groves)
	first London performance
1955	Humphrey Searle, *The Riverrun* (Scherchen)
	first London performance
1955	Veale, Overture: *The Metropolis* (Groves)
	first performance
1956	Copland, Suite: *The Red Pony* (Herrmann)
	first London performance
1956	Mahler, *Das klagende Lied* (Goehr)
	first UK performance
1956	Prokofiev, Overture: *War and Peace* (Goehr)
	first UK performance

1956   Russell Bennett, Violin Concerto [revised version] (Herrmann/Kaufmann)
        first performance

1956   Phyllis Tate, *Occasional Overture* (Herrmann)
        first performance

1957   Menotti, *Sebastian*: ballet suite (Schippers)
        first English performance

1957   Rankl, Symphony No. 5 (Rankl)
        first London performance

1957   Franz Reizenstein, *Voices of Night* (Krips)
        first London performance

1960   Goehr, *Four Songs from the Japanese* (Colin Davis/Phillips)
        first performance

1961   Britten, 'Carmen Basilienese' [*Cantata academica*] (Malcolm)
        first London performance

1962   Fricker, *Vision of Judgement* (Willcocks)
        first London performance

1962   Goehr, Violin Concerto (Boult/Parikian)
        first performance

1962   Nono, Cantata: *On the Bridge at Hiroshima* (Pritchard)
        first performance

1962   Stravinsky, *Greeting Prelude* (Colin Davis)
        first London performance

1963   Khachaturian, Concerto-Rhapsody for Cello and Orchestra
        (Hurst/Rostropovich)
        first performance

1963   Goehr, *Little Symphony* (Del Mar)
        first performance

1963   Henze, Symphony No. 5 (Henze)
        first UK performance

1963   Stravinsky, *Eight Instrumental Miniatures* (Colin Davis)
        first UK performance

1963   Tippett, *Concerto for Orchestra* (Colin Davis)
        first performance

1964   Copland, *Music for a Great City* (Copland)
        first performance *LSO

1964   Henze, *Ariosi* (Colin Davis)
        first performance

1965   Britten, *Voices for Today* (Kertész)
        first performance

1965   Khrennikov, Cello Concerto (Rozhdestvensky/Rostropovich)
        first London performance

1965   Myaskovsky, Cello Concerto (Rozhdestvensky/Rostropovich)
        first London performance

1965   Sauguet, Cello Concerto in C minor (Rozhdestvensky/Rostropovich)
        first London performance

1965   Boris Tchaikovsky, Cello Concerto in E major (Rozhdestvensky/

Rostropovich)
first London performance

1966   Banks, Horn Concerto (Colin Davis/Tuckwell)
first performance   *LSO

1966   Richard Rodney Bennett, Symphony (Kertész)
first performance   *LSO

1967   Bernstein, Symphony No. 1, 'Jeremiah' (Ozawa)
first UK performance

1967   Carrillo, *Horizontes* (Ozawa)
first UK performance

1967   Michael Haydn, Horn Concerto in D (Colin Davis/Tuckwell)
first UK performance

1967   Shostakovich, Violin Concerto No. 2 (Ormandy/Oistrakh)
first Western performance

1967   Takemitsu, *Requiem for Strings* (Ozawa)
first UK performance

1967   Xenakis, *Eonta* (Ozawa)
first London performance

1968   Lennox Berkeley, *Magnificat* (Colin Davis)
first performance

1968   Copland, *Inscape* [1967] (Copland)
first UK performance

1968   Knussen, Symphony No. 1 (Knussen)
first performance

1969   Richard Rodney Bennett, Symphony No. 2 (Previn)
first UK performance *LSO/PSF

1969   Del Tredici, *Lobster Quadrille* [*Alice in Wonderland*] (Copland)
first performance

1969   Havergal Brian, Symphony No. 14 (Downes)
first performance

1969   Knussen, *Concerto for Orchestra* (Knussen)
first performance   *FIF

1969   Knussen, *Tributum* (del Mar)
first performance

1969   Nono, Suite: *Intolleranza* (Abbado)
first performance

1969   Roussel, *Padmâvatî* (Martinon)
first UK performance

1969   Skalkottas, *Return of Ulysses* (Doráti)
first performance

1969   Webern, Three Pieces (Boulez)
first UK performance

1970   Benjamin Frankel, Symphony No. 7 (Previn)
first performance   *LSO/PSF

1970   Hoddinott, *The Sun, the Great Luminary of the Universe* (Handley)
first performance

1970	Josephs, *Variations on a Theme of Beethoven* (Previn) first UK performance
1970	Mahler, 'Waldmarchen' [*Das klagende Lied*] (Boulez) first UK performance, complete 1880 version
1970	Newson, *Twenty Seven Days* (Downes) first performance *LSO/PSF
1970	Previn, Cello Concerto (Previn/Cummings) first UK performance
1971	Henze, Symphony No. 6 (Henze) first London performance
1971	McCabe, *Notturni ed Alba* (Previn/Armstrong) first London performance
1971	Paganini, Violin Concerto No. 3 (Gibson/Szeryng) first London performance
1971	Previn, Guitar Concerto (Previn/Williams) first performance
1971	Shankar, Concerto for Sitar and Orchestra (Previn/Shankar) first performance *LSO
1971	Shostakovich, Symphony No. 13, 'Babi Yar' (Previn) first London performance
1972	Bernstein, *Three Orchestral Meditations* [from *Mass*] (Tilson Thomas) first UK performance
1972	Maw, *Odyssey* first performance of first version *LSO/AC/BBC
1972	Petrassi, *Concerto for Orchestra* No. 8 (Giulini) first UK performance
1972	Prokofiev, *Pushkiniana* (Previn) first Western performance
1972	Ruggles, *Evocations* first UK performance
1972	Tippett, Symphony No. 3 (Colin Davis/Harper) first performance *LSO
1972	John T. Williams, Symphony No. 1 (Previn) first London performance
1973	Bliss, *Metamorphic Variations* (Stokowski) first performance
1973	Gerhard, *Metamorphoses* (Atherton) first performance
1973	Penderecki, Symphony No. 1 (Penderecki) first performance *Perkins Engines
1973	William Schuman, *In Praise of Shahn* (Previn) first UK performance
1973	Simpson, Symphony No. 5 (Andrew Davis) first performance *LSO
1974	David Lord, *Incantare* (Soustrot) first performance *Rupert Foundation

1976	Crosse, *Epiphany Variations*
	first performance
1976	Panufnik, *Sinfonia di Sfere* (Atherton)
	first performance
1976	Walton, *Varii capricci* (Previn)
	first performance
1977	McCabe, *Jubilee Prelude* (Previn)
	first performance *for Queen's Silver Jubilee
1977	Previn, *Every Good Boy Deserves Favour* (Previn)
	first performance
1977	Rochberg, Concerto for Violin and Orchestra (Previn/Stern)
	first UK performance
1978	Legrand, Violin Concerto (Legrand/Gitlis)
	first performance
1979	Ferneyhough, *La terre est un homme* (Abbado)
	first London performance
1979	Panufnik, *Concerto Festivo* (Previn)
	first performance *LSO for 75th anniversary
1979	Svetlanov, *Rhapsody* No. 2 for large orchestra (Svetlanov)
	first European performance
1980	Tippett, Triple Concerto (Colin Davis/Pauk/Imai/Kirschbaum)
	first performance *RVW Trust
1980	John T. Williams, Flute Concerto (Previn/Lloyd)
	first UK performance
1980?	Panufnik, Concertino for Percussion and Strings (Previn/Thomas/Prentice)
	first performance *Shell/LSO
1982	Michael Berkeley, *Or Shall We Die?* (Hickox/LSChorus)
	first performance *LSC/Arts Council
1982	Britten, *Men of Goodwill*: Variations on a Christmas Carol (Marriner)
	first concert performance
1982	Grieg, Symphony in C minor (Dreier)
	first UK performance
1982	Henze, *Barcarola* (Henze)
	first UK performance
1982	Mayer, *Shivanataraj* (Del Mar)
	first performance *LSO/Arts Council
1982	Zamfir, *Rumanian Rhapsody* for pan-flute and orchestra (Dods/Zamfir)
	first performance
1983	Corigliano, Flute Concerto, 'Pied Piper Fantasy' (Chung/Galway)
	first London performance
1984	Bourgeois, *Fantasy for Fireworks and Orchestra* (Simon)
	first performance
1984	George Lloyd, Piano Concerto No. 4 (Lloyd/Stott)
	first performance
1984	Panufnik, Concertino for Timpani and Percussion

(Panufnik/Thomas/Prentice)
first performance

1985 Nono, *A Carla Scarpa architetto* (Abbado)
first UK performance

1985 Tommy Steele, *Portrait of Pablo* (Hickox)
first performance

1985 Tchaikovsky, Symphony No. 2, 'Little Russian' [1872 version] (Simon)
first Western performance

1988 Lukas Foss, *Renaissance Concerto* (Zinman/Galway)
first UK performance

1988 Steve Gray, Guitar Concerto (Colin Davis/Williams)
first performance

1988 Knussen, *Flourish with Fireworks* (Tilson Thomas)
first performance *LSO (for MTT's first concert as Principal Conductor)

1988 Robert Saxton, *In the Beginning* (Tate)
first performance

1989 Hoddinott, Cello Concerto, 'Noctis Equi' (Nagano/Rostropovich)
first performance *LSO

1989 Colin Matthews, *Quatrain* (Tilson Thomas)
first performance *LSO

1989 Rimsky-Korsakov, *Mlada* (Tilson Thomas)
first UK performance

1990 McCabe, Flute Concerto (Tilson Thomas/Galway)
first performance *LSO

1991 Colin Matthews, *Machines and Dreams* (Tilson Thomas)
first performance *LSO

1991 Takemitsu, Double Piano Concerto (Tilson Thomas/Serkin/Crossley)
first performance *LSO

1991 Tavener, *The Repentant Thief* (Tilson Thomas/Marriner)
first performance *LSO

1991 Wiegold, *Soft Shoe Shuffle* (Wiegold)
first performance *LSO

1992 Colin Matthews, *Hidden Variables* (Tilson Thomas)
first performance *LSO/New World SO

1992 Muldowney, Oboe Concerto (Tilson Thomas/Carter)
first performance *LSO

1992 Panufnik, Cello Concerto (Wolff/Rostropovich)
first performance *LSO

1993 Artyomov, Symphony No. 3 (Rostropovich)
first UK performance *LSO

1993 Colin Matthews, *Memorial* (Rostropovich)
first performance *LSO

1993 Robert Saxton, Cello Concerto (Knussen/Rostropovich)
first performance *LSO

1994 Adams, Violin Concerto (Nagano/Kremer)
first performance *LSO

1994	Bingham, *The Red-Hot Nail* (McNicol) first performance *LSO
1994	Ellis, *These Exalted Birds* (Nagano) first performance *LSO
1994	MacMillan, *Britannia* (Tilson Thomas) first performance *LSO
1994	Schnittke, Triple Concerto (Kremer/Bashmet/Rostropovich) first UK performance *LSO
1994	Shchedrin, Cello Concerto (Ozawa/Rostropovich) first performance *LSO
1994	Tavener, *The Myrrh Bearer* (Westrop/Bashmet/LSChorus) first performance *LSO
1995	Kirchner, *Music for Cello and Orchestra* (Kirchner/Yo Yo Ma) first UK performance
1995	Maxwell Davies, *The Three Kings* (Hickox/LSChorus) first performance *LSC/LSO
1995	Messiaen, *Concert à Quatre* (Nagano) first UK performance
1995	Schnittke, *Concerto Grosso* No. 5 (Tilson Thomas/Kremer) first UK performance
1995	Shapero, *Concerto for Classical Orchestra* (Previn) first UK performance
1995	Takemitsu, *Ceremonial* (Tilson Thomas) first UK performance
1995	Tippett, The Rose Lake (Colin Davis) first performance *LSO
1996	Holloway, *Concerto for Orchestra* No. 3 (Tilson Thomas) first performance *LSO
1996	MacMillan, Cello Concerto (Colin Davis/Rostropovich) first performance *LSO
1996	MacMillan, *The World's Ransoming* (Nagano/Pendrill) first performance *LSO/Benjamin Family/Eastern Orchestral Board
1996	Colin Matthews, Cello Concerto (Colin Davis/Rostropovich) first performance *LSO
1997	Bernstein, *A White House Cantata* (Nagano) first performance
1997	Bingham, *The Mysteries of Adad* first performance
1997	Hellawell, *Do Not Disturb* (Colin Davis/Finchley Children's Music Group) first performance *FCMG/LSO
1997	MacMillan, Symphony, 'Vigil' (Rostropovich) first performance *LSO
1997	Paul McCartney, *Standing Stone* first performance

1997 Montague/Shapcott, *The Creatures Indoors* (Placidi/Luxom)
   first performance *LSO/BT

1997 Sohal, *Satyagraha* (Mehta)
   first performance

1998 Adams, Piano Concerto, 'Century Rolls' (Adams/Ax)
   first UK performance

1998 Michael Berkeley, *Secret Garden* (Colin Davis)
   first performance

1998 Cashian, *Night Journeys* (Howarth/Percy/Carrington)
   first performance *LSO

1998 Previn, Violin Sonata (Previn/Barantschik)
   first European performance

1998 Rouse, *Der gerettete Alberich* (Alsop/Glennie)
   first European performance *LSO

1999 Gubaidulina, *Canticle of the Sun* (Numajiri/Rostropovich/London Voices)
   first UK performance

1999 Leach, *Inoh' Pokak* (McNicol)
   first performance *LSO

1999 Maazel, *Music for Violin and Orchestra* (Gieron/Maazel)
   first UK performance

1999 Penderecki, Symphony No. 5 (Penderecki)
   first UK performance

1999 Penderecki, Violin Concerto (Colin Davis/Mutter)
   first UK performance

1999 Shchedrin, *Concerto Cantabile* (Rostropovich/Vengerov)
   first UK performance

2000 Benjamin, *Palimpsest* (Boulez)
   first performance *LSO

2000 Eötvös, *zeroPoints* (Boulez)
   first performance

2000 Maazel, *Music for Cello and Orchestra* (Maazel/Rostropovich)
   first UK performance

2000 Maazel, *The Empty Pot* (Maazel/Irons)
   first performance

2000 March, *A Stirring in the Heavenlies* (Hickox)
   first performance *LSO

2000 Neuwirth, *Clinamen/Nodus* (Boulez)
   first performance *LSO

2000 Sciarrino, *Recitativo oscuro* (Boulez/Pollini)
   first performance *LSO

2002 Benjamin, Palimpsest (Parts I and II) (Benjamin)
   first performance *LSO

2002 Kancheli, *Two Great Slava from Two GKs* (Jansons/Kremer)
   first performance *LSO

2002 Previn, Violin Concerto (Previn/Mutter)
   first European performance

2002	Peter Weiner, *Happy Birthday Variations* [for Rostropovich] (Jansons/Welch) first performance *LSO
2003	Benjamin, *Shadowlines* (Benjamin) first performance
2003	Cole, *Penumbra* (Benjamin) first performance
2003	MacMillan, *A Deep But Dazzling Darkness* (MacMillan) first performance *LSO
2003	Previn, *A Streetcar Named Desire* (Previn) first UK performance
2004	Richard Bissill, Concertante for Trumpet, Horn and Clarinet first performance *LSO Centenary
2004	Karl Jenkins, Concertante for Flute, Piano and Percussion first performance *LSO Centenary
2004	Dmitri Smirnov, Concertante for Violin, Harp and Double Bass first performance *LSO Centenary
2004	Huw Watkins, Concertante for Bassoon, Violin and Harp first performance *LSO Centenary

The LSO has endeavoured to compile this list as accurately as possible. However, we would be grateful to hear of any corrections or additions – please write to Libby Rice, LSO Archivist, Barbican, London EC2Y 8DS (tel. 020 7588 1116) or email *archives@lso.co.uk*.

Film Scores performed and recorded by the LSO

In 1922 a series of silent films was shown at the Royal Opera House, Covent Garden. The scores for these were compiled by Eugene Goossens who used a variety of obscure classical music, in particular the work of August Enna. The LSO was engaged to play these scores and others that included:

1922   *The Three Musketeers* (starring Douglas Fairbanks, Snr.)
1924   *The Nibelungs* (a short German film)
1927   *The Constant Nymph*
1929   *The Life of Beethoven*

The LSO's earliest on screen credit was probably for *Eight Million*. When the producer Michael Dillon wrote in September 1934 asking permission to use the orchestra's name in his documentary, the Board of Directors agreed 'that it would be good publicity for the orchestra', but they also resolved to ask for more than the fifteen guineas offered as a fee.

The first symphonic music specifically composed for a particular film recording was Sir Arthur Bliss's score for *Things To Come*, for Alexander Korda's 1935 film based on the book by H. G. Wells. Muir Mathieson conducted the LSO for the recording, as he did for all the London Films made at Denham by Alexander Korda, which included:

1935   *Sanders of the River* (music by Mischa Spoliansky)
1937   *Elephant Boy* (music by John Greenwood)
1939   *The Four Feathers* (music by Miklós Rózsa)

In the 1940s and 1950s the orchestra recorded the music for a number of documentaries for the Crown Film Unit, Service Film Units, Ministry of Information and others, including:

1940	*Music for the People*	classical (Henry Wood)
1943	*The People's Land*	Vaughan Williams (Muir Mathieson)
1943	*Health of a Nation*	David Moule Evans (Muir Mathieson)
1944	*London Terminus*	Horace Somerville (Muir Mathieson)
1944	*Salute the Soldier*	Eric Coates (Joe Batten)
1944	*Out of Chaos*	Lennox Berkeley (Muir Mathieson)
1944	*Men of Rochdale*	John Greenwood (Muir Mathieson)
1944	*Song of the People*	Mischa Spoliansky (Muir Mathieson)
1945	*The Second Freedom*	Hubert Clifford (Muir Mathieson)

1945	*Stricken Peninsula*	Vaughan Williams (Muir Mathieson)
1945	*Burma Victory*	Alan Rawsthorne (John Hollingsworth)
1946	*A Diary for Timothy*	Richard Addinsell (Muir Mathieson)
1946	*The Way We Live*	Gordon Jacob (Muir Mathieson)
1946	*Instruments of the Orchestra (Young Person's Guide to the Orchestra)*	
		Benjamin Britten (Malcolm Sargent)
1947	*Avalanche Patrol*	Malcolm Arnold (John Hollingsworth)
1948	*University of Flying*	Francis Chagrin (John Hollingsworth)
1948	*Women in Our Time (This Modern Age)*	
		Malcolm Arnold (John Hollingsworth)
1948	*Down to the Sea*	Guy Warrack
1952	*Opus 65*	Richard Arnell (Edward Renton)
1952	*Towards Wholeness*	Temple Abady (John Hollingsworth)
1953	*A Queen is Crowned*	Guy Warrack
1954	*Flight of the White Heron*	Stanley Wicken (John Hollingsworth)

The following film soundtracks were also recorded by the LSO:

1936	*The Robber Symphony*	Friedrich Feher
1937	*Victoria the Great*	Anthony Collins (Muir Mathieson)
1938	*The Mikado*	Arthur Sullivan (Geoffrey Toye)
1940	*You Will Remember*	? (Percival Mackey)
1941	*Major Barbara*	William Walton (Muir Mathieson)
1941	*Dangerous Moonlight (Warsaw Concerto)*	
		Richard Addinsell (Mathieson, with Kentner)
1941	*Jeannie*	Mischa Spoliansky (Percival Mackey)
1941	*The Common Touch*	Tchaikovsky (Kennedy Russell)
1941	*49th Parallel (The Invaders)*	Vaughan Williams (Muir Mathieson)
1942	*The Day Will Dawn*	Richard Addinsell (Muir Mathieson)
1942	*The First of the Few (Spitfire)*	William Walton (Muir Mathieson)
1942	*In Which We Serve*	Noël Coward (Muir Mathieson)
1943	*The Gentle Sex*	John Greenwood (Muir Mathieson)
1943	*I'll Walk Beside You*	? (Percival Mackey)
1943	*Escape to Danger*	William Alwyn (Muir Mathieson)
1943	*The Flemish Farm*	Vaughan Williams (Muir Mathieson)
1943	*Yellow Canary*	Clifton Parker (Muir Mathieson)
1944	*This Happy Breed*	Noël Coward (Muir Mathieson)
1944	*Henry V* (Laurence Olivier version)	William Walton (Muir Mathieson)
1945	*For You Alone*	? (Harry Bidgood)
1945	*I Live in Grosvenor Square (A Yank in London)*	
		Anthony Collins (Muir Mathieson)
1945	*Great Day*	William Alwyn (Muir Mathieson)
1945	*Blithe Spirit*	Richard Addinsell (Muir Mathieson)
1945	*29, Acacia Avenue (The Facts of Love)*	Clifton Parker (Muir Mathieson)
1945	*The Seventh Veil*	Benjamin Frankel (Muir Mathieson)
1946	*A Musical Masquerade*	Horace Shepherd

278

1946	*I'll Turn to You*	? (Harry Bidgood)
1946	*I See a Dark Stranger*	William Alwyn (Muir Mathieson)
1946	*Green for Danger*	William Alwyn (Muir Mathieson)
1946	*Daybreak*	Benjamin Frankel (Muir Mathieson)
1946	*A Song of Thanksgiving*	William Alwyn (Muir Mathieson)
1947	*Hungry Hill*	John Greenwood (Muir Mathieson)
1947	*Odd Man Out*	William Alwyn (Muir Mathieson)
1947	*Black Narcissus*	Brian Easdale
1947	*Take My Life*	William Alwyn (Muir Mathieson)
1947	*The Brothers*	Cedric Thorpe Davie (Muir Mathieson)
1947	*The Upturned Glass*	Bernard Stevens (Muir Mathieson)
1947	*They Made Me a Fugitive*	M-F Gaillard (John Hollingsworth)
1947	*The Master of Bankdam*	Arthur Benjamin (Muir Mathieson)
1947	*The October Man*	William Alwyn (Muir Mathieson)
1947	*Uncle Silas*	Alan Rawsthorne (Muir Mathieson)
1948	*The Mark of Cain*	Bernard Stevens (Muir Mathieson)
1948	*Easy Money*	Temple Abady (Muir Mathieson)
1948	*Snowbound*	Cedric Thorpe Davie (Muir Mathieson)
1948	*Miranda*	Temple Abady (Muir Mathieson)
1948	*One Night With You*	Lambert Williamson (John Hollingsworth)
1948	*Good Time Girl*	Lambert Williamson (John Hollingsworth)
1948	*My Brother's Keeper*	Clifton Parker (John Hollingsworth)
1948	*Mr Perrin and Mr Traill*	Allan Gray (John Hollingsworth)
1948	*The Weaker Sex*	Arthur Wilkinson (Muir Mathieson)
1948	*Sleeping Car to Trieste*	Benjamin Frankel (Muir Mathieson)
1948	*It's Hard to be Good*	Anthony Hopkins (Muir Mathieson)
1948	*Portrait from Life (The Girl in the Painting)*	
		Benjamin Frankel (Muir Mathieson)
1949	*Once Upon a Dream*	Arthur Wilkinson (John Hollingsworth)
1949	*Blue Lagoon*	Clifton Parker (Muir Mathieson)
1949	*Bad Lord Byron*	Cedric Thorpe Davie (Muir Mathieson)
1949	*Floodtide*	Robert Irving
1949	*Cardboard Cavalier*	Lambert Williamson (Muir Mathieson)
1949	*It's Not Cricket*	Arthur Wilkinson (John Hollingsworth)
1949	*A Boy, a Girl and a Bike*	Kenneth Pakeman (John Hollingsworth)
1949	*Stop Press Girl*	Walter Goehr
1949	*Helter Skelter*	Francis Chagrin (Muir Mathieson)
1949	*Madness of the Heart*	Allan Gray (Muir Mathieson)
1949	*The Lost People*	John Greenwood (Muir Mathieson)
1949	*Dear Mr Prohack*	Temple Abady (Muir Mathieson)
1949	*Give Us This Day (Salt to the Devil)*	Benjamin Frankel
1949	*The Spider and the Fly*	Georges Auric (Muir Mathieson)
1949	*Boys in Brown*	Doreen Carwithen (John Hollingsworth)
1949	*Alice in Wonderland*	Sol Kaplan (Ernest Irving)
1950	*The Astonished Heart*	Noël Coward (Muir Mathieson)
1950	*They Were Not Divided*	Lambert Williamson (Muir Mathieson)

1950	*The Wooden Horse*	Clifton Parker (Muir Mathieson)
1952	*Giselle* (London Festival Ballet)	Adolphe Adam (Malcolm Sargent)
1953	*The Story of Gilbert & Sullivan*	Arthur Sullivan (Malcolm Sargent)
1953‡	*Knight of the Round Table*	Miklós Rózsa (Muir Mathieson)
1954	*Nigerian Pattern*	?(John Hollingsworth)
1955	*Out of the Clouds*	Richard Addinsell (Dock Mathieson)
1955	*The Night My Number Came Up*	Malcolm Arnold (Dock Mathieson)
1955	*The Man Who Knew Too Much*	Bernard Herrmann
1955	*The Cockleshell Heroes*	John Addison (Muir Mathieson)
1956	*1984*	Malcolm Arnold (Louis Levy)
1960	*The 3 Worlds of Gulliver*	Bernard Herrmann
1961	*Mysterious Island*	Bernard Herrmann
1969	*Song of Norway*	Grieg (Øivin Fjeldstad, with John Ogdon)
1969	*Crescendo*	Malcolm Williamson (Philip Martell)
1970	*The Music Lovers*	Tchaikovsky (André Previn)
1972*	*The Strauss Family*	J. Strauss (Cyril Ornadel)
1973	*The Great American Cowboy*	Harold Farberman
1973†	*The Exorcist*	Jack Nitzsche (David Measham)
1974†	*All This and World War II*	Lennon/McCartney (Rabinowitz/Measham)
1974*	*Edward the Seventh*	Cyril Ornadel
1975	*Rollerball*	Previn/classical (André Previn)
1977	*Star Wars, A New Hope*	John T. Williams
1978	*The Fury*	John T. Williams
1978	*Michel's Mixed-Up Musical Bird*	Michel Legrand
1978	*F. I. S. T.*	Bill Conti
1978	*Superman, The Movie*	John T. Williams
1978	*Quintet*	Tom Pierson
1979	*The Brontë Sisters*	Philippe Sarde (Carlo Savina)
1979	*The Magician of Lublin*	Maurice Jarre
1979	*Dracula*	John T. Williams
1979	*Tess*	Philippe Sarde (Carlo Savina)
1980	*Star Wars, The Empire Strikes Back*	John T. Williams
1980	*Omar Mukhtar, Lion of the Desert*	Maurice Jarre
1980†	*The Jazz Singer*	Leonard Rosenman (John Scott)
1981	*Clash of the Titans*	Laurence Rosenthal
1981	*Les Ailes de la Colombe*	Philippe Sarde (Peter Knight)
1981	*Raiders of the Lost Ark*	John T. Williams
1981	*Le Choix des Armes*	Philippe Sarde (Peter Knight)
1981	*Birgitt Haas Must Be Killed*	Philippe Sarde (Peter Knight)
1981	*Hôtel des Amériques*	Philippe Sarde (Peter Knight)
1981†	*Quest for Fire*	Philippe Sarde (Peter Knight)
1982	*The Dark Crystal*	Trevor Jones (Marcus Dods)
1982	*El Pueblo del Sol*	Lee Holdridge
1982	*Monsignor*	John T. Williams
1982	*A Royal Romance*	Richard Rodney Bennett
1982	*Twice Upon a Time*	Dawn Atkinson/Ken Melville (Atkinson)

1983	*Krull*	James Horner
1983	*Star Wars, Return of the Jedi*	John T. Williams
1983	*L'Été Meurtrier (One Deadly Summer)*	Georges Delerue
1983	*Savage Islands*	Trevor Jones (Marcus Dods)
1983	*Lovesick*	Philippe Sarde (Peter Knight)
1983	*Digital Dreams*	Mike Batt/Bill Wyman (Batt)
1983	*Never Say Never Again*	Michel Legrand
1983	*Garçon!*	Philippe Sarde (Peter Knight)
1983	*The Dresser*	James Horner
1984*	*The Last Days of Pompeii*	Trevor Jones (Marcus Dods)
1984	*Fort Saganne*	Philippe Sarde (Carlo Savina)
1984	*La Pirate*	Philippe Sarde (Carlo Savina)
1984	*Grand Canyon, the Hidden Secrets*	Bill Conti
1984	*The Masks of Death*	Malcolm Williamson (Philip Martell)
1984	*Return to Oz*	David Shire (Harry Rabinowitz)
1984	*Lifeforce*	Henry Mancini
1985	*The Dirty Dozen, the Next Mission*	Richard Harvey
1985	*Wild Geese II*	Roy Budd
1985	*Flesh and Blood*	Basil Poledouris
1985	*Plenty*	Bruce Smeaton
1985	*Eleni*	Bruce Smeaton
1985	*F/X*	Bill Conti
1986	*Aliens*	James Horner
1986	*The Nutcracker* (Pacific Northwest Ballet)	
		Tchaikovsky (Charles Mackerras)
1986	*An American Tail*	James Horner
1986	*Dancers*	Adolphe Adam (Michael Tilson Thomas)
1987*	*Noble House*	Paul Chihara
1987‡	*Madame Sousatzka*	Schumann (William Boughton)
1987	*A Summer Story*	Georges Delerue
1988	*Willow*	James Horner
1988	*Who Framed Roger Rabbit?*	Alan Silvestri
1988	*The Land Before Time*	James Horner
1988	*L'Ours (The Bear)*	Philippe Sarde (Carlo Savina)
1988	*Slipstream*	Elmer Bernstein
1988	*Honey I Shrunk the Kids*	James Horner
1989	*Rarg*	Philip Appleby (James Stobart)
1989†	*The Return of the Musketeers*	Jean-Claude Petit
1989	*Little Nemo, Adventures in Slumberland*	Tom Chase/Steve Rucker (Chase)
1989	*All Dogs Go to Heaven*	Ralph Burns
1989	*L'Autrichienne*	Didier Vasseur (David Snell)
1989*	*Romeo and Juliet*	Armando Acosta (Barry Wordsworth)
1989	*Suivez Cette Avion*	Didier Vasseur (David Snell)
1989	*Lord of the Flies*	Philippe Sarde (Harry Rabinowitz)
1990	*The Nutcracker Prince*	Victor Davies (Boris Brott)
1990	*Eve of Destruction*	Philippe Sarde (Harry Rabinowitz)

1990	*An American Tail II, Fievel Goes West* James Horner
1990	*The Josephine Baker Story* Georges Delerue
1990	*Jesuit Joe*	Philippe Sarde (Harry Rabinowitz)
1991	*Pour Sacha*	Philippe Sarde (Harry Rabinowitz)
1991†	*Rambling Rose*	Elmer Bernstein
1991†	*Cape Fear*	Bernard Herrmann (Elmer Bernstein)
1992	*Appaloosa*	Carl Davis
1992	*Once Upon a Forest (The Endangered)* James Horner
1992	*Arabian Knight (The Thief and the Cobbler)* Robert Folk
1993	*Water Traveller*	Joe Hisaishi (Nick Ingman)
1993	*The Man Without a Face* James Horner
1993	*We're Back*	James Horner
1993	*Shadowlands*	George Fenton
1993	*Viva la Blanca Paloma*	Manolo Sanlucar
1993	*Le Petit Garçon*	Philippe Sarde (Harry Rabinowitz)
1994	*Legends of the Fall*	James Horner
1994	*Immortal Beloved*	Beethoven (Georg Solti)
1994	*The Pagemaster*	James Horner
1994	*Mary of Nazareth*	Olivier Lliboutry (David Firman)
1994	*Street Fighter*	Graeme Revell (Tim Simonec)
1994	*Little Women*	Tom Newman
1994	*Last of the Dogmen*	David Arnold (Nicholas Dodd)
1995	*Braveheart*	James Horner
1995	*Balto*	James Horner
1995	*Cutthroat Island*	John Debney (David Snell)
1995	*Mary Reilly*	George Fenton
1995†	*The Fifth Element*	Donizetti (Frédéric Chaslin)
1996*	*Cold Lazarus*	Christopher Gunning
1996	*Flipper*	Joel McNeely
1996	*Meet Wally Sparks*	Michel Colombier (David Snell)
1996	*Le Jaguar*	Vladimir Cosma
1996	*Roseanna's Grave (For Roseanna)* Trevor Jones (Nick Ingman)
1996	*Le Plus Beau Métier du Monde* Vladimir Cosma
1997	*Soleil*	Vladimir Cosma
1997	*Le Bossu (On Guard!)*	Philippe Sarde (David Snell)
1997	*The Mighty*	Trevor Jones (Geoff Alexander)
1998*	*Merlin*	Trevor Jones (Geoff Alexander)
1998	*Asterix and Obelix versus Caesar* Goldman/Romanelli (David Snell)
1999	*Notting Hill*	Trevor Jones (Geoff Alexander)
1999	*Le Schpountz*	Vladimir Cosma
1999	*Star Wars, The Phantom Menace* John T. Williams
1999*	*Cleopatra*	Trevor Jones (Geoff Alexander)
1999†	*I Dreamed of Africa*	Maurice Jarre
1999	*Le Fils du Français*	Vladimir Cosma
2000	*Bored Silly*	Larry Pecorella (Arnie Roth)
2000	*The Luzhin Defence*	Alexandre Desplat

2000	*The Long Run*	Trevor Jones (Geoff Alexander)
2000	*The Body*	Serge Colbert (David Snell)
2000	*Thirteen Days*	Trevor Jones (Geoff Alexander)
2000†	*Left Behind*	James Covell
2001	*The Sedra Tree*	Mark Stevens
2001	*Final Fantasy, the Spirits Within* Elliot Goldenthal (Dirk Brossé)
2001*	*To End All Wars*	John Cameron
2001*	*Barbie in the Nutcracker*	Tchaikovsky (Arnie Roth)
2001	*Phoenix Blue*	Stewart Parsons (Chris Austin)
2001	*Asterix and Obelix: Mission Cleopatra* Philippe Chany (David Snell)
2001	*Crossroads*	Trevor Jones (Geoff Alexander)
2002	*Star Wars, Attack of the Clones* John T. Williams
2002*	*Dinotopia*	Trevor Jones (Geoff Alexander)
2002*‡	*The Gathering Storm*	Trevor Jones (Geoff Alexander)
2002	*Dreams Without Sleep*	Mark Stevens
2002*	*Barbie as Rapunzel*	Arnie Roth
2002*	*Lara Croft: Angel of Darkness* Peter Connelly/Martin Iveson (David Snell)
2002	*Conspiracy of Silence*	David Butterworth
2002	*Harry Potter and the Chamber of Secrets* John T. Williams (William Ross)
2002	*I'll Be There*	Trevor Jones (Geoff Alexander)
2003*	*Barbie of Swan Lake*	Tchaikovsky (Arnie Roth)
2003	*Inquietudes*	Alexandre Desplat
2003	*The League of Extraordinary Gentlemen* Trevor Jones (Geoff Alexander)
2004	*Around the World in Eighty Days* Trevor Jones (Geoff Alexander)
2004	*Upside of Anger*	Alexandre Desplat
2004*	*Barbie and the Pauper*	Arnie Roth

(Unless otherwise stated in brackets, the score was conducted by the composer.)
*   TV or Video productions
†   soundtracks shared with other orchestras
‡   LSO recordings intended for soundtracks, but not used

LSO festivals (1950 onwards)

1950   Sibelius cycle (Anthony Collins)
1959   Beethoven series (with Glenn Gould)
1965   Rostropovich cycle of 31 cello concertos, in London and New York
        (Rozhdestvensky)
1969   Crossroads of Twentieth-Century Music (Boulez)
1982   Music of London concerts (with RSC)
1984   Beethoven cycle (Abbado)
1983   Webern Festival (Abbado)
1985   Mahler, Vienna and the Twentieth Century (Abbado)
1986   Bernstein Festival (Bernstein et al.)
1987   Stravinsky Plus (Rozhdestvensky)
        The Gershwin Years (Tilson Thomas)
        Rostropovich 60th Birthday series (Rostropovich)
1988   A Theme with Variations – A Celebration of British Music
        (Sir Colin Davis et al.)
        International Violin series
        Shostakovich: Music from the Flames (Rostropovich)
1989   The Flight of the Firebird (Tilson Thomas)
1990   Schnittke series (Rostropovich)
        Anne-Sophie Mutter and Friends
1991   Childhood Festival (Tilson Thomas)
        Prokofiev: The Centenary Festival (Rostropovich)
1992   The Sibelius Cycle: Tender is the North (Sir Colin Davis)
1993   Festival of Britten (Rostropovich)
        Bashmet series
        Czechoslovakia (Tilson Thomas)
        Messiaen: A Commemoration (Boulez/Nagano/Howarth/London
        Sinfonietta)
1994   Jessye Norman: Impressions (Norman/Sir Colin Davis)
        Mahler Festival (Part 1) (Tilson Thomas)
1995   Schnittke series (Rostropovich)
        Boulez 70th Birthday series (Boulez)
        Tippett: Visions of Paradise (90th Birthday series) (Sir Colin Davis, also
        London Sinfonietta)
        Mahler Festival (Part 2) (Tilson Thomas)
        Solti celebrates Bartók (Solti)
1997   Bruckner/Mozart series (Sir Colin Davis)
        Brahms Centenary (Sir Colin Davis)
        Debussy: Painter of Dreams (Tilson Thomas)

	Rostropovich 70 (Rostropovich/Mehta/Ozawa)
	Ravel: Through the Looking Glass (Previn)
	Vaughan Williams: Vision of Albion (Hickox)
	The Sibelius Cycle (Sir Colin Davis)
1998	Shostakovich 1906–75 (Rostropovich)
	Boulez Celebrates Carter (Boulez)
	Bruch: The Forgotten Romantic (Hickox)
	Stravinsky Stage Works (Tilson Thomas)
	Elgar series (Sir Colin Davis)
1999	André Previn 70th Birthday Celebrations (Previn)
	Mozart/Strauss series (Haitink)
1999–2000	Berlioz Odyssey (Sir Colin Davis)
2000	Boulez 2000 (Boulez)
	Maazel at 70 (Maazel)
	Back to the Future (Mutter/Masur)
2001	Bohemian Spring (Sir Colin Davis/Belohlávek)
	Verdi Centenary (José Cura)
	Leif Ove Andsnes: Artist Portrait (Andsnes)
	Mutter plays Mozart (Sir Colin Davis/Mutter)
2002	Walton Centenary (Alsop)
	Rostropovich 75th Birthday Series (Rostropovich)
	Boulez Series (Boulez)
2002–3	By George! (George Benjamin)
2003	Berlioz Bicentenary (Sir Colin Davis)
2004	LSO Centenary Series

Recordings released on LSO Live

All recordings produced by James Mallinson with Tony Faulkner as engineer, unless otherwise stated.

January 2000
> Dvořák: Symphony No. 9, 'From the New World' (LSO 0001)
> Sir Colin Davis, conductor
> Dvořák: Symphony No. 8 (LSO 0002)
> Sir Colin Davis, conductor
> *BBC Music Magazine: Outstanding Recording*

April 2000
> Berlioz: *Roméo et Juliette* (LSO 0003)
> Sir Colin Davis, conductor
> Daniela Barcellona, Kenneth Tarver, Orlan Anastassov, London Symphony Chorus

September 2000
> Brahms: *Ein deutsches Requiem* (LSO 0005)
> André Previn, conductor
> Harolyn Blackwell, David Wilson-Johnson, London Symphony Chorus
> Berlioz: *Béatrice et Bénédict* (LSO 0004)
> Sir Colin Davis, conductor
> Enkelejda Shkosa, Kenneth Tarver, Susan Gritton, Sara Mingardo, Laurent Naouri, David Wilson-Johnson, Dean Robinson, London Symphony Chorus

February 2001
> Berlioz: *Symphonie fantastique* (LSO 0007)
> Sir Colin Davis, conductor
> *Gramophone: Editor's Choice*

April 2001
> Berlioz: *La damnation de Faust* (LSO 0008)
> Sir Colin Davis, conductor
> Giuseppe Sabbatini, Enkelejda Shkosa, Michele Pertusi, David Wilson-Johnson, London Symphony Chorus
> *Gramophone: Editor's Choice*

July 2001
> Berlioz: *Les Troyens* (LSO 0010)
> Sir Colin Davis, conductor
> Ben Heppner, Michelle de Young, Petra Lang, Sara Mingardo, Peter Mattei, Stephen Milling, Kenneth Tarver, London Symphony Chorus (Engineer: Simon Rhodes)

Grammy Awards 2002: Best Classical Album winner, Best Opera winner
Gramophone Awards: Best Opera 2002; Classical Brits 2002: Critics'
Choice; Charles Cros 2002: Orphée d'Or; Academie du disque lyrique
2003: Orphée Charles Munch; Gramophone: Editor's Choice

October 2001

Dave Brubeck and the LSO (LSO 0011)
Russell Gloyd, conductor
(Engineer: Jack Renner)

February 2002

Elgar: Symphony No. 1 (LSO 0017)
Sir Colin Davis
Gramophone: Editor's Choice

April 2002

Elgar Symphony No. 2 (LSO 0018)
Sir Colin Davis, conductor

May 2002

Elgar/Payne Symphony No. 3 (LSO 0019)
Sir Colin Davis, conductor
BBC Music Magazine: Discs of the Decade

August 2002

Shostakovich: Symphony No. 11 (LSO 0030)
Mstislav Rostropovich, conductor
Gramophone: Editor's Choice and Record of the Month
Grammy Awards 2003: three nominations
Classical Brits 2003: one nomination

November 2002

Bruckner: Symphony No. 9 (LSO 0023)
Sir Colin Davis, conductor

February 2003

Bruckner: Symphony No. 6 (LSO 0022)
Sir Colin Davis, conductor
BBC Music Magazine: Benchmark Recording

March 2003

Dvořák: Symphony No. 7 (LSO 0014)
Sir Colin Davis, conductor

May 2003

Holst: *The Planets* (LSO 0029)
Sir Colin Davis, conductor
Ladies of the London Symphony Chorus

July 2003

Berlioz: *Harold en Italie* (LSO 0040)
Sir Colin Davis, conductor
Tabea Zimmermann, viola
Gramophone: Editor's Choice and Record of the Month

August 2003

Mahler: Symphony No. 6 (LSO 0038)

Mariss Jansons, conductor
Gramophone: Editor's Choice

January 2004

Brahms: Symphony No. 2, Double Concerto (LSO 0043)
Bernard Haitink, conductor
Gordan Nikolitch, violin
Tim Hugh, cello
(Engineer: Jonathan Stokes for Classic Sound Ltd)
Gramophone: Editor's Choice

March 2004

Sibelius: Symphonies Nos. 3 & 7 (LSO0051)
Sir Colin Davis, conductor
(Engineer: Neil Hutchinson for Classic Sound Ltd)
Gramophone: Editor's Choice
Le mon-de de la musique: CHOC

April 2004

Brahms: Symphony No 1, Tragic Overture (LSO0045)
Bernard Haitink, conductor
(Engineer: Jonathan Stokes for Classic Sound Ltd)

June 2004

Sibelius: Symphonies Nos. 5 & 6 (LSO0037)
Sir Colin Davis, conductor
(Engineer – Symphony No 5: Jonathan Stokes for Classic Sound Ltd
Engineer – Symphony No 6: Tony Faulkner for Green Room Productions)
Classic FM Magazine: Disc of the Month

July 2004

Britten: Peter Grimes (LSO0054)
Sir Colin Davis, conductor
Glenn Winslade, Janice Watson, Anthony Michaels-Moore, Catherine
Wyn-Rogers, Jill Grove, James Rutherford, Jonathan Lemalu, Sally
Matthews, Alison Buchanan, Christopher Gillett, Ryland Davies, Nathan
Gunn, London Symphony Chorus
(Engineers: Jonathan Stokes and Neil Hutchinson for Classic Sound Ltd)

List of sources

Aldous, R., *Tunes of Glory: the Life of Malcolm Sargent*, London, Hutchinson, 2001

Arts Council of Great Britain, *Committee on the London Orchestras* (Goodman Report), London, ACGB, 1965

Arts Council of Great Britain, *Report of the Advisory Committee of the London Orchestras* (Hoffman Report), London, ACGB, 1993

Arts Council of Great Britain, *Report on Orchestral Resources in Great Britain* (Peacock Report), London, ACGB, 1970

Bailey, P. (ed.), *Music Hall: The Business of Pleasure*, Milton Keynes, Open University Press, 1986

Barbirolli, E., *Life with Glorious John: A Portrait of Sir John Barbirolli*, London, Robson, 2002

Beecham, T., *A Mingled Chime*, London, Hutchinson, 1944

Blackwood, A., *Sir Thomas Beecham: the Man and the Music*, London, 1994

Blandford, L., *The LSO: Scenes from Orchestra Life*, London, Michael Joseph, 1984

Boult, A., *My Own Trumpet*, Hamish Hamilton, London 1973

Carpenter, H., *Benjamin Britten: a Biography*, London, Faber, 1992

Doráti, A., *Notes of Seven Decades*, London, Hodder and Stoughton, 1979

Ehrlich, C., *The Music Profession in Britain since the Eighteenth Century: a Social History*, Oxford, Clarendon Press, 1985

Elkin, R., *Queen's Hall: 1893–1941*, London, Rider, 1944

Fifeld, C., *True Artist and True Friend: a Biography of Hans Richter*, Oxford University Press, 1993

Foss, H., and Goodwin, N., *London Symphony: Portrait of an Orchestra*, London, Naldrett Press, 1954

Freedland, M., *André Previn*, London, 1991

Gaisberg, F. W., *Music on Record*, London, Hale, 1946

Goossens, E., *Overture and Beginners*, London, Methuen, 1951

Hayes, M. (ed.), *The Selected Letters of William Walton*, London, Faber, 2002

Heath, E., *Music: a Joy for Life*, London, Sidgwick and Jackson, 1976

House, J., *Impressionism for England : Samuel Courtauld as Patron and Collector*, London, Courtauld Institute, 1994

Huntley, J., *British Film Music*, London, Skelton Robinson, 1947

Jackson, G., *First Flute*, London, Dent, 1968

Kennedy, M., *Portrait of Elgar*, Oxford University Press, 1968

Kenyon, N., *The BBC Symphony Orchestra 1930–1980*, London, BBC, 1981

Kenyon, N., *Simon Rattle*, London, Faber, 2001

Moore, J. N., *Elgar on Record: the Composer and the Gramophone*, Oxford University Press, 1974

Nettel, R., *The Orchestra in England*, London, Cape, 1948

Pearton, M., *The London Symphony Orchestra at 70: a History of the Orchestra*, London, Gollancz, 1974

Peters, C., *England and the English*, London, 1904

Pettitt, S. J., *Philharmonia Orchestra: a Record of Achievement 1945–1985*, London, Robert Hale, 1985

Pound, R., *Sir Henry Wood*, London, Cassell, 1969

Priestley, J. B., *Trumpets over the Sea*, London, Heinemann, 1968

Reed, W. H., *Elgar as I Knew Him*, London, Gollancz, 1936

Reid, C., *Beecham: an Independent Biography*, London, 1961

Ronald, L., *Myself and Others*, London, 1931

Russell, T., *Philharmonic Decade*, London, Hutchinson, 1945

Sachs, H. (ed.)., *The Letters of Arturo Toscanini*, London, Faber, 2002

Sinclair, A., *Arts and Cultures: The History of the 50 Years of the Arts Council of Great Britain*, London, Sinclair Stevenson, 1995

Schneer, J., *London 1900: the Imperial Metropolis*, Yale University Press, 2001

Scholes, P., *The Mirror of Music 1844–1944*, London, Novello/Oxford University Press, 1947

Schonberg, H., *The Great Conductors*, New York, 1967

Shore, B., *The Orchestra Speaks*, London, Longmans, Green and Co., 1938

Smyth, A., (ed.), *To Speak for Ourselves*, London, Kimber, 1970

Smyth, E., *What Happened Next*, London, 1940

Stevenson, J., *British Society 1914–45* [The Pelican Social History of Britain], London, Penguin, 1984

Strutt, W. M., *The Reminiscences of a Musical Amateur*, London, 1915

Witts, R., *Artist Unknown: An Alternative History of the Arts Council*, London, 1998

Wood, H., *About Conducting*, London, Sylvan Press, 1945

Wood, H., *My Life of Music*, London, Gollancz, 1938

Index

Abbado, Claudio *114*, 144, 172, *194*, 233
  LSO's principal guest conductor 190
  becomes the LSO's principal conductor
    (1979) 191, 212
  and the Barbican 201, 202
  Beethoven cycle 203
  Mahler/Vienna project 206–7, 210
  Gillinson on 212–13
  communication problems 213, 216
  rehearsals with the LSO 122, 213–14
  musical understanding 214
  loyalty issues 214–15
  Murphy on 122
  music director of Vienna State Opera 215
Abbey Road studios, St John's Wood, London
  42, 43
Academy of Ancient Music 229
Academy of St Martin-in-the-Fields 148
Adams, John 226
Addinsell, Richard: *Warsaw Concerto* 177–8
Adès, Thomas 226
  Asyla 229
Aldeburgh, Suffolk 142, 189
Aldwych Theatre, London 197
Alldis, John 181, 182
Ambrosian Singers 181
Anderson, George 33
André Previn's Music Night (television pro-
  gramme) 179–80
Anne, HRH The Princess 78
Antwerp 38
Archer, Thomas 238
Arnold, Sir Malcolm 102, *168*
Arrau, Claudio 101
Arts Council of Great Britain 94, 96, 97, 100,
  104, 148–53, 198, 199, 202, 204, 205,
  211, 232, 241, 248, 251
Arts Florissants, Les 229
Athens Festival 155
Atkins, Ivor 55, 116
Atterberg, Kurt 48

Bach, J. C. 144
Bach, Johann Sebastian 28, 89, 229
  Mass in B minor 15
  St Matthew Passion 226
  Suite in D 25

Ballets Russes 135
Baltic, SS 32, 45
Banks, Don 141
Bantock, Granville 57
  Omar Khayyám 52–3
Barbican Arts Centre, City of London xi, 2,
  107, 189, *194*, 211
  a public building fiasco 195–6, 199–200
  arts centre idea first mooted 196–7
  LSO's plans 197–9
  LSO's residency invitation 191
  opens in March 1982 195, 200
  a leading international arts centre 195
  acoustics 105, 195, 200–201, 217, 221
  LSO's catastrophic losses in its first months
    there xi, 44, 202–4
  described 200
  Pit theatre 200
  month-long 'festivals' 201–2
  Duncan's suggestion 152, 205
  'Detta affair' 219–20
  Tusa replaces O'Cathain 220–21
  summer music jamboree 240
Barbican Estate 196
Barbirolli, Sir John 53, 58, 100
Barenboim, Daniel 151
Barry, Gerald 105
Bartók, Béla 139, 148
  The Miraculous Mandarin 122
Bashmet, Yuri 249
Bath Festival 182
Bavarian Radio Symphony Orchestra 218
Bax, Sir Arnold 102, 177
  Malta GC film music 177
  Symphony No.1 in E flat major 57–8
Bayreuth Festival 25, 181, 217
BBC Concert Orchestra 74–5, 150
BBC Northern Orchestra 7
BBC Philharmonic Orchestra 74
BBC Symphony Orchestra 29, 64, 70, 72–4, 75,
  81, 82, 148, 150, 161, 173, 174, 176,
  188, 206, 217
BBC World Service 220
BBC2 145
Beard, Paul 80
Beaverbrook, Lord 65, 66
Beecham, Joseph 51